Lecture Notes in Computer Science　　10129

Commenced Publication in 1973
Founding and Former Series Editors:
Gerhard Goos, Juris Hartmanis, and Jan van Leeuwen

More information about this series at http://www.springer.com/series/7412

Maria A. Zuluaga · Kanwal Bhatia
Bernhard Kainz · Mehdi H. Moghari
Danielle F. Pace (Eds.)

Reconstruction, Segmentation, and Analysis of Medical Images

First International Workshops, RAMBO 2016 and HVSMR 2016
Held in Conjunction with MICCAI 2016
Athens, Greece, October 17, 2016
Revised Selected Papers

 Springer

Editors

Maria A. Zuluaga
University College London
London
UK

Kanwal Bhatia
King's College London
London
UK

Bernhard Kainz
Imperial College London
London
UK

Mehdi H. Moghari
Harvard Medical School and Boston
  Children's Hospital
Boston, MA
USA

Danielle F. Pace
MIT
Cambridge, MA
USA

ISSN 0302-9743   ISSN 1611-3349 (electronic)
Lecture Notes in Computer Science
ISBN 978-3-319-52279-1   ISBN 978-3-319-52280-7   (eBook)
DOI 10.1007/978-3-319-52280-7

Library of Congress Control Number: 2016963670

LNCS Sublibrary: SL6 – Image Processing, Computer Vision, Pattern Recognition, and Graphics

Printed on acid-free paper

This Springer imprint is published by Springer Nature
The registered company is Springer International Publishing AG
The registered company address is: Gewerbestrasse 11, 6330 Cham, Switzerland

Preface

This book gathers the works presented at the Workshop on Reconstruction and Analysis of Moving Body Organs (RAMBO) and the Workshop on Whole-Heart and Great Vessel Segmentation from 3D Cardiovascular MRI in Congenital Heart Disease (HVSMR), which were held in conjunction with MICCAI on October 17, 2016.

RAMBO

Physiological motion is an important factor in several medical imaging applications. For instance, the speed of motion may inhibit the acquisition of high-resolution images needed for effective visualization and analysis, for example, in cardiac or respiratory imaging or in functional magnetic resonance imaging (fMRI) and perfusion applications. Additionally, in cardiac and fetal imaging, the variation in frame of reference may confound automated analysis pipelines. The underlying motion may also need to be characterized either to enhance images or for clinical assessment. Techniques are therefore needed for faster or more accurate reconstruction or for analysis of time-dependent images. Despite the related concerns, few meetings have addressed the issues caused by motion in medical imaging, without restriction on the clinical application area or methodology used. RAMBO 2016 was set up to provide a discussion forum for researchers for whom motion and its effects are critical in image analysis or visualization. By inviting contributions across all application areas, the workshop aimed to bring together ideas from different areas of specialization, without being confined to a particular methodology. In particular, the recent trend to move from model-based to learning-based methods of analysis has resulted in increased transferability between application domains. A further goal of this workshop was to enhance the links between image analysis (including computer vision and machine learning techniques) and image acquisition and reconstruction, which generally tends to be addressed in separate meetings. The presented contributions can be broadly categorized into segmentation, registration, and reconstruction, while application areas include cardiac, abdominal, fetal, and brain perfusion, showing the breadth of interest in the topic. Research from both academia and industry is presented. We hope that this workshop enables the cross-fertilization of ideas across application domains with the aim of tackling and taking advantage of the problems and opportunities arising from motion in medical imaging.

October 2016

Bernhard Kainz
Kanwal Bhatia
Ghislain Vaillant
Maria A. Zuluaga

HVSMR

Congenital heart disease (CHD) affects approximately 1.2% of children and is the leading cause of birth defect-related deaths. About 6 to 19 per 1,000 cause moderate to severe problems requiring immediate surgical repair. Clinicians currently rely on two-dimensional imaging (2D) for monitoring and procedural planning. However, 2D images cannot depict the 3D spatial relationships of intracardiac anatomy, and reliance on them limits efficient decision-making.

Compared with conventional 2D imaging techniques, it has been recently shown that 3D virtual and physical heart models convey several benefits when visualizing intracardiac anatomy in 3D and in producing consensus around a surgical plan.

Three-dimensional images can be generated by segmenting the cardiac muscle and blood in 3D images acquired from echocardiography, X-ray, or magnetic resonance imaging (MRI). MRI has many advantages including better image quality compared with echocardiography, and unlike X-ray is not associated with ionizing radiation. However, segmentation of cardiac MR images is challenging owing to intensity inhomogeneities (due to the motion of the heart and blood), poor contrast, the presence of thin walls separating cardiac chambers, and the wide anatomical variability in congenital heart disease patients.

Manual segmentation has been the most robust technique for delineating the cardiac muscle and blood in cardiac MR datasets. This technique, however, is time intensive (4–8 h of work), prone to error, and subject to intra- and inter-observer variability. As of yet, there is no robust automatic segmentation algorithm developed for cardiac MR segmentation for congenital heart disease.

The HVSMR workshop gathered researchers from around the world to tackle this challenging problem, sharing a newly released open dataset of cardiac MR images from patients with various forms of congenital heart disease. The ultimate goal is to improve surgical planning for patients with complex congenital heart disease. We believe this workshop provided a snapshot of the current progress in the field of cardiac MR segmentation for this patient cohort.

October 2016

Mehdi H. Moghari
Danielle F. Pace
Alireza Akhondi-Asl
Andrew J. Powell

Organization

RAMBO: Conference Chairs

Bernhard Kainz	Imperial College London, UK
Kanwal Bhatia	King's College London, UK
Maria A. Zuluaga	University College London, UK
Ghislain Vaillant	Imperial College London, UK

HVSMR: Conference Chairs

Mehdi Hedjazi Moghari	Boston Children's Hospital and Harvard Medical School, USA
Danielle F. Pace	Massachusetts Institute of Technology, USA
Alireza Akhondi-Asl	Boston Children's Hospital and Harvard Medical School, USA
Andrew Powell	Boston Children's Hospital and Harvard Medical School, USA

RAMBO: Program Committee

Wenjia Bai	Imperial College London, UK
Olivier Bernard	CREATIS, France
Wolfgang Birkfellner	Medical University Vienna, Austria
Lucilio Cordero-Grande	King's College London, UK
Ali Gholipour	Boston Children's Hospital, USA
Alberto Gomez	King's College London, UK
Matthias Heinrich	Universität zu Lübeck, Germany
Karim Lekadir	Stanford University, USA
Herve Lombaert	Inria, France
Bartlomiej Papiez	University of Oxford, UK
Francois Rousseau	Telecom Bretagne, France
Martin Urschler	Graz University of Technology, Austria
Wolfgang Wein	ImFusion GmbH, Germany

HVSMR: Program Committee

Polina Golland	Massachusetts Institute of Technology, USA
Terry Peters	Western University, Canada
Caroline Petitjean	University of Rouen, France
Martin Rajchl	Imperial College London, UK
Daniel Rueckert	Imperial College London, UK

Alistair Young   The University of Auckland, New Zealand
Xiahai Zhuang   Shanghai Jiao Tong University, China

Additional Reviewers

Jan Egger   Graz University of Technology, Austria
Vikash Gupta   University of Southern California, USA
Matthew Chung Hai Lee   Imperial College London, UK
Steven McDonagh   University of Edinburgh, UK

Contents

RAMBO: Registration

Point-Spread-Function-Aware Slice-to-Volume Registration: Application
to Upper Abdominal MRI Super-Resolution   3
   Michael Ebner, Manil Chouhan, Premal A. Patel, David Atkinson,
   Zahir Amin, Samantha Read, Shonit Punwani, Stuart Taylor,
   Tom Vercauteren, and Sébastien Ourselin

Motion Correction Using Subpixel Image Registration   14
   Amir HajiRassouliha, Andrew J. Taberner, Martyn P. Nash,
   and Poul M.F. Nielsen

Incompressible Phase Registration for Motion Estimation from Tagged
Magnetic Resonance Images   24
   Fangxu Xing, Jonghye Woo, Arnold D. Gomez, Dzung L. Pham,
   Philip V. Bayly, Maureen Stone, and Jerry L. Prince

RAMBO: Reconstruction

Robust Reconstruction of Accelerated Perfusion MRI Using Local
and Nonlocal Constraints   37
   Cagdas Ulas, Pedro A. Gómez, Felix Krahmer, Jonathan I. Sperl,
   Marion I. Menzel, and Bjoern H. Menze

Graph-Based 3D-Ultrasound Reconstruction of the Liver in the Presence
of Respiratory Motion   48
   Houssem-Eddine Gueziri, Sebastien Tremblay, Catherine Laporte,
   and Rupert Brooks

Whole-Heart Single Breath-Hold Cardiac Cine: A Robust
Motion-Compensated Compressed Sensing Reconstruction Method   58
   Javier Royuela-del-Val, Muhammad Usman, Lucilio Cordero-Grande,
   Marcos Martin-Fernandez, Federico Simmross-Wattenberg,
   Claudia Prieto, and Carlos Alberola-López

Motion Estimated-Compensated Reconstruction with Preserved-Features
in Free-Breathing Cardiac MRI   70
   Aurélien Bustin, Anne Menini, Martin A. Janich, Darius Burschka,
   Jacques Felblinger, Anja C.S. Brau, and Freddy Odille

RAMBO and HVSMR: Deep Learning for Heart Segmentation

Recurrent Fully Convolutional Neural Networks for Multi-slice MRI
Cardiac Segmentation   83
   Rudra P.K. Poudel, Pablo Lamata, and Giovanni Montana

Dilated Convolutional Neural Networks for Cardiovascular MR
Segmentation in Congenital Heart Disease   95
   Jelmer M. Wolterink, Tim Leiner, Max A. Viergever, and Ivana Išgum

3D FractalNet: Dense Volumetric Segmentation for Cardiovascular
MRI Volumes.   103
   Lequan Yu, Xin Yang, Jing Qin, and Pheng-Ann Heng

Automatic Whole-Heart Segmentation in Congenital Heart Disease
Using Deeply-Supervised 3D FCN   111
   Jinpeng Li, Rongzhao Zhang, Lin Shi, and Defeng Wang

RAMBO and HVSMR: Discrete Optimization and Probabilistic Intensity Modeling

A GPU Based Diffusion Method for Whole-Heart and Great
Vessel Segmentation   121
   Philipp Lösel and Vincent Heuveline

Fully-Automatic Segmentation of Cardiac Images Using 3-D MRF Model
Optimization and Substructures Tracking   129
   Georgios Tziritas

HSVMR: Atlas-Based Strategies

Strengths and Pitfalls of Whole-Heart Atlas-Based Segmentation
in Congenital Heart Disease Patients   139
   Maria A. Zuluaga, Benedetta Biffi, Andrew M. Taylor, Silvia Schievano,
   Tom Vercauteren, and Sébastien Ourselin

Automated Cardiovascular Segmentation in Patients with Congenital Heart
Disease from 3D CMR Scans: Combining Multi-atlases and Level-Sets   147
   Rahil Shahzad, Shan Gao, Qian Tao, Oleh Dzyubachyk,
   and Rob van der Geest

HSVMR: Random Forests

Automatic Heart and Vessel Segmentation Using Random Forests
and a Local Phase Guided Level Set Method   159
   Chunliang Wang, Qian Wang, and Örjan Smedby

Total Variation Random Forest: Fully Automatic MRI Segmentation
in Congenital Heart Diseases 165
    Anirban Mukhopadhyay

Author Index 173

RAMBO: Registration

Point-Spread-Function-Aware Slice-to-Volume Registration: Application to Upper Abdominal MRI Super-Resolution

Michael Ebner[1]([✉]), Manil Chouhan[2,3], Premal A. Patel[1,4],
David Atkinson[2], Zahir Amin[3], Samantha Read[3], Shonit Punwani[2,3],
Stuart Taylor[2,3], Tom Vercauteren[1], and Sébastien Ourselin[1]

[1] Translational Imaging Group, CMIC, University College London, London, UK
michael.ebner.14@ucl.ac.uk
[2] Centre for Medical Imaging, University College London, London, UK
[3] Radiology Department, University College London Hospitals
NHS Foundation Trust, London, UK
[4] Radiology Department, Great Ormond Street Hospital
for Children NHS Foundation Trust, London, UK
http://cmictig.cs.ucl.ac.uk

Abstract. MR image acquisition of moving organs remains challenging despite the advances in ultra-fast 2D MRI sequences. Post-acquisition techniques have been proposed to increase spatial resolution a posteriori by combining acquired orthogonal stacks into a single, high-resolution (HR) volume. Current super-resolution techniques classically rely on a two-step procedure. The volumetric reconstruction step leverages a physical slice acquisition model. However, the motion correction step typically neglects the point spread function (PSF) information. In this paper, we propose a PSF-aware slice-to-volume registration approach and, for the first time, demonstrate the potential benefit of Super-Resolution for upper abdominal imaging. Our novel reconstruction pipeline takes advantage of different MR acquisitions clinically used in routine MR cholangio-pancreatography studies to guide the registration. On evaluation of clinically relevant image information, our approach outperforms state-of-the-art reconstruction toolkits in terms of visual clarity and preservation of raw data information. Overall, we achieve promising results towards replacing currently required CT scans.

Keywords: Super-resolution reconstruction · Point spread function · Registration · Scattered data approximation · MRCP study

1 Introduction

In recent years, volumetric magnetic resonance (MR) reconstruction and analysis of moving body organs have attracted increasing clinical interest in numerous areas where subject motion cannot be avoided but the excellent tissue contrast of MR imaging (MRI) is still required. In this context, ultra-fast 2D MRI is

© Springer International Publishing AG 2017
M.A. Zuluaga et al. (Eds.): RAMBO 2016/HVSMR 2016, LNCS 10129, pp. 3–13, 2017.
DOI: 10.1007/978-3-319-52280-7_1

the method of choice for many applications [7,13,15]. However, a balance has to be struck between a short scanning time to avoid motion artefacts, and the signal-to-noise ratio which must be maintained at an acceptable level.

MR cholangio-pancreatography (MRCP) is one typical use of ultra-fast 2D MR and provides a series of sequences to define the upper gastrointestinal tract and particularly the biliary anatomy [1]. Typically, one axial and one coronal single-shot T2-weighted stack of low-resolution (LR) slices are acquired at inhaled breath-hold. Even though this provides valuable anatomical information, the anisotropic voxel dimensions with their inherently large slice thickness come at a cost. Small structures relevant for clinical diagnosis can be obscured due to partial volume averaging effects (PVEs). Inter-slice motion during image acquisition also limits geometric integrity of the corresponding stack of bundled slices. Additionally, a heavily T2-weighted volume, gated by respiratory motion, is acquired at high resolution. The gain in resolution of liquid-filled structures comes at the cost of structural information from the surrounding structures compared to single-shot slice, as shown in Fig. 1. Consequently, MR alone may not be sufficient for diagnosis and additional contrast-enhanced computed tomography (CT) imaging at higher resolution is performed. However, CT does not have the inherent high soft tissue contrast resolution available on T2-weighted MRI and carries risks of radiation exposure, iodinated contrast exposure and the need for additional investigation increases healthcare costs.

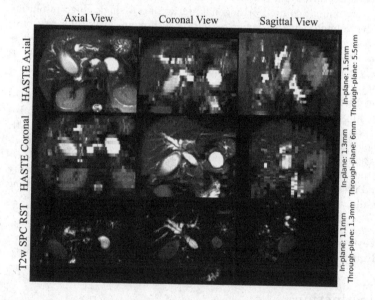

Fig. 1. Visualization of typical MR data acquired in MRCP studies showing anatomy of the biliary tree. Motion is visible throughout the HASTE stacks. The heavily T2-weighted volume (T2w SPC RST) has approximately five times higher resolution compared to the HASTE through-plane direction. However, the heavily T2-weighted volume loses valuable tissue contrast in the surrounding anatomy.

Recent advances in image post-processing have demonstrated the potential to increase the resolution a posteriori by combining several orthogonal MRI stacks of LR 2D slices into a single, HR 3D volume – a method called *Super-Resolution Reconstruction* (SRR). Its application ranges from adult studies on the tongue [15] and thorax [13] to fetal applications [7,10]. To our knowledge, Super-Resolution (SR) has not yet been applied to MRCP studies to define upper gastrointestinal tract and biliary anatomy. An SRR technique needs to overcome several challenges in this context. Firstly, stacks are acquired consecutively and cannot be regarded as motion-free given the non-periodic respiratory motion [8], tissue deformation due to cardiac motion and arterial pulsation, peristaltic and other complex motion affecting the upper gastrointestinal anatomy, as shown in Fig. 1. Secondly, accurate registration and reconstruction are complicated by the fact that in current clinical protocols usually only two single-shot T2-weighted stacks are available (in axial and coronal planes) with a slice thickness approximately five times higher than the in-plane resolution. Existing respiratory motion models require the availability of respiratory surrogate data [8] which are currently not available for MRCP studies. Using an SRR approach such as the iterative two-step registration-reconstruction approach used in fetal MRI [7,10], applied to only two stacks, is prone to generate a strongly biased volume and the currently used rigid motion models might not be sufficient. Additionally, current motion correction techniques do not take into account the PSF for registration. This is particularly problematic since neglecting the PSF during resampling introduces aliasing and subsequently results in additional loss of information [2,3].

In this paper, our contributions are three-fold: (i) introduction of a novel PSF-aware slice-to-volume registration (SVR) method which takes into consideration the physical slice acquisition process, (ii) use of a novel SRR framework to reconstruct upper abdominal MRI using a single, consistent model to incorporate the PSF in both registration and reconstruction steps and (iii) novel use of an existing heavily T2-weighted volume available in MRCP studies to guide registration.

2   PSF-Aware Slice-to-Volume Registration for SRR

In this section, we describe the proposed framework for reconstructing the upper abdominal anatomy based on two orthogonal single-shot T2-weighted stacks and a heavily T2-weighted volume ("3D reference") to guide the motion correction. We use a single, uniform approach which incorporates a PSF-aware model for both the registration and reconstruction steps. Additionally, we apply an efficient scattered data approximation approach to initialize the SRR algorithm with a regular grid volume from scattered slices.

Slice Acquisition Model and Algorithm Overview. Starting from the classical slice acquisition model [5,7]

$$\mathbf{y}_k = \mathbf{D}_k\,\mathbf{B}_k\,\mathbf{W}_k\,\mathbf{x} + \mathbf{n}_k \tag{1}$$

a relationship between the (vectorized) acquired LR 2D slice $\mathbf{y}_k \in \mathbb{R}^{N_k}$ and the unknown (vectorized) HR volume $\mathbf{x} \in \mathbb{R}^N$ can be established whereby $N_k \ll N$ due to the LR 2D image acquisition. The remaining variables in (1) include the linear downsampling operator $\mathbf{D}_k$, the linear blurring operator $\mathbf{B}_k$ carrying the PSF information, the linear motion operator $\mathbf{W}_k$ and the image noise $\mathbf{n}_k \in \mathbb{R}^N$ for each slice $k \in \{1, \ldots, K\}$, respectively.

The following is assumed: (i) the resolution of the heavily T2-weighted volume is sufficiently high to act as a 3D reference volume, (ii) the occurring deformation can be captured by deforming the slice only in the in-plane direction; the contribution in the orthogonal slice-select direction can therefore be neglected given the thick slices and the associated intensity information uncertainty due to PVEs. Based on those assumptions, we propose the following non-iterative 3-step motion correction algorithm for upper abdominal anatomy whereby each step fully respects the assumed physical acquisition model (1):

1. Multimodal volume-to-volume registration: Rigid registration is applied between each stack and the 3D reference.
2. Multimodal slice-to-volume registration: Each individual slice of each stack is rigidly registered to the 3D reference.
3. In-plane deformation: Based on the intersection of the slices with the 3D reference, each slice is deformed in-plane to compensate for non-rigid deformations.

A volumetric reconstruction based on Tikhonov regularization is then applied. In summary, the algorithm only requires one motion correction cycle consisting of three steps to register the slices with the heavily T2-weighted volume before one SRR step is performed to reconstruct a single, isotropic HR volume from motion corrected, scattered, single-shot slices.

Point-Spread-Function-Aware Slice-to-Volume Registration. The intent of using a PSF-aware registration is to blur the moving image (3D reference) with the PSF defined by the relative position between fixed image (LR 2D slice) and moving image in order to make them comparable during the registration process [2,3]. However, although the classical slice acquisition model provides an intuitive understanding about the physical process, the direct computation with the large matrices involved would cause a substantial memory cost even for sparse representation. Avoiding the explicit storage of matrix-coefficients allows for a more efficient iterative computational scheme [4]. Therefore, we chose to represent (1) *pointwise* as a *matrix-free* formulation

$$\mathbf{y}_k(i) = A_k(i, \mathbf{x}) \in \mathbb{R} \quad \text{for all} \quad i = 1, \ldots, N_k \tag{2}$$

with a linear operator $A_k(i, \cdot)$ acting as PSF-defined intensity interpolator in the floating space at a (transformed) physical position of voxel i of slice $\mathbf{y}_k$. The PSF itself is defined by the MR acquisition protocol. In practice, a reasonable approximation for single-shot sequences in the slice-coordinate system has been found to be a 3D Gaussian defined by the variance-covariance matrix $\widetilde{\mathbf{B}}_k := \operatorname{diag}\left(\frac{(1.2\,s_1)^2}{8\ln(2)}, \frac{(1.2\,s_2)^2}{8\ln(2)}, \frac{s_3^2}{8\ln(2)}\right)$ with s_1, s_2 being the spacing in-plane and s_3 through-plane [2,6]. For the registration, this variance-covariance matrix needs to be expressed in the coordinate system of the moving image in order to accommodate the interpolation in the moving space accordingly. Slices are rigidly motion corrected to find the best rigid motion estimate within the 3D reference before the non-rigid deformation step is applied. Hence, a basis transform with orthogonal matrix $\mathbf{U}_k$, accounting for the rotation between the LR slice and the HR volume, expresses the PSF by $\mathbf{U}_k^T \widetilde{\mathbf{B}}_k \mathbf{U}_k$ for each single point with respect to the floating space. That means, a PSF-aware SVR can be implemented by providing an *oriented Gaussian interpolator* A_k for each slice k to a generic registration framework which updates the PSF depending on the current transformation parameters. The operation $A_k(i, \cdot)$ can be efficiently computed as a matrix-vector multiplication without storing a matrix explicitly by iterating over the $N_k \ll N$ voxels in a multi-threaded fashion while considering the oriented Gaussian-weighted 3D reference volume voxel intensities.

Similarly, the multimodal volume-to-volume registration is made PSF-aware by blurring the 3D reference with an oriented Gaussian filter considering the PSF defined by slice-select direction and slice dimensions for each stack.

Super-Resolution Reconstruction. Once the slices are PSF-aware motion corrected, a reconstruction step based on (1) and similar to that described by [5] can be deployed. With a mask operator $\mathbf{M}_k$ used to select the region of interest within each slice k, the minimization problem reads

$$\min_{\mathbf{x}} \left(\sum_{k=1}^{K} \frac{1}{2} \|\mathbf{M}_k(\mathbf{y}_k - \mathbf{A}_k \mathbf{x})\|_{\ell^2}^2 + \frac{\alpha}{2} \|\mathbf{D}\mathbf{x}\|_{\ell^2}^2 \right) \quad \text{subject to} \quad \mathbf{x} \geq 0 \qquad (3)$$

where $\mathbf{A}_k \mathbf{x}$ denotes the application of (2) stacked to a vector in $\mathbb{R}^{N_k}$, α the regularization parameter and $\mathbf{D}$ the differential operator applied on the HR reconstruction estimate $\mathbf{x}$. In this application, we chose a L-BFGS-B algorithm to deal with this large linear system and its positivity constraints to solve the corresponding normal equations. The required adjoint oriented Gaussian operator $\mathbf{A}_k^*$ can be computed in a similar matrix-free fashion as $\mathbf{A}_k$, which can be shown by elementary transformations. Using a first-order Tikhonov regularization term in (3) has the advantage of introducing a correlation between neighbouring voxels, which is especially useful since only two orthogonal stacks with thick slices are available and it is likely that certain areas of the volume are not sufficiently sampled after having registered each slice individually to the 3D reference.

Scattered Data Approximation. In order to initialize the SRR solver with a regular grid volume from motion corrected slices we propose a *scattered data approximation* (SDA) approach. We use a discrete variant of Nadaraya-Watson kernel regression as an efficient SDA scheme for irregularly sampled inputs [14].

It is based on nearest neighbour sampling onto a regular grid followed by a subsequent Gaussian blurring operation for each single slice.

3   Data, Evaluation Methodology and Results

Data and Data Preprocessing. MRCP studies of four anonymized patients, scanned at the University College London Hospital, London, were used for this study. Among the clinically acquired scans for MRCP studies, a set of axial and coronal 2D HASTE sequences and a 3D heavily T2-weighted SPC RST volume acquisition were performed, as shown in Fig. 1. The acquisition parameters for the coronal stack were TE = 91 ms, TR = 1350 ms, flip angle of 170° with resolution of 1.25 mm × 1.25 mm × 6 mm. The respective parameters for the axial stack were TE = 91 ms, TR = 1200 ms, flip angle of 160° with resolution of 1.48 mm × 1.48 mm × 5.50 mm. The heavily T2-weighted volume was acquired in coronal direction with dimensions of 1.09 mm × 1.09 mm × 1.30 mm. HASTE images were preprocessed via an ITK bias field correction filter step [12]. Rectangular masks were provided for both axial and coronal stacks to mark a region of clinical interest.

Parametrization of Reconstruction Pipeline. Both the multimodal volume-to-volume and slice-to-volume PSF-aware registration approaches use mutual information as the similarity measure and are implemented in ITK. The PSF-aware in-plane deformation was performed with the NiftyReg software using a fast free-form deformation algorithm [9]. Given the different acquisition parameters of the HASTE sequences, a linear model was used for intensity normalization prior to the volumetric reconstruction. The corresponding SRR step was performed with the regularization parameter $\alpha = 0.03$ selected via L-curve studies. The initial value was computed by the SDA approach with $\sigma = 4$ to avoid the problem of inpainting during SRR.

Evaluation Methodology. The algorithm was run with and without the consideration of the oriented PSF for all registration steps (PSF_0 or PSF_1) and with and without usage of the in-plane deformation model (DM_0 or DM_1) resulting in four different reconstructions for analysis. The reconstructions were initially quantitatively assessed by evaluating the residual via a normalized cross correlation metric, instead of the ℓ^2-norm, in order to be insensitive to the intensity normalization step used to compensate for the different acquisition protocols. Following this, subjective assessment in a clinical context was made including direct comparison to reconstructions obtained by open-source toolkits successfully employed in the challenging problem of fetal MRI reconstructions (BTK-toolkit [11], version from 6 Jan 2016, and the IRTK-based toolkit [7], version from 11 Jun 2015). Two radiologists, blinded to the reconstruction methods, individually assessed reconstruction side-by-side and in comparison to the original HASTE data. The final score is a joint agreement of the radiologists' individual results. Scores were given for:

1. Clinical usefulness: based on how well common bile duct (CBD), left and right hepatic duct (LHD & RHD) were visualized and the degree of visible motion artefacts
2. Reconstruction quality: inferred by assessment of preservation of original structural information and the amount of additionally introduced artefactual structures
3. Radiologists' preferred reconstruction

Results. The evaluation of the residuals (1) for all four subjects are visualized in Fig. 2. The best agreement between the observed slice y_k and simulated slice $M_k A_k x$ was obtained for the reconstruction which used the most comprehensive model including PSF-aware registration and in-plane deformable model ($PSF_1 DM_1$). This is confirmed by calculating the mean of the residuals which rank $PSF_1 DM_1$ ahead of all other variants. $PSF_1 DM_1$ yields consistently better agreement for subjects 3 and 4 compared to other approaches which show less accurate registration results for some slices.

The radiologists' evaluation, shown in Table 1, indicates that the blinded radiologists had a clear preference for our novel PSF-aware SVR reconstructions. Additionally, our proposed reconstruction framework yields reconstructions of similar clarity of CBD, LHD and RHD as the original HASTE data. The reconstructions obtained via IRTK score slightly lower and it was felt that the images would not be suitable for making a clinical diagnosis. Furthermore, all reconstruction approaches demonstrate their ability to correct for motion visible in the HASTE data. With regards to preservation of information in the original HASTE stacks, our novel PSF-aware SVR reconstructions are close to the originals' whereas IRTK and BTK[1] perform less satisfactorily. All reconstruction methods, to some degree, introduce structures which cannot be directly visualized by the original HASTE data.

In Fig. 3 our reconstruction variant $PSF_1 DM_1$ and the reconstructions based on IRTK and BTK of one subject are provided along with the linearly resampled original data for comparison. This demonstrates that our proposed reconstruction framework largely preserves axial and coronal HASTE data information with minor degradation in image quality as opposed to both IRTK and BTK reconstructions. Moreover, it reveals sharp tissue delineation also in sagittal section where no image stack information is provided.

4   Discussion

In this work, we present for the first time a single, consistent SRR framework which takes into consideration the PSF for both the motion correction and volumetric reconstruction steps. We put a particular focus on efficient implementation details like the matrix-free approach to efficiently compute the oriented

---

[1] The BTK-results used in here do not include the SRR step. Using the standard parametrization of BTK, the SRR outcome was less satisfying and of poorer quality than the reconstruction obtained via local neighbourhood oriented Gaussian interpolation [10].

Gaussian and adjoint oriented Gaussian operators for slice-to-volume registration and the PSF-aware volume-to-volume registration step. We test our framework by reconstructing upper abdominal MRI purely based on existing data available in current clinical MRCP studies. We propose a novel motion correction approach by using the existing heavily T2-weighted volume to guide the slice-to-volume registration to address the challenge of having only two orthogonal stacks with thick slices affected by deformable motion. Despite the high degree of undersampling, we achieve remarkable results which outperform current state-of-the-art techniques developed for fetal MRI, as shown in Fig. 3. Further improvements in the current implementation include the incorporation of the oriented PSF for the gradient computation. This shortcoming could also describe the drop in accuracy for some slices observed in Fig. 2. Overall, the obtained results are promising and may have the potential to avoid CT scans for further evaluation of this area. Existing limitations are assuming and only accounting for in-plane deformation and sparseness of available data. In the future, we expect to make further improvements using more orthogonal stacks for higher anatomy sampling in combination with a more refined motion model. This will also allow increasing the field of view of the reconstruction to assess the entire biliary tree of clinical interest.

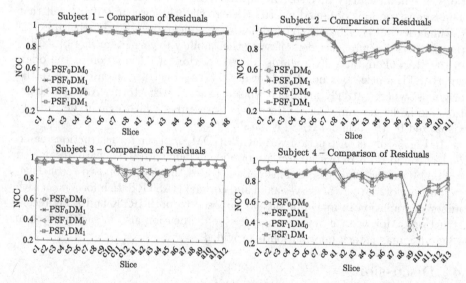

Fig. 2. Evaluation of the residuals for all subjects and modes of our proposed reconstruction framework visualized for all axial slices (a) and coronal slices (c). The associated NCC mean and standard deviation over all subjects for each mode are 0.88 ± 0.10 for PSF_0DM_0, 0.89 ± 0.08 for PSF_0DM_1, 0.88 ± 0.11 for PSF_1DM_0 and 0.90 ± 0.08 for PSF_1DM_1, respectively.

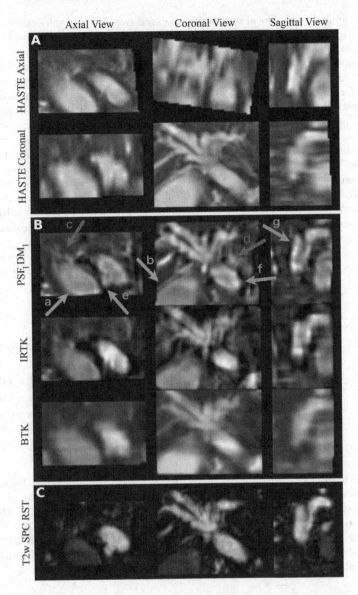

Fig. 3. Qualitative comparison between linearly resampled original HASTE data (A) and reconstructions obtained by BTK, IRTK and our proposed approach (B). Reconstructions are based on one axial and one coronal HASTE stack only. Several arrows on our reconstruction show examples of successfully preserved raw data information (blue *a* and *b*), introduction of artefacts (red *c* and *d*) and resolution improvement (green *e*, *f* and *g*) in direct comparison with the other reconstruction approaches. Artefacts are explained by similar intensities in the original data (*c*) in addition to the complex deformation occurred between axial and coronal stack acquisition (*d*). Resolution improvement was achieved by the combined usage of SR and the incorporated heavily T2-weighted volume information (C) as reference during motion correction. (Color figure online)

Table 1. Summary of clinical evaluation averaged over all four subjects. Evaluation included original HASTE data, four modes of our proposed reconstruction framework and reconstructions by other toolkits (BTK, IRTK). Clarity of anatomical structure score indicates how well CBD, LHD and RHD are visualized in each image with ratings 0 (structure not seen), 1 (poor depiction), 2 (suboptimal visualization; image not adequate for diagnostic purposes), 3 (clear visualization of structure but reduced tissue contrast; image-based diagnosis feasible) and 4 (excellent depiction; optimal for diagnostic purposes). Visible motion score rates the amount of visible non-corrected motion from score 0 (complete motion) to 3 (no motion). Preserved structural information score indicates how well original HASTE data information has been preserved with grades 0 (structures not identified), 1 (poor visualization of structures), 2 (clear visualization but not as good as originals) and 3 (as good as original). Introduced artefacts score rates the amount of additional artefactual structures from 0 (lots of new artefacts) to 2 (no new artefact). Radiologists' preference ranks the subjectively preferred reconstructions from 1 (least preferred) to 6 (most preferred) reconstruction.

	Clinical usefulness		Reconstruction quality		Radiologists' preference
	Clarity of anatomical structures	Visible motion	Preserved structural information	Introduced artefacts	
HASTE Ax & Cor	2.9 ± 0.3	1.8 ± 0.5	—	—	—
PSF_0DM_0	2.9 ± 0.3	2.8 ± 0.5	2.0 ± 0.0	0.8 ± 0.5	4.2 ± 0.9
PSF_0DM_1	2.9 ± 0.3	2.5 ± 0.5	1.8 ± 0.5	1.0 ± 0.0	5.5 ± 1.0
PSF_1DM_0	2.9 ± 0.3	2.8 ± 0.5	2.0 ± 0.0	0.5 ± 0.5	3.5 ± 1.0
PSF_1DM_1	2.9 ± 0.3	2.8 ± 0.5	2.0 ± 0.0	0.5 ± 0.5	4.5 ± 0.5
IRTK	2.4 ± 0.5	2.8 ± 0.5	1.2 ± 0.1	0.0 ± 0.0	1.8 ± 0.5
BTK	1.9 ± 0.3	2.0 ± 0.0	1.0 ± 0.0	1.0 ± 0.0	1.2 ± 0.5

Acknowledgements. This work is supported by the EPSRC-funded UCL Centre for Doctoral Training in Medical Imaging (EP/L016478/1), the Department of Healths NIHR-funded Biomedical Research Centre at University College London Hospitals and Innovative Engineering for Health award by the Wellcome Trust [WT101957] and Engineering and Physical Sciences Research Council (EPSRC) [NS/A000027/1]. Furthermore, this work was funded by NIHR Clinical Lectureship and NIHR Senior Investigator grant.

References

1. Barish, M.A., Yucel, E.K., Ferrucci, J.T.: Magnetic resonance cholangiopancreatography. N. Engl. J. Med. **341**(4), 258–264 (1999)
2. Cardoso, M.J., Modat, M., Vercauteren, T., Ourselin, S.: Scale factor point spread function matching: beyond aliasing in image resampling. In: Navab, N., et al. (eds.) MICCAI 2015. LNCS, vol. 9350, pp. 675–683. Springer, Cham (2015)
3. Chacko, N., Chan, K.G., Liebling, M.: Intensity-based point-spread-function-aware registration for multi-view applications in optical microscopy. In: 2015 IEEE 12th International Symposium on Biomedical Imaging (ISBI), pp. 306–309. IEEE (2015)

4. Diamond, S., Boyd, S.: Convex optimization with abstract linear operators. In: IEEE International Conference on Computer Vision (ICCV), pp. 675–683, no. 1. IEEE (2015)
5. Gholipour, A., Estroff, J.A., Warfield, S.K.: Robust super-resolution volume reconstruction from slice acquisitions: application to fetal brain MRI. IEEE Trans. Med. Imaging **29**(10), 1739–1758 (2010)
6. Jiang, S., Xue, H., Glover, A., Rutherford, M., Rueckert, D., Hajnal, J.V.: MRI of moving subjects using multislice snapshot images with volume reconstruction (SVR): application to fetal, neonatal, and adult brain studies. IEEE Trans. Med. Imaging **26**(7), 967–980 (2007)
7. Kainz, B., Steinberger, M., Wein, W., Kuklisova-Murgasova, M., Malamateniou, C., Keraudren, K., Torsney-Weir, T., Rutherford, M., Aljabar, P., Hajnal, J.V., Rueckert, D.: Fast volume reconstruction from motion corrupted stacks of 2D slices. IEEE Trans. Med. Imaging **34**(9), 1901–1913 (2015)
8. McClelland, J.R., Hawkes, D.J., Schaeffter, T., King, A.P.: Respiratory motion models: a review. Med. Image Anal. **17**(1), 19–42 (2013)
9. Modat, M., Ridgway, G.R., Taylor, Z.A., Lehmann, M., Barnes, J., Hawkes, D.J., Fox, N.C., Ourselin, S.: Fast free-form deformation using graphics processing units. Comput. Methods Program. Biomed. **98**(3), 278–284 (2010)
10. Rousseau, F., Glenn, O.A., Iordanova, B., Rodriguez-Carranza, C., Vigneron, D.B., Barkovich, J.A., Studholme, C.: Registration-based approach for reconstruction of high-resolution in utero fetal MR brain images. Acad. Radiol. **13**(9), 1072–1081 (2006)
11. Rousseau, F., Oubel, E., Pontabry, J., Schweitzer, M., Studholme, C., Koob, M., Dietemann, J.L.: BTK: an open-source toolkit for fetal brain MR image processing. Comput. Methods Program. Biomed. **109**(1), 65–73 (2013)
12. Tustison, N.J., Avants, B.B., Cook, P.A., Zheng, Y., Egan, A., Yushkevich, P.A., Gee, J.C.: N4ITK: improved N3 bias correction. IEEE Trans. Med. Imaging **29**(6), 1310–1320 (2010)
13. Van Reeth, E., Tan, C.H., Tham, I.W., Poh, C.L.: Isotropic reconstruction of a 4-D MRI thoracic sequence using super-resolution. Magn. Reson. Med. **73**(2), 784–793 (2015)
14. Vercauteren, T., Perchant, A., Malandain, G., Pennec, X., Ayache, N.: Robust mosaicing with correction of motion distortions and tissue deformations for in vivo fibered microscopy. Med. Image Anal. **10**(5), 673–692 (2006)
15. Woo, J., Murano, E.Z., Stone, M., Prince, J.L.: Reconstruction of high-resolution tongue volumes from MRI. IEEE Trans. Biomed. Eng. **59**(12), 3511–3524 (2012)

Motion Correction Using Subpixel Image Registration

Amir HajiRassouliha[1]([⊠]), Andrew J. Taberner[1,2], Martyn P. Nash[1,2],
and Poul M.F. Nielsen[1,2]

[1] Auckland Bioengineering Institute (ABI),
The University of Auckland, Auckland, New Zealand
ahaj975@aucklanduni.ac.nz
[2] Department of Engineering Science,
The University of Auckland, Auckland, New Zealand

Abstract. Several methods have been proposed to correct motion in medical and non-medical applications, such as optical flow measurements, particle filter tracking, and image registration. In this paper, we designed experiments to test the accuracy and robustness of a recently proposed algorithm for subpixel image registration. In this case, the algorithm is used to correct the relative motion of the object and camera in pairs of images. This recent algorithm (named phase-based Savitzky-Golay gradient-correlation (P-SG-GC)) can achieve very high accuracies in finding synthetically applied translational shifts.

Experiments were performed using a camera, a flat object, a manual translational stage, and a manual rotational stage. The P-SG-GC algorithm was used to detect the flat object motion from the initial and shifted images for a set of control points on the surface of the object, which were automatically matched in subimages of 128 pixel $\times$ 128 pixel. A least-squares method was used to estimate the image transformation matrix that can register the shifted image to the initial image.

The results demonstrated that the P-SG-GC algorithm can accurately correct for the relative motion of the object and camera for a large range of applied shifts with a registration error less than 1 pixel. Furthermore, the P-SG-GC algorithm could detect the images in which the motion could not be corrected due to poorly matched control points between the initial and shifted images. We conclude that the P-SG-GC algorithm is an accurate and reliable algorithm that can be used to correct for object or camera motion.

Keywords: Motion correction · Subpixel image registration · Translational tests · Rotational tests

1 Introduction

Motion artefacts between pairs of images can arise due to unwanted movements of either the imaging device or the imaging target. Motion artefacts are problematic in many applications. In medical images, breathing and movement of patients can cause distortions and artefacts that can confound diagnosis. Motion artefacts are also an issue in camera-based systems, especially where it is necessary to have a stabilised recording.

© Springer International Publishing AG 2017
M.A. Zuluaga et al. (Eds.): RAMBO 2016/HVSMR 2016, LNCS 10129, pp. 14–23, 2017.
DOI: 10.1007/978-3-319-52280-7_2

For example, the use of a hand-held stereoscopic device (such as [1]) to record surface deformations of living skin is challenging, due to movement of the subjects' limbs or the stereoscopic device. Correcting for such relative motion can improve the analysis of medical images and can increase the accuracy of measurements. For example, human knee cartilage mapping was improved after motion correction [2]. Motion correction has been performed using several methods, such as optical flow [3], particle filter tracking [4], adaptive block motion vectors filtering [5], and, most commonly, image registration [6–11]. However, most of the existing methods for subpixel image registration lack accuracy or robustness to large shifts. To address these limitations, a new method for subpixel image registration has been recently proposed by HajiRassouliha et al. [12]. This is a phase-based method that uses Savitzky-Golay differentiators in gradient correlation (P-SG-GC) [12]. The P-SG-GC algorithm can achieve high accuracies in finding synthetically applied shifts. The registration error of this algorithm was shown to be less than 0.0002 pixel, which is 60 times better than state-of-the-art algorithms [12]. Furthermore, the P-SG-GC algorithm is computationally efficient and performs well in low-textured images [12], which makes it suitable for motion correction in real-time applications.

In this study, a variety of manual translational and rotational shifts were applied to a flat object, which was imaged using a camera. The relative shifts between pairs of images were estimated using the P-SG-GC algorithm in a set of control points (centres of subimages of size 128 pixel × 128 pixel) in the initial and shifted images. The displacements of these control points were used to estimate the image transformation matrix using a least-squares method. Each shifted image was registered to the initial image and the registration error was calculated to indicate the accuracy of the P-SG-GC algorithm in correcting the motion.

2   Method

Figure 1 shows the experimental setup used to test the ability of the P-SG-GC algorithm in measuring rigid motion. A single monochrome CMOS USB 3 camera (Flea3 FL3-U3-13Y3 M-C, Point Grey, Canada) equipped with a 12.5 mm lens was attached to a photographic stand in a position perpendicular to the surface of a flat target object. The target was attached to a manual linear translational stage, which was itself attached to a manual rotational stage. The combination of the two stages enabled the application of rigid in-plane shifts to the target, and the camera stand enabled moving the camera in the direction perpendicular to the surface of the object (Fig. 1) to provide a scaling effect in the camera images.

The following five experiments (E1 to E5) were designed and performed to test the ability of the P-SG-GC algorithm in detecting and measuring the relative motion of the target and camera:

E1. Translational shifts of the target: the target was shifted at 1 mm steps to a maximum of 5 mm (i.e. five translational shift values) using the translational stage.
E2. Rotational shifts of the target: The target was rotated at 0.5° steps to a maximum of 3° (i.e. six rotational shift values) using the rotational stage.

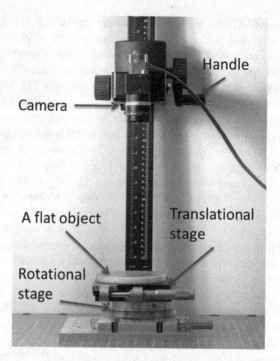

Fig. 1. The experimental setup

E3. Translational and rotational shifts of the target: the target was shifted at 1 mm
    steps, and at each step was rotated by 0.25° to a maximum of 5 mm and 1.25° (i.e.
    five combinations of rotational and translational shift values) using the transla-
    tional and rotational stages.
E4. Translational shifts of the camera: the camera was shifted in the direction per-
    pendicular to the surface of the target at 2 mm steps to a maximum of 10 mm (i.e.
    to provide five scaling effects) using the photographic stand handle (Fig. 1).
E5. Translational shifts of the camera and the target: the camera was shifted as
    described in E4, but at 1 mm steps, and at each step 0.5 mm translational shifts
    were applied to the target using the translational stage (i.e. to provide five com-
    binations of scaling and translation).

The images of E1 to E5 were divided into subimages of size 128 pixel × 128 pixel to
measure localised motion of the object. These subimages were distributed uniformly
across the surface of the target with a step increment of 20 pixel. The subimage size
determines the maximum shift that the algorithm could identify. The number of steps
and the maximum shift values in E1 to E5 were chosen according to the pixel size, the
subimage size, and the ability of the P-SG-GC algorithm in estimating that type of
motion. Note that this algorithm was developed for registration of images with translational shifts, but here was tested in a wider set of test conditions.

In the first step, the P-SG-GC algorithm was used to measure shifts between all
subimages of the initial and shifted images in the x and y directions (d_x and d_y) at each

step of E1 to E5. The centres of the subimages in the initial image (C_s) were considered as control points. Thus, the corresponding control points (i.e. centres of subimages) in the shifted image (C_s) are given by Eq. 1.

$$C_s(n)\begin{bmatrix} x \\ y \end{bmatrix} = C_i(n)\begin{bmatrix} x \\ y \end{bmatrix} + \begin{bmatrix} d_x(n) \\ d_y(n) \end{bmatrix} \quad (n \in \{1, 2, \ldots, N\}) \tag{1}$$

where, n is the subimage number, and N is the total number of subimages. The accuracy of the P-SG-GC algorithm in estimating d_x and d_y values for subimages of an image (and consequently $C_s(n)$) depends on several factors, including the subimage texture level, the magnitude of subimage shift, and the nature of the shift between the subimages. The integer error metric of the P-SG-GC algorithm (defined in [12]) was used as an indication of the level of confidence in estimating the shift between subimages. The threshold value of the integer error was set to 4 to provide an acceptable accuracy, and the control points with an error less than this threshold were considered as control points with a precise match (i.e. $\hat{C}_s(n)$ and $\hat{C}_i(n)$).

The next step for correcting the motion between the initial and the shifted images is to find a geometric image transformation (T) that registers the images. Equation 2 shows the relation between the control points in the initial and the shifted image that can be used for registration [13].

$$\hat{C}_s(n)\begin{bmatrix} x \\ y \\ 1 \end{bmatrix} = T \times \hat{C}_i(n)\begin{bmatrix} x \\ y \\ 1 \end{bmatrix} \quad (n \in \{1, 2, \ldots, M\}) \tag{2}$$

where, T is a 3×3 matrix given in Eq. 3 [13], and M is the number of subimages that had an acceptable match (i.e. integer errors less than 4).

$$T = \begin{bmatrix} a_1 & a_2 & a_3 \\ a_4 & a_5 & a_6 \\ a_7 & a_8 & 1 \end{bmatrix} \tag{3}$$

In the transformation matrix, T, $\begin{bmatrix} a_3 \\ a_6 \end{bmatrix}$ is the translation vector, $[a_7, a_8]$ is the projection vector, and $\begin{bmatrix} a_1 & a_2 \\ a_4 & a_5 \end{bmatrix}$ defines rotation, scaling and shearing [13]. The values of these elements identify the type of transformation, i.e. rigid, similarity, affine, projective, or some combination of these transformation types. Considering the applied shifts in E1 to E5, affine and projective image transformations are suitable for the registration of the images in this study. Affine transformations are able to describe translational, rotational, scaling, and shearing differences between the images. However, the projection vector is zero for affine transformations, so they preserve the parallelism between lines and cannot correct perspective effects. This issue was solved in projective transformations by adding the projection vector to the transformation matrix of affine transformations. Therefore, projective transformations are able to correct perspective effects, at the cost of introducing two additional parameters to the projection vector (i.e.

$[a_7, a_8]$). The elements of T ($[a_1, \ldots, a_8]$) were estimated using a least-squares method based on control points from the initial and shifted images. The least-squares method was only used for the images in which the percentage of the control points with an integer error less than 4 ($\hat{C}_s(n)$ and $\hat{C}_i(n)$) was more than 80% of the total number of control points ($C_s(n)$ and $C_i(n)$). Otherwise, this method detects the insufficiency of precise control points for finding an accurate transformation. This will help to avoid an incorrect registration of the images.

Two methods were used to assess the accuracy of registration between the initial and shifted images. The first method was a qualitative assessment performed by overlaying the registered and the initial images and subtracting their intensity values. The second method was a quantitative method for estimating the registration error. The 2D subpixel displacements (D) between the control points of the registered and the initial images ($\hat{C}_s(n)$ and $\hat{C}_i(n)$) were estimated using Eq. 4, and were averaged in all the subimages to find the registration error (Eq. 5).

$$D(n) = \sqrt{d_x^2 + d_y^2} \ (pixel) \quad (n \in \{1, 2, \ldots, M\}) \tag{4}$$

$$RE = \frac{\sum_{n=1}^{M} D(n)}{M} \ (pixel) \tag{5}$$

The accuracy of motion correction in a camera system is effected by optical distortions of the camera lens, especially the radial distortion [14]. Lens distortion causes non-uniform pixel displacements over the image. Thus, the appearance of an object changes when the object is positioned in different locations of a camera image. This effect becomes evident in the estimation of registration error. We reduced this effect by undistorting the images using radial and tangential lens distortion coefficients estimated through a camera calibration process [14].

3   Results and Discussion

The results of experiments E1 to E5 are presented in Figs. 2, 3, 4, 5 and 6. In each figure, the initial image and the final image for that experiment were overlaid following and prior to correction to provide a qualitative indication of the accuracy of the P-SG-GC algorithm in correcting for the relative motion of the target and camera. The intensity values of the initial and the final images for each experiment were subtracted and were colour-coded with and without motion correction to illustrate the effect of motion correction. The registration error (Eq. 5) was found at each step of experiments E1 to E5, and is provided as a quantitative estimate of the accuracy of the P-SG-GC algorithm. The vertical axis of the graphs in Figs. 2, 3, 4, 5 and 6(e) shows the average displacement of all subimages for that particular applied shift. In the final image of E3, the control points with an integer error less than 4 ($\hat{C}_s(n)$ and $\hat{C}_i(n)$) were less than 80% of the total number of control points. The P-SG-GC algorithm could thus detect the insufficiency of control points for correcting the motion in this case. For this reason, the result of the final image of this experiment is not presented in Fig. 4.

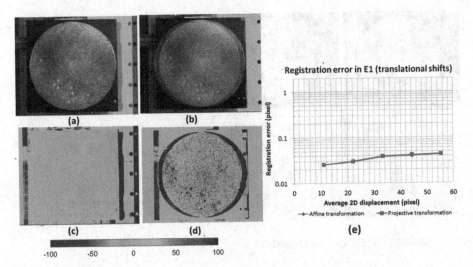

Fig. 2. The results of the translational shift in experiment E1. The final image for this experiment (5 mm shift of the target) is overlaid on the initial image with (a) and without (b) motion correction. The subtraction of the intensity values for the initial and final images with and without motion correction is shown in (c) and (d), respectively, and the values are colour-coded. The registration error is shown in (e).

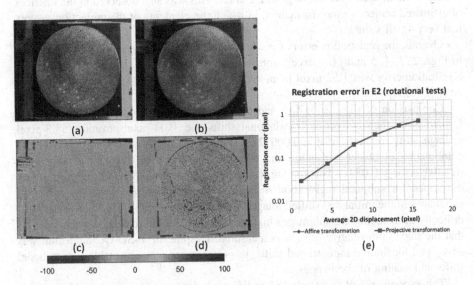

Fig. 3. The results of the rotational tests in experiment E2 involving a 3° rotation of the target. See Fig. 2 caption for explanation of the panels.

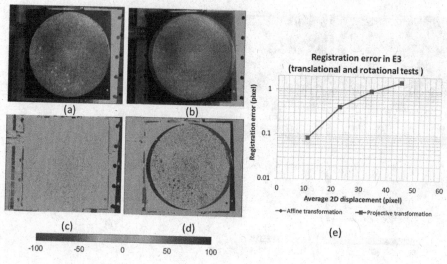

Fig. 4. The results of the translational and rotational tests in experiment E3 involving a 5 mm translation and 1.25° rotation of the target. See Fig. 2 caption for explanation of the panels. The P-SG-GC algorithm detected that the proportion of matched control points with an acceptable error was insufficient for correcting the motion in the final image of this experiment (i.e. 5 mm translation and 1.25° rotation of the target). For this reason, the result does not include this image.

The comparison of Figs. 2, 3, 4, 5 and 6(e) illustrates that the affine and projective transformations have had very close registration errors, indicating that the perspective effects of the images were not large in E1 to E5. This was also observed in the matrices of estimated projective transformation, in which the elements of the projection vectors had very small values.

Overall, the registration errors were less than 1 pixel for all motion correction tests in Figs. 2, 3, 4, 5 and 6(e), except for the fourth image of E3 (Fig. 4), for which the registration error was 1.52 pixel in an average displacement of 45.2 pixel (the relative error is 0.034).

Comparison of Figs. 2, 3, 4, 5 and 6(e) shows that the P-SG-GC algorithm performed best when correcting translational shifts (i.e. 0.04 pixel error for 55.3 pixel average shift (relative error = 0.00072)). The largest registration error was for the combination of object translation and rotation (i.e. 1.52 pixel for 45.2 average shift (relative error = 0.034)). This finding was expected, since the P-SG-GC algorithm was developed for subpixel registration of images with translational shifts by matching subimages of the initial and shifted images. Therefore, the P-SG-GC will have the most difficulty in matching the subimages that are both rotated and translated, such as in E3 that the maximum relative error was measured. Despite the P-SG-GC algorithm was developed for finding translational shifts, its performance was acceptable for rotational shifts and scaling of the images.

The experiments of this study (E1 to E5) were designed to cover typical scenarios of motion correction problems. Even though the shifts were applied using translational and rotational stages, it is expected that the P-SG-GC algorithm could perform similarly in correcting motion in practical applications.

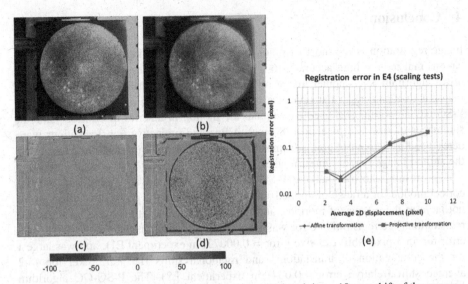

Fig. 5. The results of the camera shifts in experiment E4 involving a 10 mm shift of the camera. See Fig. 2 caption for explanation of the panels.

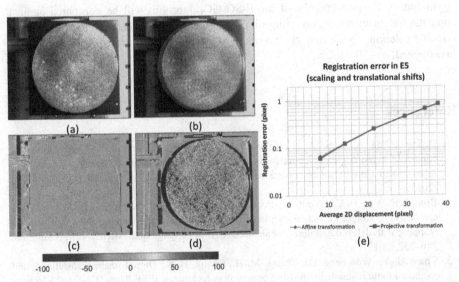

Fig. 6. Results of the camera and translational shifts in experiment E5 involving a 5 mm shift of the camera and 2.5 mm shift of the target. See Fig. 2 caption for explanation of the panels.

4 Conclusion

Image registration is the most common technique for correcting for motion in applications that require high accuracy [6–11]. In this paper, we tested the capability of a novel algorithm for subpixel image registration (P-SG-GC) using a series of experiments with a camera, a flat object, a translational stage, and a rotational stage. The P-SG-GC algorithm was used to estimate the motion in a series of control points in subimages of size 128 pixel × 128 pixel. Affine and projective transformations were determined using control points from subimages and a least-squares method to register the shifted images to the initial images.

The results showed that the P-SG-GC algorithm could accurately and reliably correct motion for a range of applied shifts. We found that the perspective effects were not large in these types of motions, and that affine transformations were sufficient for registration. The registration error was least for pure translational shifts (i.e. 0.04 pixel error for 55.3 pixel shift (relative error = 0.00072) in experiment E1), and was largest for the combination of translational and rotational shifts (i.e. 1.52 pixel for 45.2 average shift (relative error = 0.034) in experiment E3). The P-SG-GC algorithm detected that precisely matched control points were insufficient for correcting the motion for the final image in E3. The result of this study indicates that P-SG-GC may be used as a reliable algorithm for correcting for the relative motion between a camera system and the target object. In particular, the P-SG-GC algorithm could be an accurate algorithm for correcting translational shifts.

In future, the performance of the P-SG-GC algorithm will be compared against competing algorithms for correcting motions in practical applications. In addition, the possible solutions to improve the accuracy of the algorithm in rotational tests will be investigated.

References

1. Hajirassouliha, A., Kmiecik, B., Taberner, A.J., Nash, M.P., Nielsen, P.M.F.: A low-cost, hand-held stereoscopic device for measuring dynamic deformations of skin in vivo. In: 30th International Conference on Image and Vision Computing New Zealand (IVCNZ 2015) (2015)
2. Bron, E.E., Van Tiel, J., Smit, H., Poot, D.H.J., Niessen, W.J., Krestin, G.P., Weinans, H., Oei, E.H.G., Kotek, G., Klein, S.: Image registration improves human knee cartilage T1 mapping with delayed gadolinium-enhanced MRI of cartilage (dGEMRIC). Eur. Radiol. **23**, 246–252 (2013)
3. Chang, J.-Y., Wen-Feng, H., Cheng, M.-H., Chang, B.-S.: Digital image translational and rotational motion stabilization using optical flow technique. IEEE Trans. Consum. Electron. **48**, 108–115 (2002)
4. Yang, J., Schonfeld, D., Mohamed, M.: Robust video stabilization based on particle filter tracking of projected camera motion. IEEE Trans. Circuits Syst. Video Technol. **19**, 945–954 (2009)
5. Vella, F., Castorina, A., Mancuso, M., Messina, G.: Digital image stabilization by adaptive block motion vectors filtering. IEEE Trans. Consum. Electron. **48**, 796–801 (2002)

6. Crum, W.R., Hartkens, T., Hill, D.L.G.: Non-rigid image registration: theory and practice. Br. J. Radiol. **77**, S140–S153 (2004)
7. Chang, H.-C., Lai, S.-H., Lu, K.-R.: A robust real-time video stabilization algorithm. J. Vis. Commun. Image Represent. **17**, 659–673 (2006)
8. Kumar, S., Azartash, H., Biswas, M., Nguyen, T.: Real-time affine global motion estimation using phase correlation and its application for digital image stabilization. IEEE Trans. Image Process. **20**, 3406–3418 (2011)
9. Erturk, S.: Digital image stabilization with sub-image phase correlation based global motion estimation. IEEE Trans. Consum. Electron. **49**, 1320–1325 (2003)
10. Jenkinson, M., Bannister, P., Brady, M., Smith, S.: Improved optimization for the robust and accurate linear registration and motion correction of brain images. Neuroimage **17**(2), 825–841 (2002)
11. Xue, H., Shah, S., Greiser, A., Guetter, C., Littmann, A., Jolly, M.P., Arai, A.E., Zuehlsdorff, S., Guehring, J., Kellman, P.: Motion correction for myocardial T1 mapping using image registration with synthetic image estimation. Magn. Reson. Med. **67**, 1644–1655 (2012)
12. Hajirassouliha, A., Taberner, A.J., Nash, M.P., Nielsen, P.M.F.: Subpixel phase-based image registration using Savitzky-Golay differentiators in gradient-correlation. IEEE Transactions on Image Processing (2016). (Under Review)
13. Goshtasby, A.: Chapter 9: transformation functions. In: Image Registration. Springer, London (2012)
14. Wöhler, C.: 3D Computer vision: efficient methods and applications. Part 1, Chap. 1 (2013)

Incompressible Phase Registration for Motion Estimation from Tagged Magnetic Resonance Images

Fangxu Xing[1(✉)], Jonghye Woo[1], Arnold D. Gomez[2], Dzung L. Pham[3], Philip V. Bayly[4], Maureen Stone[5], and Jerry L. Prince[2]

[1] Department of Radiology, Massachusetts General Hospital/
Harvard Medical School, Boston, MA, USA
fxing1@mgh.harvard.edu
[2] Department of Electrical and Computer Engineering, Johns Hopkins University,
Baltimore, MD, USA
[3] Center for Neuroscience and Regenerative Medicine, Henry Jackson Foundation,
Bethesda, MD, USA
[4] Department of Mechanical Engineering and Materials Science,
Washington University in St. Louis, St. Louis, MO, USA
[5] Department of Neural and Pain Sciences,
University of Maryland School of Dentistry, Baltimore, MD, USA

Abstract. Tagged magnetic resonance imaging has been used for decades to observe and quantify motion and strain of deforming tissue. Three-dimensional (3D) motion estimation has been challenging due to a tradeoff between slice density and acquisition time. Typically, sparse collections of tagged slices are processed to obtain two-dimensional motion, which are then combined into 3D motion using interpolation methods. This paper proposes a new method by reversing this process: first interpolating tagged slices and then directly estimating motion in 3D. We propose a novel image registration framework that uses the concept of diffeomorphic registration with a key novelty that defines a similarity metric involving the simultaneous use of three harmonic phase volumes. The other novel aspect is the use of the harmonic magnitude to enforce incompressibility in the tissue region. The final motion estimates are dense, incompressible, diffeomorphic, and invertible at a 3D voxel level. The approach was evaluated using simulated phantoms and human tongue motion data in speech. Compared with an existing method, it shows major advantages in reducing processing complexity, improving computation speed, allowing running motion calculations, and increasing noise robustness, while maintaining a good accuracy.

Keywords: Motion · Tagged MRI · Phase · Registration · Incompressible

1 Introduction

Various methods for estimating tissue motion and strain using tagged magnetic resonance (MR) imaging have been proposed in the past with applications in

© Springer International Publishing AG 2017
M.A. Zuluaga et al. (Eds.): RAMBO 2016/HVSMR 2016, LNCS 10129, pp. 24–33, 2017.
DOI: 10.1007/978-3-319-52280-7_3

cardiac imaging and speech and brain injury studies [1, 7, 10]. Tagged imaging is widely used because the tag patterns reveal the internal motion of the tissue in addition to motion on the surface. However, tagged images by themselves provide only two-dimensional (2D) in-plane motion information, which is a limitation since three-dimensional (3D) motion is typically desired for more advanced studies.

Many methods have been proposed for estimating 3D motion from tagged slices. They can be broadly classified into two types: (1) acquire a large number of closely spaced image slices to directly achieve a 3D volume, or (2) interpolate information gleaned from sparsely acquired image slices. Although the former offers a dataset that enables direct computation of 3D motion [9], the large amount of time that it costs in acquisition makes it impractical for routine clinical use. Therefore, most of the proposed methods have focused on the latter: acquisition and processing of sparse slices followed by interpolation into 3D motion [2,5]. These methods are generally quite complex involving multiple steps such as 2D motion estimation, tissue segmentation, and 3D splines or finite elements interpolation. Further, when additional features of the estimated motion field such as incompressibility, running displacements, and inverse fields are desired, extra processing steps are needed that further increases complexity, time, and potential numerical error.

In this work, we propose a new method for 3D motion estimation using sparse tagged MR slices that aims to incorporate various processing stages in one algorithm. We first interpolate raw tagged slices onto a denser grid, then apply the harmonic phase (HARP) method [6] to yield 3D phase volumes, and finally incorporate them in an image registration framework based on iLogDemons algorithm [3] with two novel aspects: (1) developing a new phase vector similarity metric and update force to drive the registration process, and (2) using a harmonic magnitude to define where to enforce incompressibility. The estimation result benefits from the diffeomorphic properties of the model since it produces an automatic inverse field and enables motion computation between any two time frames. The method is evaluated using simulation and real MR speech data of the human tongue. We compare its performance with an existing method called incompressible deformation estimation algorithm (IDEA) [2]. Evaluations demonstrate a comparable accuracy and major improvements in reducing processing complexity and increasing speed and noise robustness.

2   Methods

2.1   Acquisition of Tagged Images

A subject's tagged data is acquired at multiple time frames during tissue deformations. While sparse parallel slices are imaged to cover the tissue region (typical resolution: 1.88 mm in-plane and 6.00 mm through-plane), orthogonal magnetic tag planes are applied from three directions to ensure the capture of all x, y, and z components. For example, on sagittal image slices, axial and coronal tag planes are used to capture inferior–superior motion and anterior–posterior motion, and the remaining left–right motion is captured with sagittal tag planes on axial image slices.

2.2   Interpolation of Tagged Slices

Due to the nature of tagged imaging, the tag period (distance between two crests or troughs in the tag pattern) is typically much higher than the image resolution (e.g., 1.88 mm resolution with 12.00 mm tag period), which causes a low frequency contribution from the tag patterns. Thus, it is reasonable to interpolate more tagged slices between the acquired sparse data. We use tricubic b-spline interpolation to produce an arbitrarily dense 3D grid $\mathbf{x}$ covering the tissue region, as illustrated with red dots in Fig. 1(a). Let $\mathbf{x}_s$ denote the locations of the sparsely acquired sagittal images $I_a(\mathbf{x}_s)$ with horizontal tag planes, shown with blue dots in Fig. 1(a). Subscript a is used because the tag planes in this scenario are axial. Tricubic b-spline finds the values $I_a(\mathbf{x})$ by

$$I_a(\mathbf{x}) = \sum_{\mathbf{x}_s} c(\mathbf{x}_s)\beta^3(\mathbf{x} - \mathbf{x}_s), \tag{1}$$

where $\beta^3(\mathbf{x})$ is the interpolation kernel and $c(\mathbf{x}_s)$ are coefficients computed from $I_a(\mathbf{x}_s)$. Interpolated slice examples are shown in Fig. 1(c). In a similar fashion, the remaining two cardinal acquisitions with orthogonal tags can be interpolated onto the same dense 3D grid to create the image $I_c(\mathbf{x})$ having coronal tag planes and the image $I_s(\mathbf{x})$ having sagittal tag planes at every time frame, yielding a sequence of 3D vector-valued tagged volumes.

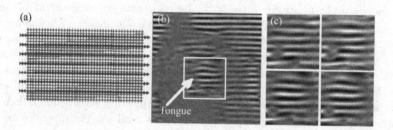

Fig. 1. (a) Side view of the spatial locations of the acquired slices with pixels in blue and the dense 3D grid with voxels in red. (b) Acquired sagittal slice of the head. (c) Interpolated sagittal slices near the tongue region. (Color figure online)

2.3   Harmonic Volumes

The HARP method [6] applies a bandpass filter on one of the second harmonic peaks in the Fourier domain of the tagged images, yielding a complex-valued image, where motion information is contained in the phase part and anatomical information is contained in the magnitude part (see Fig. 2). We perform 3D

HARP filtering on the three interpolated tag volumes I_a, I_c, and I_s, respectively. For example, for the volume $I_a(\mathbf{x})$, the complex image after HARP filtering can be denoted as

$$J_a(\mathbf{x}) = M_a(\mathbf{x})e^{j\Phi_a(\mathbf{x})}, \tag{2}$$

where $M_a(\mathbf{x})$ is the HARP magnitude volume and $\Phi_a(\mathbf{x})$ is the HARP phase volume. The same notation applies for coronally and sagittally tagged volumes, yielding $M_c(\mathbf{x})$, $\Phi_c(\mathbf{x})$, $M_s(\mathbf{x})$, and $\Phi_s(\mathbf{x})$.

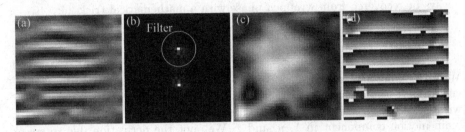

Fig. 2. HARP processing of a tagged image. (a) Tagged slice. (b) Filtering in the Fourier domain. (c) Harmonic magnitude. (d) Harmonic phase.

2.4   Registration of Phase Volumes

Since harmonic phase is a material property, it can be used instead of brightness to associate voxels between time frames. At each time frame, tracking all three linearly independent phase values solves the aperture problem of optical flow. We introduce a diffeomorphic registration framework for this task in order to incorporate regularization, incompressibility, and inverse computation—properties necessary for most biological applications. The classic diffeomorphic demons registration is an iterative method alternating between force-driven stepwise update and deformation field regularization [11], providing a diffeomorphic deformation field that can be used as motion estimate. In the log domain (implying stationary velocity fields), a symmetric velocity update [4] is given at each step by

$$\delta\mathbf{v}(\mathbf{x}) = \frac{2(I_0(\mathbf{x}) - I_t(\mathbf{x}))(\nabla I_0(\mathbf{x}) + \nabla I_t(\mathbf{x}))}{||\nabla I_0(\mathbf{x}) + \nabla I_t(\mathbf{x})||^2 + (I_0(\mathbf{x}) - I_t(\mathbf{x}))^2/K} , \tag{3}$$

where $I_0(\mathbf{x})$ is the fixed image, $I_t(\mathbf{x})$ is the moving image at the current step, and K is a normalization factor. Note that the method ensures a freedom of reference, i.e., $I_0(\mathbf{x})$ can be either at the first time frame or at any of the neighboring time frames with respect to the target time frame t.

In terms of phase, a key difference from regular intensity images is that the phase value is wrapped into the range of $[-\pi, \pi)$ by

$$\Phi(\mathbf{x}) = W(\Theta(\mathbf{x})) := \mathrm{mod}(\Theta(\mathbf{x}) + \pi, 2\pi) - \pi, \tag{4}$$

where $\Theta(\mathbf{x})$ is the true phase hidden because of wrapping. Since only wrapped phase $\Phi(\mathbf{x})$ is available, we must reformulate to account for wrapping. Given two phases $\Phi_1 = W(\Theta_1)$ and $\Phi_2 = W(\Theta_2)$, the difference computation

$$\Theta_1 - \Theta_2 = W(\Phi_1 - \Phi_2) \tag{5}$$

holds when $|\Theta_1 - \Theta_2| < \pi$. This is typically true for such motions where tags do not deform more than half a period—the so-called *small motion assumption*. On the other hand, in the gradient computation, the true phase's gradient can always be recovered from wrapped phase with a mathematical trick [6]:

$$\nabla\Theta(\mathbf{x}) = \nabla^*\Phi(\mathbf{x}) := \begin{cases} \nabla\Phi(\mathbf{x}), & \text{if } |\nabla\Phi(\mathbf{x})| \le |\nabla W(\Phi(\mathbf{x}) + \pi)|, \\ \nabla W(\Phi(\mathbf{x}) + \pi), & \text{otherwise.} \end{cases} \tag{6}$$

With the difference and gradient operators redefined, we minimize the demon energy in a fashion similar to that in [8,11]. All three pairs of phase volumes with three tag directions are used simultaneously because each pair provides a main motion component in x, y, and z. We omit the derivation due to space limitation. This yields the proposed velocity update in the demons registration framework:

$$\begin{aligned}
\delta\mathbf{v}(\mathbf{x}) &= \frac{2\mathbf{v}_0(\mathbf{x})}{\alpha_1(\mathbf{x}) + \alpha_2(\mathbf{x})/K} \text{, where} \\
\mathbf{v}_0(\mathbf{x}) &= W(\Phi_{a0}(\mathbf{x}) - \Phi_{at}(\mathbf{x}))(\nabla^*\Phi_{a0}(\mathbf{x}) + \nabla^*\Phi_{at}(\mathbf{x})) \\
&\quad + W(\Phi_{s0}(\mathbf{x}) - \Phi_{st}(\mathbf{x}))(\nabla^*\Phi_{s0}(\mathbf{x}) + \nabla^*\Phi_{st}(\mathbf{x})) \\
&\quad + W(\Phi_{c0}(\mathbf{x}) - \Phi_{ct}(\mathbf{x}))(\nabla^*\Phi_{c0}(\mathbf{x}) + \nabla^*\Phi_{ct}(\mathbf{x})), \\
\alpha_1(\mathbf{x}) &= ||\nabla^*\Phi_{a0}(\mathbf{x}) + \nabla^*\Phi_{at}(\mathbf{x})||^2 + ||\nabla^*\Phi_{s0}(\mathbf{x}) + \nabla^*\Phi_{st}(\mathbf{x})||^2 \\
&\quad + ||\nabla^*\Phi_{c0}(\mathbf{x}) + \nabla^*\Phi_{ct}(\mathbf{x})||^2 \text{, and} \\
\alpha_2(\mathbf{x}) &= W(\Phi_{a0}(\mathbf{x}) - \Phi_{at}(\mathbf{x}))^2 + W(\Phi_{s0}(\mathbf{x}) - \Phi_{st}(\mathbf{x}))^2 \\
&\quad + W(\Phi_{c0}(\mathbf{x}) - \Phi_{ct}(\mathbf{x}))^2.
\end{aligned} \tag{7}$$

2.5   Incorporation of Incompressibility

iLogDemons [3] is a variation of the diffeomorphic demons that incorporates incompressibility, which is achieved by solving Poisson's equation $\nabla^2 p = \nabla \cdot \mathbf{v}(\mathbf{x})$ for the current stationary velocity estimate $\mathbf{v}(\mathbf{x})$ to find its "divergence part" $\mathbf{v}_d(\mathbf{x}) = \nabla p$ and removing it by $\mathbf{v}(\mathbf{x}) - \mathbf{v}_d(\mathbf{x})$. Since only the tissue region is incompressible, we normalize the previously generated HARP magnitudes $M_a(\mathbf{x})$, $M_c(\mathbf{x})$, and $M_s(\mathbf{x})$ to the range of $[0,1]$ and use their mean $M(\mathbf{x})$ as a weighted mask to specify the region of incompressibility. Then $\mathbf{v}(\mathbf{x})$ is updated by

$$\mathbf{v}(\mathbf{x}) \longleftarrow \mathbf{v}(\mathbf{x}) - M(\mathbf{x})\mathbf{v}_d(\mathbf{x}). \tag{8}$$

When tissue is present, $M(\mathbf{x}) \approx 1$ and we see from (8) that incompressibility is enforced. In regions that are not incompressible such as the airway around the tongue, $M(\mathbf{x}) \approx 0$ and the "divergence part" of the velocity field is kept. Since HARP magnitude is automatically computed with phase, this strategy removes the requirement of any manual or automated segmentation step, as is often required in other approaches.

2.6 PVIRA

We name the proposed method Phase Vector Incompressible Registration Algorithm (PVIRA). It includes: (1) interpolation of tagged slices, (2) HARP processing for phase and magnitude, and (3) motion estimation using a phase-adaptive force and a magnitude-orientated incompressibility constraint in the demons registration framework. The iteration steps for demons are standard [0] and we omit the details due to space limitation. A simultaneous inverse displacement field can be found by reversing the sign of the final estimate of the stationary velocity field and computing its exponential map.

3 Results

Since the true motion of tissue deformation is difficult to know accurately by an independent method, it is essential to use simulation to evaluate PVIRA. First, we simulated the deformation of a soft tissue in a mild rotation. A $64 \times 64 \times 64$ volume was generated with 1.0 mm voxel resolution and 10.0 mm tag period. The tissue exists on a cylinder-shaped region with a circular cross-section in the x–y plane. The outer boundary of the cylinder was subjected to a half-sinusoidal angular acceleration pulse, and synthetic displacement fields were generated by a finite element simulation (COMSOL v4.3), which were in-plane rotations in 18 time frames around the center, as shown in Fig. 3(b). The motion fields were used to deform simulated tagged volumes, as shown in Fig. 3(a) at the x–y cross section before and after deformation. These volumes were processed with PVIRA, yielding the motion estimate shown in Fig. 3(c) and its error magnitude from the truth shown in Fig. 3(d). The internal voxels have an error below 0.2 mm. Figure 3(e) shows the Jacobian determinant on this cross section. The values are close to 1 except for some boundary effects, which indicates incompressibility (mean: 1.01 ± 0.03). Besides this particular time, the errors of all 18 frames with increasing rotation are box-plotted in Fig. 3(i), where the center bar indicates the median that are all lower than 0.1 mm (mean: 0.07 ± 0.06 mm).

To compare, we used the previously reported IDEA method (based on 2D HARP) [2] on the same dataset. The estimation error is 0.08 ± 0.07 mm and the Jacobian is 1.00 ± 0.05. The proposed algorithm has a similar accuracy. We also studied the effect of noise by adding normally distributed Gaussian noise to the tags, as shown in Fig. 3(f). The corresponding motion estimates from both methods are shown in Figs. 3(g) and (h). PVIRA was able to recover the truth due to the contribution from its stepwise velocity field regularization inherited from diffeomorphic demons, while IDEA suffers from noise due to a lack of global regularization. We tested ten scenarios when the noise energy was

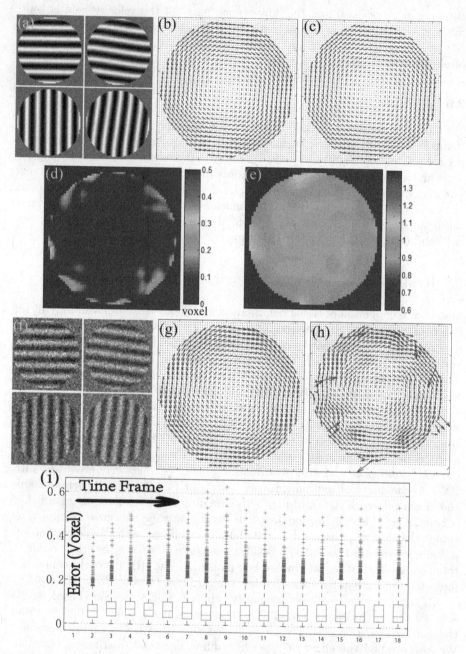

Fig. 3. Test of PVIRA on simulated data. (a) Simulated tagged data. (b) Simulated true motion. (c) Estimated motion. (d) Estimation error. (e) Jacobian determinant of estimate. (f) Simulation with noise. (g) PVIRA estimate under noise. (h) IDEA estimate under noise. (i) Box-plotted error with increasing motion.

raised step-wisely from 0.1 to 1.0. The mean and median of error from PVIRA (0.12 ± 0.10 mm) are lower than IDEA (0.32 ± 0.39 mm) on all noise levels, indicating a better noise robustness (a student t-test yields $p < 0.01$).

Next we applied PVIRA and IDEA on fifteen subjects' tongue MR data in speech, each with 26 time frames. The tongue motion was controlled by a speech phrase that includes both a forward motion and an upward motion. Figures 4(a) to (d) show the motion fields of one subject at two time frames—one for forward motion and one for upward motion—resulting from the two algorithms. Qualitatively, we see that PVIRA yields similar results to IDEA. Note that these motions were all relative to the first time frame because of the limitations of IDEA. It uses 2D motion as basis for interpolation and assumes them as in-plane projections of the 3D motion. Thus IDEA must be relative to time frame 1 where the tag planes are flat. However, in practice the so-called *running displacements*—i.e., motions between consecutive time frames t and $t + 1$—are often needed. IDEA requires another numerical method to find the inverse motion from t back to 1 and compose it with motion from 1 to $t+1$ to yield motion from t to $t+1$. These extra inversion and composition steps can introduce numerical errors especially on the boundary, as shown in Figs. 4(f) and (h). However, PVIRA is not limited to time frame 1 and running displacements can be directly computed, as shown in Figs. 4(e) and (g). The results are smoother and visually interpretable with less boundary error. This is a very important feature of PVIRA that greatly improves on much past work in tracking from tagged MR images.

Finally, we report on the computation times of IDEA and PVIRA. IDEA requires preprocessing several steps, including 2D HARP tracking, computing 3D super-resolution volumes, and segmenting the tongue using a semi-automatic method. These steps took about three hours per subject. IDEA itself took about 5.6 hours per subject, which means that the whole IDEA process took about 8.6 hours. On the other hand, PVIRA processes all steps in one algorithm which took about 33 min per subject. PVIRA is therefore over ten times faster than IDEA. (All computations were carried out on a double-core workstation with 2.2 GHz processor and 8 GB of RAM.)

4   Conclusion and Discussion

We proposed a novel motion estimation method for tagged MR images. A phase-based driving force specifically designed for HARP phase registration was developed, yielding a field estimate that is 3D, diffeomorphic, and incompressible. Compared with IDEA, the new method maintains comparable accuracy but has better noise robustness, allows running displacement calculation, and is over ten times faster.

Current method is still in development and needs further validation. Although true motion is hard to learn from real human data, application of PVIRA to more areas such as cardiac study, traumatic brain injury study, and body muscle motion estimation can provide more information on the properties of the algorithm. Moreover, applying PVIRA on groups of healthy and patient

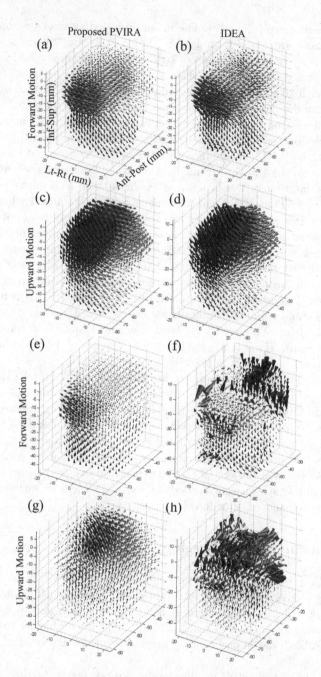

Fig. 4. (a) to (d) show displacement estimates from PVIRA and IDEA at two critical times. (e) to (h) show running displacement estimates between two neighboring times. Note: *cones* are used to visualize fields (cone size: magnitude, cone color: red for left–right, green for front–back, blue for up–down). (Color figure online)

subjects can be carried out to test its ability to separate different classes. Previous classification work using IDEA has been reported with success [12]. Thus this experiment can provide further comparisons between IDEA and PVIRA. Lastly, to successfully interpolate a 3D tagged volume using sparse acquisitions, the sparsity of input data (minimum number of 2D slices) needs to be tested to study the limit for PVIRA to be effective.

Acknowledgments. This work was supported by Grants NIH/NIDCD 1R01DC014717, NIH/NINDS 4R01NS055951, and NIH/NIDCD R00DC012575.

References

1. Ibrahim, E.: Myocardial tagging by cardiovascular magnetic resonance: evolution of techniques-pulse sequences, analysis algorithms, and applications. J. Cardiovasc Magn. Reson. **13**, 36 (2011)
2. Liu, X., Abd-Elmoniem, K., Stone, M., Murano, E., Zhuo, J., Gullapalli, R., Prince, J.: Incompressible deformation estimation algorithm (IDEA) from tagged MR images. IEEE Trans. Med. Imag. **31**(2), 326–340 (2012)
3. Mansi, T., Pennec, X., Sermesant, M., Delingette, H., Ayache, N.: iLogdemons: a demons-based registration algorithm for tracking incompressible elastic biological tissues. Int. J. Comput. Vis. **92**(1), 92–111 (2011)
4. Nithiananthan, S., Brock, K., Daly, M., Chan, H., Irish, J., Siewerdsen, J.: Demons deformable registration for CBCT-guided procedures in the head and neck: convergence and accuracy. Med. Phys. **36**(10), 4755–4764 (2009)
5. O'Dell, W., Moore, C., Hunter, W., Zerhouni, E., McVeigh, E.: Three-dimensional myocardial deformations: calculation with displacement field fitting to tagged MR images. Radiology **195**(3), 829–835 (1995)
6. Osman, N., McVeigh, E., Prince, J.: Imaging heart motion using harmonic phase MRI. IEEE Trans. Med. Imaging **19**(3), 186–202 (2000)
7. Parthasarathy, V., Prince, J.L., Stone, M., Murano, E., NessAiver, M.: Measuring tongue motion from tagged Cine-MR using harmonic phase (HARP) processing. J. Acoust. Soc. Am. **121**(1), 491–504 (2007)
8. Peyrat, J., Delingette, H., Sermesant, M., Xu, C., Ayache, N.: Registration of 4D cardiac CT sequences under trajectory constraints with multichannel diffeomorphic demons. IEEE Trans. Med. Imaging **29**(7), 1351–1368 (2010)
9. Ryf, S., Spiegel, M., Gerber, M., Boesiger, P.: Myocardial tagging with 3DCSPAMM. J. Magn. Reson. Imaging **16**, 320–325 (2002)
10. Sabet, A., Christoforou, E., Zatlin, B., Genin, G., Bayly, P.: Deformation of the human brain induced by mild angular head acceleration. J. Biomech **41**(2), 307–315 (2008)
11. Vercauteren, T., Pennec, X., Perchant, A., Ayache, N.: Diffeomorphic demons: effcient non-parametric image registration. NeuroImage **45**(1), S61–S72 (2009)
12. Xing, F., Woo, J., Lee, J., Murano, E., Stone, M., Prince, J.: Analysis of 3-D tongue motion from tagged and cine magnetic resonance images. J. Speech Lang. Hear. Res. **59**(3), 468–479 (2016)

RAMBO: Reconstruction

Robust Reconstruction of Accelerated Perfusion MRI Using Local and Nonlocal Constraints

Cagdas Ulas[1,3]([✉]), Pedro A. Gómez[1,3], Felix Krahmer[2], Jonathan I. Sperl[3], Marion I. Menzel[3], and Bjoern H. Menze[1,4]

[1] Computer Science, Technische Universität München, Munich, Germany
cagdas.ulas@tum.de
[2] Applied Numerical Analysis, Technische Universität München, Munich, Germany
[3] GE Global Research, Munich, Germany
[4] Institute for Advanced Study, Technische Universität München, Munich, Germany

Abstract. Dynamic perfusion magnetic resonance (MR) imaging is a commonly used imaging technique that allows to measure the tissue perfusion in an organ of interest via assessment of various hemodynamic parameters such as blood flow, blood volume, and mean transit time. In this paper, we tackle the problem of recovering perfusion MR images from undersampled k-space data. We propose a novel reconstruction model that jointly penalizes spatial (local) incoherence on temporal differences obtained based on a reference image and the patchwise (nonlocal) dissimilarities between spatio-temporal neighborhoods of MR sequence. Furthermore, we introduce an efficient iterative algorithm based on a proximal-splitting scheme that solves the joint minimization problem with fast convergence. We evaluate our method on dynamic susceptibility contrast (DSC)-MRI brain perfusion datasets as well as on a publicly available dataset of in-vivo breath-hold cardiac perfusion. Our proposed method demonstrates superior reconstruction performance over the state-of-the-art methods and yields highly accurate estimation of perfusion time profiles, which is very essential for the precise quantification of clinically relevant perfusion parameters.

1 Introduction

Medical diagnosis and research heavily employ perfusion-weighted magnetic resonance imaging (MRI) techniques to estimate the blood flow and volume through examination of the spatio-temporal changes of the signal intensities following the injection of a blood bolus via exogenous paramagnetic tracers. In neuroimaging, these techniques have become widespread clinical tools in the diagnosis of stroke – for the assessment of the tissue at risk –, and the treatment of patients with cerebrovascular disease. One of the major obstacles in the clinical use of perfusion imaging is the need to track the rapid kinetics of contrast agent (tracer) uptake for accurate perfusion quantification [6]. Moreover, the short scanning

© Springer International Publishing AG 2017
M.A. Zuluaga et al. (Eds.): RAMBO 2016/HVSMR 2016, LNCS 10129, pp. 37–47, 2017.
DOI: 10.1007/978-3-319-52280-7_4

time available for each frame often results in limited spatial and temporal resolution, or poor signal-to-noise ratio (SNR) images. In order to improve the spatial or temporal resolution, one widely used approach is to accelerate the acquisition of each frame through the undersampling of k-space by acquiring only a subset of k-space lines [3,15]. However, the undersampling often results in aliasing artifacts in image space and in the context of perfusion MRI, accurate reconstruction of the complete temporal perfusion signal with its peak and high dynamics becomes an even more challenging task.

In recent years, various approaches have been proposed to solve the reconstruction problem in related dynamic imaging tasks, considering, such as piecewise smoothness in the spatial domain [17], high correlation and sparsity in the temporal domain [3,4,10], sparse representations of local image regions via learned dictionaries [3] and low-rank property of MR sequences in the full spatiotemporal space [10,14,17]. Although these methods allow highly accurate reconstructions from fewer k-space data, the main drawback is that their performance is very sensitive to motion and rapid intensity changes occurring over the duration of image acquisition as encountered in perfusion MRI. In addition, these methods often result in over smooth and blurry image regions that are lacking finer details when the acquired data are contaminated with high noise.

In this paper, we integrate two fundamentally different approaches that both increase the robustness of the reconstruction for perfusion MRI: (i) we enforce pixel-wise local sparsity constraint on the temporal differences that limits the overall dynamic of the perfusion time series, (ii) we enforce patch-wise similarity constraint on the spatio-temporal neighborhoods of whole MR sequence, which provides smooth spatial image regions with less temporal blurring especially when there is significant inter-frame motion and noise. We present the main optimization problem in a joint formal framework and introduce a new proximal splitting strategy that benefits from the weighted-average of proximals – thus, overcome a key limitation of the widely used Fast Composite Splitting Algorithm (FCSA) [9] –, and efficiently solves the joint minimization problem with fast convergence. The proposed method is validated on different types of MR perfusion datasets in comparison with the state-of-the-art methods and extensive experiments demonstrate the superior performance of our method in terms of reconstruction accuracy and accurate estimation of perfusion time profiles from undersampled k-space data even when being presented with high noise levels.

Contributions. Our main contributions are four-fold: (1) We present a new reconstruction scheme which cannot only produce high-quality spatial images for dynamic MRI but also enable to reconstruct the complete temporal signal dynamics for perfusion MRI from undersampled k-space data (Sect. 2). (2) We introduce an efficient proximal-splitting algorithm based on a generalized forward-backward splitting scheme [13]. This algorithm provides fast convergence and can be easily applied to various medical image applications that consider optimization problems where the objective function is the sum of several convex regularization terms (Sect. 3). (3) We demonstrate the efficiency and effectiveness of our method by comparing with state-of-the-art techniques on clinical datasets (Sect. 4). (4) Our proposed reconstruction model can enable accurate quantification of clinically useful perfusion parameters while accelerating the acquisition through the use of fewer k-space samples.

2 Formulation

Throughout the paper we consider the reconstruction problem only on 2D+t data (i.e., on a single slice followed over time), however the idea presented here can also easily be extended to 3D+t data. We assume that $X^{3D} \in \mathbb{C}^{M \times N \times T}$ is a 2D perfusion image series represented as a spatio-temporal 3D volume. Let $x_t \in \mathbb{C}^{M \times N}$ denote one perfusion MR frame at time t with $M \times N$ pixels, y_t is the corresponding undersampled k-space measurements of x_t, and $\mathbb{T} = \{1, 2, ..., T\}$ is the set of frame number indices in the sequence. The main goal is to recover all x_t's from the collected k-space measurements y_t's. The observation model between x_t and y_t can be mathematically formulated as

$$y_t = R_t(\mathcal{F}_{2D}x_t + \eta) \tag{1}$$

where R_t denotes the undersampling mask to acquire only a subset of k-space, $\mathcal{F}_{2D}$ is the 2D Fourier Transform operator and η is additive Gaussian noise in k-space. We also denote the partial 2D Fourier operator for frame t as $\mathcal{F}_t = R_t \mathcal{F}_{2D}$, and stack the $\mathcal{F}_t$ for all frames of the sequence as $\mathcal{F}_u = \text{diag}\{\mathcal{F}_1, \mathcal{F}_2, .., \mathcal{F}_T\}$.

We propose solving the following optimization problem for the reconstruction of perfusion MR sequences:

$$\hat{X} = \arg\min_X \left\{ \frac{1}{2}\|\mathcal{F}_u X - Y\|_2^2 + \lambda_1 \mathcal{G}_1(X) + \lambda_2 \mathcal{G}_2(X) \right\} \tag{2}$$

where $X \in \mathbb{C}^{MN \times T}$ denotes the whole perfusion MRI sequence and $Y \in \mathbb{C}^{MN \times T}$ represents the collection of all the k-space measurements. λ_1 and λ_2 are the tuning parameters for two regularization terms.

Local ($\mathcal{G}_1$) regularizer: The first regularization term in (2) penalizes the sum of spatial finite differences on the difference images calculated based on a reference for every image frame $x_t \in \mathbb{C}^{M \times N}$, and this term is named as dynamic total variation (TV) [4] and for the whole MR sequence, it can be defined as

$$\mathcal{G}_1(X) = \sum_{t \in \mathbb{T}} \sum_{n=1}^{M \times N} \sqrt{\left(\nabla_x(x_t - \bar{x})_n\right)^2 + \left(\nabla_y(x_t - \bar{x})_n\right)^2} \tag{3}$$

where $\bar{x}$ is the reference image computed by averaging all the frames in MR sequence, ∇_x and ∇_y represent the finite-difference operators along the x and y dimensions, respectively. The intuition behind using dynamic TV over standard TV is that it is better adjusted to the variation in time, and this regularizer serves as a penalty on the overall dynamic of the temporal perfusion signal.

Nonlocal ($\mathcal{G}_2$) regularizer: The second regularization term in (2) penalizes the weighted sum of ℓ_2 norm distances between spatio-temporal neighborhoods (patches) of MR sequence, and this penalty term can be specified by [16]

$$\mathcal{G}_2(X) = \sum_{(p_x,p_y,p_t)\in\Omega} \sum_{(q_x,q_y,q_t)\in\mathcal{N}_p} w(p,q)\|P_p(X^{3D}) - P_q(X^{3D})\|_2^2 \qquad (4)$$

where $p = (p_x, p_y, p_t)$ and $q = (q_x, q_y, q_t)$ are two voxels, and the voxel of interest is $p \in \Omega$, where $\Omega = [0, M] \times [0, N] \times [0, T]$. The term $P_p(X^{3D})$ denotes a spatio-temporal 3D patch of the MR sequence centered at voxel p. We represent $\mathcal{N}_p$ as a 3D search window around voxel p, and the size of the patch should be smaller than the size of the search window. We simply denote N_p and N_w as the size of a patch and search window, respectively. The weights $w(p,q)$ are determined based on ℓ_2 norm distance between the patches and calculated as

$$w(p,q) = e^{-\frac{\|P_p(X^{3D})-P_q(X^{3D})\|_2^2}{h^2}} \qquad (5)$$

where h is a smoothing parameter controlling the decay of the exponential function. The use of exponential weighting ensures that a voxel which is more similar to the voxel of interest in terms of Euclidean distance receives higher weight.

This regularizer is capable of exploiting the similarities between patch pairs in adjacent frames and it can enforce smooth solutions in the spatio-temporal neighbourhoods of MR sequence even when there is significant inter-frame motion and high noise introduced during acquisition.

3   Algorithm

To efficiently solve the primal problem (2), we propose to apply a proximal-splitting framework to this problem. Before describing our proximal-splitting based algorithm, we should first give the definition of a proximal map.

Proximal map: Given a continuous convex function $g(x)$ and a scalar $\rho > 0$, the proximal operator associated to convex function g can be defined as [9]

$$prox_\rho(g)(z) := \underset{x\in\mathcal{H}}{\arg\min} \left\{ \frac{1}{2\rho}\|x - z\|_2^2 + g(x) \right\} \qquad (6)$$

Now we can reformulate the problem (2) as the following denoising problem

$$\hat{X} = \underset{X}{\arg\min} \left\{ \frac{1}{2}\|X - X_g\|_2^2 + \rho\lambda_1\mathcal{G}_1(X) + \rho\lambda_2\mathcal{G}_2(X) \right\} \qquad (7)$$

Since each of the regularization term in the cost function (2) is convex, the problem (7) can be represented as the proximal map of the sum of two regularization terms as described in Fast Composite Splitting Algorithm (FCSA) [9]

$$\hat{X} = prox_\rho(\lambda_1\mathcal{G}_1 + \lambda_2\mathcal{G}_2)(X_g) \qquad (8)$$

The problem (7) admits to a unique solution as given in (8). However, the proximity operator of the sum of two functions is usually intractable. To compute it iteratively, one can adopt an efficient proximal-splitting method to this problem. Proximal-splitting methods are first-order iterative algorithms that solve relatively large-scale optimization problems with several nonsmooth penalties. They operate by splitting the convex objective function to minimize and generating individual subproblems which are evaluated easily via proximal operators.

To solve our main problem in (7), we split the objective function into two individual subproblems that we term $\mathcal{G}_1$-subproblem and $\mathcal{G}_2$-subproblem.

$\mathcal{G}_1$-**subproblem:** The proximal map for this subproblem can be defined as

$$X_{\mathcal{G}_1} = prox_\rho(\lambda_1\mathcal{G}_1)(X_g) = \arg\min_X \left\{ \frac{1}{2\rho}\|X - X_g\|_2^2 + \lambda_1\mathcal{G}_1(X) \right\} \qquad (9)$$

In order to solve the subproblem (9), we first reformulate it by introducing new variables $d_t = x_t - \bar{x}$ and $d_g^t = X_g^t - \bar{x}$, in this way the problem turns into

$$\hat{d} = \arg\min_d \left\{ \sum_{t\in\mathbb{T}} \left(\frac{1}{2\rho}\|d_t - d_g^t\|_2^2 + \lambda_1\|d_t\|_{TV} \right) \right\} \qquad (10)$$

where $d = \{d_1, ..., d_T\}$ and $\|d_t\|_{TV} = \|[Q_1d_t, Q_2d_t]\|_{2,1}$, where Q_1 and Q_2 are two $MN \times MN$ first order finite difference matrices in vertical and horizontal directions, and $\ell_{2,1}$ norm is the sum of the ℓ_2 norm of each row of given matrix.

Given a reference image $\bar{x}$, the cost function in (10) can be minimized individually for every frame x_t of MR sequence. This guarantees that the sum of the costs in (10) is also minimized. The cost function can be efficiently minimized by using the fast iteratively reweighted least squares (FIRLS) algorithm [5] based on preconditioned conjugate gradient method. This algorithm enables fast convergence and low computational cost by adopting a new preconditioner which can be accurately approximated using the diagonally dominant structure of the matrix $\mathcal{F}_t^H\mathcal{F}_t$, where H is the conjugate transpose. Once the problem (10) is solved, the estimated solution for problem (9) can be calculated as

$$\hat{X}_{\mathcal{G}_1} = \left[\hat{d}_1 + \bar{x}, \hat{d}_2 + \bar{x}, ..., \hat{d}_T + \bar{x} \right] \qquad (11)$$

$\mathcal{G}_2$-**subproblem:** The proximal map for $\mathcal{G}_2$ subproblem can be specified by

$$X_{\mathcal{G}_2} = prox_\rho(\lambda_2\mathcal{G}_2)(X_g) = \arg\min_X \left\{ \frac{1}{2\rho}\|X - X_g\|_2^2 + \lambda_2\mathcal{G}_2(X) \right\} \qquad (12)$$

The problem (12) can be solved using a two-step alternating minimization scheme in an iterative projections onto convex sets (POCS) framework [11]. In each iteration, the first step involves the projection of image estimate onto the data fidelity term via a steepest descend update and the second step performs the minimization of the neighborhood penalty term on the projected data. The minimization of the penalty function in (12) is equivalent to applying non-local means (NLM) filter [2] to the projected images. This is mathematically derived in [12] with a single assumption that only one sub-iteration of the penalty term is performed with constant and predetermined weights. The mathematical formulation of a NLM filter is given as [12]

$$\hat{X}(p_x, p_y, p_t) = \frac{\sum_{(q_x, q_y, q_t) \in \mathcal{N}_p} w(p, q) X(q_x, q_y, q_t)}{\sum_{(q_x, q_y, q_t) \in \mathcal{N}_p} w(p, q)} \tag{13}$$

We have now iterative solvers for each subproblem $\mathcal{G}_1$ and $\mathcal{G}_2$. In this work, we have developed an efficient algorithm by adopting a generalized forward-backward splitting (GFBS) framework [13] that minimizes the sum of multiple convex functions. Basically, FCSA and GFBS are operator-splitting algorithms and they both use forward-backward schemes. The main difference between GFBS and FCSA is that GFBS enables the use of weighted-average of the outputs of individual proximal mappings for finitely many convex functions, whereas FCSA only applies simple averaging. The weighted-average of the outputs of proximals may practically yield better results depending on the effectiveness of each penalty (regularization) term employed in various applications.

We further accelerate the convergence of the algorithm with an additional acceleration step similar to the Fast Iterative Shrinkage-Thresholding Algorithm (FISTA) [1]. This step adaptively increases the value of step size parameter (α_k) through iterations and make it sufficiently close to 1. Our proposed reconstruction algorithm is outlined in Algorithm 1. The most computationally expensive step of our algorithm is solving each proximal map. Fortunately, the computation of proximal maps can be done in parallel since there is no dependency between the inputs of proximity operators. All the other steps involve adding and multiplying vectors or scalars, and are thus very cheap in terms of computational complexity. The GFBS method has been shown to converge when $\gamma < 2/L$ if the convex function $f = \frac{1}{2}\|X - X_g\|_2^2$ has a Lipschitz continuous gradient with constant L [13]. We refer the readers to original GFBS paper [13] for details concerning the proof of the convergence of the algorithm.

4   Experiments

Experimental Setup: We evaluate our method on two different types of perfusion MRI datasets. We use three DSC-MRI brain perfusion sequences ($128 \times 128 \times 60$) and one in-vivo breath-hold cardiac perfusion sequence[1] ($192 \times 192 \times 40$) from [4] with normalized intensities. All the perfusion datasets used in the experiments are acquired with full-sampling and the fully-sampled sequences are artificially corrupted by multiplying its corresponding k-space representation with a binary undersampling mask and subsequently adding Gaussian white noise. To simulate undersampling, we retrospectively apply a time-varying variable density Cartesian mask in our experiments (see Fig. 1). The sampling ratio is set to 1/4 for brain sequences and 1/6 for cardiac sequence.

---

[1] Available at: http://web.engr.illinois.edu/~cchen156/SSMRI.html.

Algorithm 1. Proposed algorithm

Input: Undersampled k-space data Y, $\mathcal{F}_u$, λ_1, λ_2

Initialize: $z_1^0 = z_2^0 = \mathcal{F}_u^H Y$, w_1, w_2, $X^0 = \sum_{i=1}^2 w_i z_i^0$, $\alpha_0 = 0.5$, $\gamma = 1$, $k = 0$

while *stopping criteria not met* **do**

$\quad X_g = X^k - \gamma \mathcal{F}_u^H (\mathcal{F}_u X^k - Y)$;

$\quad z_1^{k+1} = z_1^k + \alpha_k (prox_{\frac{\gamma}{w_1}} (2\lambda_1 \mathcal{G}_1)(X^k + X_g - z_1^k) - X^k)$;

$\quad z_2^{k+1} = z_2^k + \alpha_k (prox_{\frac{\gamma}{w_2}} (2\lambda_2 \mathcal{G}_2)(X^k + X_g - z_2^k) - X^k)$;

$\quad X^{k+1} = w_1 z_1^{k+1} + w_2 z_2^{k+1}$;

$\quad \alpha_{k+1} = 1 + 2(\alpha_k - 1)/(1 + \sqrt{1 + 4(\alpha_k)^2})$;

$\quad k \leftarrow k + 1$;

end

Output: Reconstructed image data X

We compare our method with three state-of-the-art reconstruction methods: the dynamic total variation (DTV) [4], (k,t)-space via low-rank plus sparse prior (kt-RPCA) [14], and fast total variation and nuclear norm regularization (FTVNNR) [17]. To ensure fair comparison, similar to the experiments presented in [3], we empirically fine-tune the optimal regularization parameters for all methods individually for each dataset and depending on noise level. For our proposed method, we specifically set $\lambda_2 = 0.25$ for all noise levels and set $\lambda_1 = 0.025$ for relatively high level noise and $\lambda_1 = 0.001$ for low noise levels. We test the following noise levels and report the results: $\sigma = \{10^{-1}, 5 \times 10^{-2}, 10^{-2}, 5 \times 10^{-3}, 10^{-3}\}$. For the proposed method, we set $N_w = 7 \times 7 \times 7$, $N_p = 5 \times 5 \times 5$, and $w_1 = w_2 = 0.5$ for all sequences. We consider using small cubic neighborhoods for N_w and N_p since large neighborhoods drastically increase the computation time. To reduce the computational burden, we also employ an optimized blockwise version of the non-local means filter that was proposed by Coupé et al. [7] for 3D medical data. We adopt the Peak Signal-to-Noise Ratio (PSNR) as the metric for quantitative evaluation. Instead of directly calculating PSNR on a whole image or 3D sequence, we employ a region-based analysis by calculating the PSNR on randomly selected 100 image blocks (50×50) in 2D frames. This allows us to test for statistical differences using paired t-test when comparing different methods.

Results: Figures 1 and 2 demonstrate a single reconstructed frame of the first and third brain perfusion dataset, respectively, and the estimation of perfusion time profiles averaged over voxels inside a small region of interest. The results in Fig. 1 reveal that kt-RPCA and FTVNNR show quite similar performances, and the DTV yields both better reconstruction and estimation of perfusion signal compared to these two methods. Compared with all three methods, our proposed method can achieve the best reconstruction and very accurate estimation of perfusion time profiles even when the k-space measurements are contaminated with a relatively high level noise ($\sigma = 5 \times 10^{-2}$). The reconstruction results of our method are also statistically significant (p-value $< 10^{-5}$) when compared with all other methods. Moreover, both kt-RPCA and FTVNNR result in over spatial

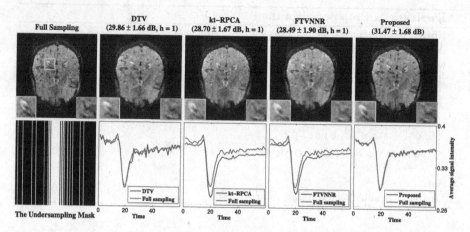

Fig. 1. (Top) Results (mean±std, h-value) of the 22nd frame of the first brain dataset and close-up views of two regions of interest (yellow and green square). h = 1 specifies the statistical significance between the results of proposed and compared method, (Bottom) An exemplary undersampling mask and for each method, estimation of perfusion time profiles averaged over the voxels inside the red square shown in top-left figure. The standard deviation of added Gaussian noise is $\sigma = 5 \times 10^{-2}$. Our method achieves both the best frame-based reconstruction and the most accurate estimation of peaks and temporal pattern of perfusion signal. (Color figure online)

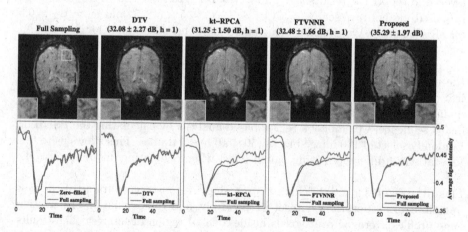

Fig. 2. (Top) Results (mean±std, h-value) of the 15th frame of the third brain dataset and close-up views of two regions of interest (yellow and green square), (Bottom) For each method, estimation of perfusion time profiles averaged over the voxels inside the red square shown in top-left figure. The standard deviation of added Gaussian noise is $\sigma = 10^{-3}$. Our method again achieves both the best frame-based reconstruction and the most accurate estimation of peaks and temporal pattern of perfusion signal. (Color figure online)

smoothing (see close-up views in Fig. 1) and along time as well, which can be clearly seen from smoothening of the perfusion peaks in the third-fourth column of Fig. 1. In contrast, the proposed method reconstructs a perfusion pattern that is in good agreement with the pattern of the fully sampled data (see Fig. 1 bottom fifth column), and produces less blurry image regions and sharper edges. The perfusion time profiles obtained from the third dataset (see Fig. 2 bottom plots) also demonstrate the success of our proposed method. Considering the spatial outputs, when looking at details in close-up views of Fig. 2, the reconstructions obtained by kt-RPCA and FTVNNR are more blurry and thus lacking some finer details in yellow region, whereas the reconstruction obtained by proposed method involves more finer information in yellow region and provides sharper edges in green region.

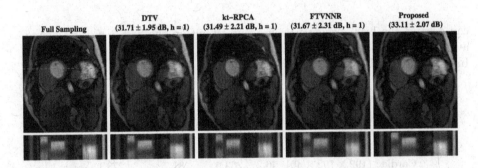

Fig. 3. (Top) Results of the 18th frame of the cardiac dataset with added noise $\sigma = 10^{-2}$, (Bottom) Temporal cross sections by the red dashed line. All methods can produce high quality spatial frames, however, our method yields less noisy and blurry temporal profiles, and the aliasing artifacts are also mostly removed. (Color figure online)

We also validate our method on a cardiac perfusion data from [4] and the results are presented in Fig. 3. All methods here can produce high quality images, however, when looking temporal cross sections at bottom, it can be observed that our method gives less noisy and with lower aliasing artifacts reconstruction on myocardium surface while FTVNNR provides more blurry result. The reason is that our method can utilize both local consistency in temporal differences and nonlocal similarities between spatio-temporal neighborhoods of MR sequence while the FTVNNR does not explicitly exploit sparsity in temporal domain.

Quantitative results of different reconstruction methods on both brain and cardiac perfusion datasets are shown in Fig. 4. Note that the NLM only solves the $\mathcal{G}_2$-subproblem of Sect. 3. From the figure, one can clearly see that our proposed method achieves the highest mean PSNR for all noise levels applied. The running time of all methods on the brain and cardiac datasets is provided in Table 1. Compared with the other three methods, our method needs the highest amount of processing time. However, due to its faster convergence, our method

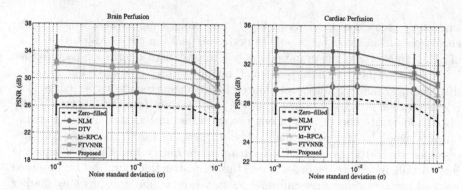

Fig. 4. PSNR results versus noise std (σ) for (left) Brain, (right) Cardiac datasets. Our joint local and nonlocal regularization based method performs the best.

can achieve the best reconstruction accuracy within the first 3–4 iterations on average, which approximately takes 4.5 min for cardiac dataset on a desktop with Intel Xeon CPU E3-1226 v3 Processor.

Table 1. The time cost of different reconstruction methods.

Time (Seconds)	DTV	kt-RPCA	FTVNNR	Proposed
Brain ($128 \times 128 \times 60$)	54.5	194.5	74.3	304.6
Cardiac ($192 \times 192 \times 40$)	46.2	263.9	81.7	278.1

5   Conclusion

We have presented a robust reconstruction model for perfusion MRI, which is based on a joint regularization of pixel-wise and patch-wise spatio-temporal constraints. Numerical experiments validate the efficiency of our method over the state-of-the-art methods in terms of reconstruction accuracy and estimation of perfusion time profiles in varying noise conditions. We also introduce an iterative algorithm that efficiently solves convex optimization problems with mixtures of regularizers. Our algorithm provides fast convergence and can be easily extended to other medical image applications, in particular denoising and super-resolution. The proposed method can be also extended to parallel MR imaging [8] and be applied to multi-coil data. Future work will aim at expanding our work with the fitting of pharmacokinetic models and quantitative analysis of perfusion parameters on 3D+t brain perfusion data using partial k-space measurements.

Acknowlededgments. The research leading to these results has received funding from the European Union's H2020 Framework Programme (H2020-MSCA-ITN-2014) under grant agreement no 642685 MacSeNet. We also thank Dr. Christine Preibisch (Neuroradiology, Klinikum rechts der Isar der TU München) for providing brain perfusion datasets.

References

1. Beck, A., Teboulle, M.: A fast iterative shrinkage-thresholding algorithm for linear inverse problems. SIAM J. Imag. Sci. **2**(1), 183–202 (2009)
2. Buades, A., Coll, B., Morel, J.M.: A non-local algorithm for image denoising. In: IEEE Conference on Computer Vision and Pattern Recognition (CVPR), vol. 2, pp. 60–65 (2005)
3. Caballero, J., Price, A.N., Rueckert, D., Hajnal, J.: Dictionary learning and time sparsity for dynamic MR data reconstruction. IEEE Trans. Med. Imag. **33**(4), 979–994 (2014)
4. Chen, C., Li, Y., Axel, L., Huang, J.: Real time dynamic MRI with dynamic total variation. In: Golland, P., Hata, N., Barillot, C., Hornegger, J., Howe, R. (eds.) MICCAI 2014. LNCS, vol. 8673, pp. 138–145. Springer, Heidelberg (2014). doi:10.1007/978-3-319-10404-1_18
5. Chen, C., et al.: Preconditioning for accelerated iteratively reweighted least squares in structured sparsity reconstruction. In: IEEE Conference on Computer Vision and Pattern Recognition (CVPR), pp. 2713–2720 (2014)
6. Conturo, T.E., et al.: Arterial input functions for dynamic susceptibility contrast MRI: requirements and signal options. J. Mag. Reson. Imag. **22**, 697–703 (2005)
7. Coupé, P., Yger, P., Prima, S., Hellier, P., Kervrann, C., Barillot, C.: An optimized blockwise nonlocal means denoising filter for 3-D magnetic resonance images. IEEE Trans. Med. Imag. **27**(4), 425–441 (2008)
8. Deshmane, A., Gulani, V., Griswold, M.A., Seiberlich, N.: Parallel MR imaging. J. Mag. Reson. Imag. **36**(1), 55–72 (2012)
9. Huang, J., Zhang, S., Metaxas, D.N.: Efficient MR image reconstruction for compressed MR imaging. Med. Imag. Anal. **15**(5), 670–679 (2011)
10. Lingala, S.G., Hu, Y., DiBella, E., Jacob, M.: Accelerated dynamic MRI exploiting sparsity and low-rank structure: k-t SLR. IEEE Trans. Med. Imag. **30**(5), 1042–1054 (2011)
11. Marks, R.J.: Alternating projections onto convex sets. In: Jansson, P.A. (ed.) Deconvolution of Images and Spectra, 2nd edn. Academic Press, Orlando (1996)
12. Protter, M., Elad, M., Takeda, H., Milanfar, P.: Generalizing the nonlocal-means to super-resolution reconstruction. IEEE Trans. Imag. Proc. **18**(1), 36–51 (2009)
13. Raguet, H., Fadili, J., Peyré, G.: A generalized forward-backward splitting. SIAM J. Imag. Sci. **6**(3), 1199–1226 (2013)
14. Trémoulhéac, B., Dikaios, N., Atkinson, D., Arridge, S.R.: Dynamic MR image reconstruction-separation from undersampled (k-t)-space via low-rank plus sparse prior. IEEE Trans. Med. Imag. **33**(8), 1689–1701 (2014)
15. Ulas, C., Gómez, P., Sperl, J.I., Preibisch, C., Menze, B.H.: Spatio-temporal MRI reconstruction by enforcing local and global regularity via dynamic total variation and nuclear norm minimization. In: IEEE 13th International Symposium on Biomedical Imaging (ISBI), pp. 306–309 (2016)
16. Yang, Z., Jacob, M.: Nonlocal regularization of inverse problems: a unified variational framework. IEEE Trans. Imag. Proc. **22**(8), 3192–3203 (2013)
17. Yao, J., Xu, Z., Huang, X., Huang, J.: Accelerated dynamic MRI reconstruction with total variation and nuclear norm regularization. In: Navab, N., Hornegger, J., Wells, W.M., Frangi, A.F. (eds.) MICCAI 2015. LNCS, vol. 9350, pp. 635–642. Springer, Heidelberg (2015). doi:10.1007/978-3-319-24571-3_76

Graph-Based 3D-Ultrasound Reconstruction of the Liver in the Presence of Respiratory Motion

Houssem-Eddine Gueziri[1][(✉)], Sebastien Tremblay[2], Catherine Laporte[1], and Rupert Brooks[2]

[1] École de technologie supérieure, Montreal, QC, Canada
houssem-eddine.gueziri.1@ens.etsmtl.ca
[2] Elekta Ltd., Montreal, QC, Canada

Abstract. In this paper, we explore the feasibility of 3D ultrasound (US) reconstruction of the liver in the presence of respiratory motion using a minimally cumbersome acquisition protocol involving a commonly available tracked 2D+t wobbler US probe. We exploit measurements of the probe's displacement against the skin to coarsely assign frames to their corresponding respiratory states. These assignments are refined using a graph representation of the spatial adjacency relationships and appearance continuity between the frames. Finally, frames providing the smallest motion variation, within a respiratory state, are first selected using a shortest path strategy, then passed to the reconstruction algorithm. Our method is fully based on tracked US imaging and does not require a pre-operative reference image. Moreover, no breath-control effort is required on the part of the patient, thereby limiting the complexity of the acquisition protocol. We tested our approach with an intercostal acquisition protocol, demonstrating enhancements in stability and the quality of liver reconstruction at different respiratory states, compared to a naive gating approach.

1 Introduction

1.1 Background

Image-guided radiation therapy (IGRT) is a good alternative to minimally-invasive surgery for tumour treatment. Typically, the IGRT workflow involves a pre-operative planning session followed by several treatment sessions. A few weeks before the beginning of the treatment sessions, a 3D computed tomography (CT) reference image is acquired during the planning session to determine the tumour location and the radiation dosage required. Prior to each treatment session, a rapid imaging scan of the tumour region, typically a cone beam CT (CBCT) scan, is acquired and registered to the reference image to compensate for the change in tumour location since the planning session.

Recently, ultrasound (US) image guidance has been considered as an alternative solution to CBCT for pre- and intra-operative motion correction during radiotherapy. Organ repositioning was successfully employed using 2D and 3D

M.A. Zuluaga et al. (Eds.): RAMBO 2016/HVSMR 2016, LNCS 10129, pp. 48–57, 2017.
DOI: 10.1007/978-3-319-52280-7_5

US image-guided procedures for prostate treatment, where small or nonexistent motion occurred during the radiation delivery [5,6]. However, organs subject to respiratory motion, in particular abdominal and thoracic organs, are prone to a higher risk of undesired healthy tissue radiation due to localization errors caused by misalignment with the CT reference images.

Moreover, 3D US acquisition in the presence of respiratory motion raises several challenges. Direct volume acquisition through a 2D array transducer generally results in poor image resolution, which may affect the registration and localization procedures. In contrast, a mechanically swept 1D-array transducer, i.e., a wobbler probe, referred to as 2D+t US imaging, maintains standard 2D US resolution at the cost of low temporal resolution. Unfortunately, in the presence of motion, the volume acquired with a single sweep is corrupted, since frame t and frame $t' \neq t$ are not acquired in the same respiratory state.

This paper presents a method for sorting the images from multi-sweep 2D+t US for volume reconstruction in the presence of respiratory motion. We tested our approach for 3D+t liver reconstruction through the intercostal US acquisition technique. Our contributions are twofold. First, we introduce a novel graph-based image selection method for 3D+t reconstruction. Second, we demonstrate the feasibility of our approach for liver reconstruction through a minimally cumbersome image-guided US acquisition protocol. Indeed, during the acquisition, we only consider the use of a tracked 2D+t probe and no specific patient effort in breath-control, thereby significantly reducing the procedure's complexity compared to current practice.

1.2 Related Work

To deal with respiratory motion during imaging, the *breath-hold* technique, wherein the patient interrupts breathing while being imaged is the most common strategy. However, it is impracticable in some situations. Alternatively, *gating* strategies consider only the frames at a particular phase of the breathing cycle that is determined through an external surrogate respiratory measurement (e.g., respiratory belt, spirometer, skin surface displacement, etc.).

While surrogate data are useful for breath monitoring [1,4], the information provided by the surrogates does not necessarily reflect the internal motion of the organs. To address this shortcoming, image-based similarity measures have been employed to describe the internal organ motion, e.g., by Nakamoto et al. [7] using successive 2D-US sagittal slices to build a 3D deformation field, by Preiswerk et al. [8] using a statistical model based on the principal component analysis of pre-operative Magnetic Resonance Imaging (MRI) data of different patients, and by Wein et al. [13] using the normalized cross-correlation (NCC) similarity measure to register the current frame to a pre-operative reference volume. All aforementioned approaches require a reference volume acquired during a breath-hold procedure. Our approach differs in that it operates in regular breathing conditions and requires no reference image at all.

In related work [11], Siebenthal et al. proposed a MRI-based 3D+t reconstruction by analyzing temporal frame continuity in the acquisition sequence.

They looked at similarity changes before and after each frame to determine the transitional motion describing the respiratory state. The approach was fully image-based and no surrogate was utilized, therefore requiring that feature points be tracked in the MRI sequence. This approach does not generalize well to US image guidance. Due to the restricted field of view of the US images, feature points may be lost or occluded by shadowing artifacts during the acquisition, rendering tracking inaccurate.

Wachinger et al. [12] proposed to reconstruct series of US volumes based on a 2D+t wobbler acquisition probe. Their approach associates a respiratory state to each frame using the lower dimensional manifold learning [2] representation of the frames, i.e., a 1D signal response. Based on the response of every angular position of the wobbler probe, the respiratory state is estimated by associating the frame with its interpolated response in the lower dimensional space. Although the approach is fully image-based, it does not account for probe motion during the acquisition nor for shadowing artifacts. To compensate for these types of artifacts, we exploit a combination of surrogate data and image information using a graph-based model to extract sequences of frames corresponding to the same respiratory state. This results in the reconstruction of 3D US volumes at different respiratory states acquired in regular breathing conditions.

2   Graph-Based 3D+t Ultrasound Reconstruction

In this section, we first describe our 2D+t US image acquisition setup and technique (Sect. 2.1). During acquisition, each frame is associated with a coarsely defined respiratory state based on the displacement of the probe (Sect. 2.2). For each such state, we create a directed acyclic graph describing the neighbourhood relationships between adjacent frames in space (Sect. 2.3). A weight is associated to each edge based on pairwise frame similarity. Finally, a three-stage shortest-path strategy is used to extract frames with minimum motion-induced variations within each respiratory state (Sect. 2.4).

2.1   Materials and Acquisition Approach

Image acquisition is performed using a Clarity[1] Autoscan probe (Elekta AB, Stockholm, Sweden). It consists of a 2D-US probe mounted on a mechanical rotary motor allowing automated 2D sweeps. The probe is tracked using a Polaris camera (Northern Digital Inc., Waterloo, ON, Canada) so that the position and the orientation of each frame is known with respect to the isocenter room coordinates. The probe is attached to an adjustable rigid arm fixed to the table (see Fig. 1a). Since the probe is tracked, we exploit the displacement of the probe in 3D space as surrogate data for respiratory monitoring, as suggested by Nakamoto et al. [7]. A tracked marker placed on the surface of the abdomen [1], would provide a much clearer respiratory signal, since abdominal motion is larger than that

---

[1] Using the Anticosti system for investigation purposes only.

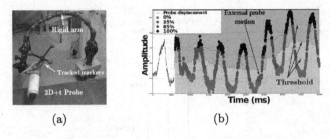

Fig. 1. Acquisition setups: (a) 2D+t US probe attached to an adjustable rigid arm, and (b) respiratory signal acquired with the displacement of the tracked probe, frames are assigned to their respective respiratory states using $T_w = 6.1\,s$.

of the thoracic cage. In this paper, we investigate the feasibility of monitoring breath using the thoracic motion of the probe during an intercostal acquisition protocol. This configuration provides a less cumbersome solution for capturing patient respiration. More importantly, it requires no additional temporal calibration to synchronize an external surrogate signal with the acquired images.

2.2 Respiratory State Assignment

We divide the respiratory cycle into $N \geq 2$ non-overlapping finite states $\Phi_{k=1...N}$, where Φ_0 and Φ_N are the end-exhalation and the end-inhalation states, respectively. We want to associate each frame to its corresponding state based on probe position. During breathing, the pressure applied by the motion of the rib cage against the probe allows to capture the respiratory signal. The respiratory signal $r(t)$ associated to a frame t is then given by the magnitude of the probe's displacement $||P_t||_2$ in the 3D room coordinate reference, where P_t is the 3D position of the probe and $||.||_2$ is the Euclidean norm. However, $||P_t||_2$ depends on the ultrasound acquisition procedure, e.g., a probe placed against the patient's ribs results in smaller displacement than a probe placed against the abdomen. Therefore, $r(t)$ is normalized by the range of the probe's displacement $R_{amp} = \max_{\{\forall t,t' \in T_w\}} |r(t) - r(t')|$ within a time period T_w.

The range R_{amp} is divided into N equal intervals corresponding to the respiratory states. For each new sample of the respiratory signal, R_{amp} is updated for the current period T_w. Then, the corresponding US frame is assigned to the nearest state Φ_k. This approach has two main benefits. First, it allows automatic correction for respiratory signal drift in time. This can occur when the probe is subject to external motion (see Fig. 1b). Second, discretizing the respiratory cycle provides a natural robustness to amplitude noise present in the signal, i.e., the frames which are prone to assignment errors occur near the threshold separating two states. This constitutes the *pre-selection* step. Once the frames are assigned, a graph-based *post-selection* refinement step is applied for each respiratory state. Therefore, assignment errors do not result in drastic changes in the reconstructed volume.

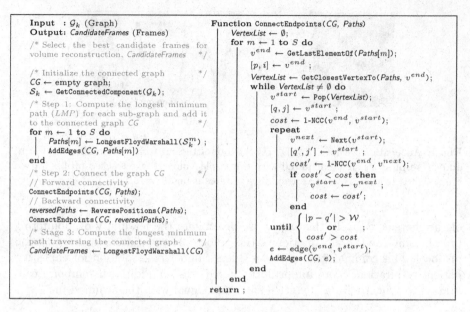

Algorithm 1. Pseudo-code for graph-based frame selection.

2.3   Graph Modelling

Using all the frames of the state Φ_k for reconstruction may result in a discontinuous/noisy volume because of probe tracking imprecision and/or assignment errors. In order to enforce continuity between consecutive frames, we perform a graph-based post-selection refinement for each state. Considering the acquisition technique described in Sect. 2.1, a frame $I(p, i)$ is defined by its position $p = 1 \dots M$ within the sweep, where M is the total number of images in one sweep, and $i \in \mathbb{N}$ is the sequential number of the sweep. Let $\mathcal{G}_k = \langle \mathcal{V}_k, \mathcal{E}_k \rangle$ denote a directed graph where the set of vertices $\mathcal{V}_k = \{I(p, i)\}$ contains the frames assigned to Φ_k, and $\mathcal{E}_k = \{(I(p, i), I(p', i')) \in \mathcal{V}_k^2\}$ represents the edges connecting pairs of vertices. For readability, we write $e_{I,I'} = (I(p, i), I(p', i'))$. For each edge $e_{I,I'}$, we associate a *transitional cost* $w_{I,I'}$ representing a dissimilarity measure between the two frames. The NCC measure was shown to provide satisfactory results for US images [3,7]. Therefore, we define our cost function as

$$w_{I,I'} = 1 - NCC(I, I'). \tag{1}$$

Each newly acquired frame $I(p, i)$, is added to the corresponding graph $\mathcal{G}_k$ and the associated edge $e_{I,I'}$ or $e_{I',I}$ is created $\forall I' = I(p', i') \in \mathcal{V}_k$ such that

$$|i - i'| < L \quad \text{and} \quad \begin{cases} p' - p = 1 & \text{for } e_{I,I'} \\ p' - p = -1 & \text{for } e_{I',I} \end{cases}, \tag{2}$$

where $L \in \mathbb{N}^\star$ is a threshold precluding the association of frames too distant in time (Fig. 2a). This is because the US imaging conditions may vary during the acquisition, affecting, for instance, the global image luminance and quality.

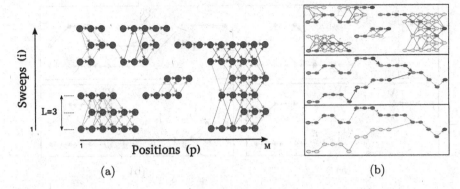

Fig. 2. Example of frame selection: (a) graph representation of a respiratory state, edge color represents the cost ranging from low (blue) to high (red), (b) shortest path computation, (top) *LMPs* of the connected components, (middle) the connected simplified graph, and (bottom) the selected frames using the longest minimum path through the graph approach (Color figure online).

2.4 Selecting Frames for Volume Reconstruction

The approach described above might result in a disconnected graph $\mathcal{G}_k$ (see Fig. 2a). In this section, we describe a three-stage strategy, summarized in Algorithm 1, to connect the graph such as to extract the *candidate frames* for volume reconstruction that generate minimal variation with respect to the cost function.

By construction, $\mathcal{G}_k$ is acyclic, and its vertices are topologically ordered along the same direction. Therefore, we can define v^{start} and v^{end} as starting and ending endpoints, respectively. Because each sub-graph can contain multiple start- and end-vertices, a straightforward connection between all start-to-end vertices could be computationally expensive. To avoid this, we simplify the graph before connecting the endpoints.

Stage 1 – Simplifying the graph: First, we divide the graph into S connected components. Each component is a sub-graph $\mathcal{S}_k^m = \mathcal{G}_k[\mathcal{C}_m], m \in \{1, \dots, S\}$ induced by the subset of connected vertices $C_m \subset \mathcal{V}_k$. For each $\mathcal{S}_k^m$ we compute the longest path traversing the sub-graph that provides the minimum cost, i.e., the *Longest-Minimum-Path* (*LMP*). This is done by selecting the longest path among the pairwise shortest paths returned by the Floyd-Warshall algorithm [10]. Finally, each $\mathcal{S}_k^m$ is replaced with its corresponding *LMP* simplified version $\mathcal{S}_k^m$ (Fig. 2b (top)).

Stage 2 – Connecting the graph: Connecting each endpoint of the *LMPs* to the closest frame could result in violating the constraint $|i - i'| < L$ from Eq. (2). Instead, we connect the graph's endpoints as follows (see Fig. 3): (i) for each end vertex of a *LMP*, find all the *LMPs* with potential *start* vertices within a tolerance window $\mathcal{W}$ of missing frames, (ii) if no start vertex is found within $\mathcal{W}$, connect the end vertex to the nearest start vertex; otherwise, for each *LMP*

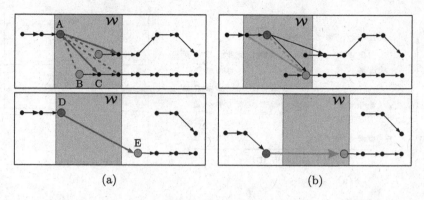

(a) (b)

Fig. 3. Endpoint connectivity example: (a) forward connectivity (end vertices to start vertices), (b) backward connectivity (start vertices to end vertices). Dashed lines indicate that the cost is not minimal, e.g., connecting end vertex A to start vertex C within $\mathcal{W}$ (greyed region), vertex B is not connected. connecting vertices outside $\mathcal{W}$, e.g., vertex D to the closest vertex E.

found, connect the end and start vertices with the minimum cost within $\mathcal{W}$. The role of $\mathcal{W}$ is to discard outlier endpoints if a sufficiently close frame on the same LMP generates a lower cost, e.g., in Fig. 3a, A is connected directly to C even if B is closer. The new connected vertices are labelled as endpoints and the procedure is repeated to connect the $LMPs$ from the other side, i.e., to connect each *start* vertex to the closest *end* vertices (Fig. 3b). This can be achieved by reversing the order of the vertex positions and applying the same procedure.

Stage 3 – Selecting the candidate frames: To find the selected frames for volume reconstruction, we compute the LMP over the final connected graph. This approach results in selecting at most one frame for each sweep position. Finally, the volume is interpolated considering the 3D position of each frame [9].

3 Results

We tested our reconstruction approach on two intercostal liver scans of a healthy volunteer acquired at 45 fps and a sector angle of 44.6°, and at 75 fps with a sector angle of 22.4°, respectively. The algorithm parameters L and $\mathcal{W}$ were empirically set to 3 and 5, respectively. Figure 4a shows the volume reconstruction without respiratory gating, i.e., from a single probe sweep, and with respiratory gating using our graph-based approach, over an acquisition duration of 30 s. The images are nearly perpendicular to the coronal plane, highlighting motion artifacts in this view, e.g., along the diaphragm. To assess the effect of the graph-based refinement, we reconstructed volumes of the liver in different respiratory states using: (i) a naive gating approach that considers all the frames pre-selected by the surrogate data, which is referred to as the average volume (ii) the frames post-selected by the graph-based approach. Figures 4c–f compare cross-sectional

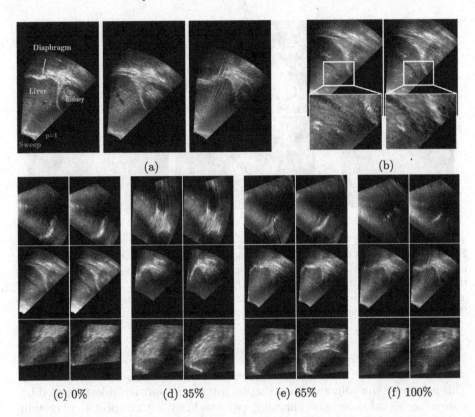

Fig. 4. Volume reconstruction results of 4 respiratory states: (a) Coronal view of the reconstructed volume without motion gating (left), at end-exhalation (middle) and end-inhalation (right), (b) zoom on the reconstructed volumes, average volume (left) graph-based approach (right) we can see artifact correction, (c–f) examples of cross-sections of the reconstructed volumes, average volume (left columns) graph-based approach (right columns), arrows point at artifacts, Axial view (top), Coronal view (middle) and Sagittal view (bottom).

images obtained with both approaches for the same volunteer. Although the average volume provides consistent information because of the surrogate data, it does not provide sharp images. In contrast, graph-based refinement helps ensure image continuity while preserving structural information integrity (see Fig. 4b).

The respiratory signal measured by the probe's displacement might be subject to external perturbations. In order to assess the sensitivity of the reconstruction to the quality of the respiratory signal, a Gaussian noise with $\sigma_{10\%} = 10\%$ and $\sigma_{30\%} = 30\%$ of the total amplitude range was added to the respiratory signal before performing the reconstruction. Figure 5a shows a boxplot of the peak signal to noise ratio (PSNR) comparing the volumes reconstructed from the noisy signal with their corresponding volumes reconstructed from the original signal. For both $\sigma_{10\%}$ and $\sigma_{30\%}$, our approach provides a higher PSNR

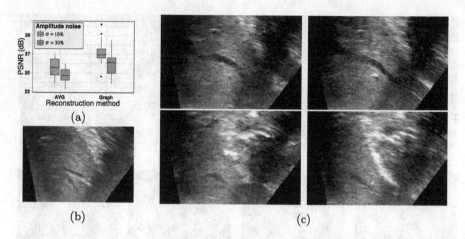

(a)

(b)   (c)

Fig. 5. Comparison of the volumes reconstructed with noisy respiratory signal: (a) box-plot of the PSNR comparing reconstruction with noisy signal to reconstruction with the original signal, (b) breath-hold reconstruction example, and (c) example of end-exhalation (bottom) and end-inhalation (top) reconstructions using average volume (left) and our graph-based approach (right).

($PSNR_{10\%} = 27.17 \pm 0.18$ and $PSNR_{30\%} = 25.94 \pm 0.18$) than the average volume reconstruction ($PSNR_{10\%} = 25.56 \pm 0.17$ and $PSNR_{30\%} = 24.67 \pm 0.13$). This is because the volume reconstruction using our approach is less affected by respiratory signal noise, providing improved stability with respect to uncertain surrogate data. Figure 5b shows an example of reconstruction in which the acquisition was performed under breath-hold. Comparatively, reconstruction artifacts, due to the noise added to the probe displacement signal, can be observed in Fig. 5c. Image continuity is preserved when using our graph-based refinement approach.

4   Conclusion

This paper demonstrated the feasibility of 3D+t US reconstruction of the liver in the presence of respiratory motion. The image acquisition technique involves the use of a 2D+t autoscan US probe and no breath-holding on part of the patient, rendering the procedure minimally cumbersome and suitable for intra-operative interventions. The proposed approach combines the usage of breath surrogate data and a pairwise image similarity measure to reduce motion-induced variations within the same discrete respiratory state. First, we assign each frame to a respiratory state based on the probe's displacement. Then, for each respiratory state a directed acyclic graph is created such that adjacent frames are connected through edges with the associated weights corresponding to the image dissimilarities. Finally, a shortest path strategy based on the Floyd-Warshall algorithm is used to find the longest path traversing the graph that minimizes variation between frames, ensuring a globally optimal solution with respect to the edge weights. We tested our approach with a intercostal liver image acquisition protocol in regular breathing conditions. Results show significant enhancement of reconstruction quality and robustness to surrogate measurement noise, compared to a naive gating approach. We believe that our approach could be an interesting alternative for 4D imaging to compensate for respiratory motion during intra-operative procedures.

References

1. Atkinson, D., Burcher, M., Declerck, J., Noble, J.: Respiratory motion compensation for 3-D freehand echocardiography. Ultrasound Med. Biol. **27**(12), 1615–1620 (2001)
2. Belkin, M., Niyogi, P.: Laplacian eigenmaps for dimensionality reduction and data representation. Neural Comput. **15**(6), 1373–1396 (2003)
3. Harris, E.J., Miller, N.R., Bamber, J.C., Evans, P.M., Symonds-Tayler, J.R.N.: Performance of ultrasound based measurement of 3D displacement using a curvilinear probe for organ motion tracking. Phys. Med. Biol. **52**(18), 5683 (2007)
4. Koshani, R., Balter, J.M., Hayman, J.A., Henning, G.T., van Herk, M.: Short-term and long-term reproducibility of lung tumor position using active breathing control (ABC). Int. J. Radiat. Oncol. **65**(5), 1553–1559 (2006)
5. Lachaine, M., Falco, T.: Intrafractional prostate motion management with the clarity autoscan system. Med. Phys. Int. **1**(1), 72–80 (2013)
6. Langen, K., Pouliot, J., Anezinos, C., Aubin, M., Gottschalk, A., Hsu, I.C., Lowther, D., Liu, Y.M., Shinohara, K., Verhey, L., Weinberg, V., Roach III, M.: Evaluation of ultrasound-based prostate localization for image-guided radiotherapy. Int. J. Radiat. Oncol. **57**(3), 635–644 (2003)
7. Nakamoto, M., Hirayama, H., Sato, Y., Konishi, K., Kakeji, Y., Hashizume, M., Tamura, S.: Recovery of respiratory motion and deformation of the liver using laparoscopic freehand 3D ultrasound system. Med. Image Anal. **11**(5), 429–442 (2007)
8. Preiswerk, F., De Luca, V., Arnold, P., Celicanin, Z., Petrusca, L., Tanner, C., Bieri, O., Salomir, R., Cattin, P.C.: Model-guided respiratory organ motion prediction of the liver from 2D ultrasound. Med. Image Anal. **18**(5), 740–751 (2014)
9. Scheipers, U., Koptenko, S., Remlinger, R., Falco, T., Lachaine, M.: 3-D ultrasound volume reconstruction using the direct frame interpolation method. IEEE Trans. Ultrason. Ferroelectr. Freq. Control **57**(11), 2460–2470 (2010)
10. Sedgewick, R.: Algorithms in C, Part 5: Graph Algorithms. Addison-Wesley, Boston (2002)
11. von Siebenthal, M., Székely, G., Gamper, U., Boesiger, P., Lomax, A., Cattin, P.: 4D MR imaging of respiratory organ motion and its variability. Phys. Med. Biol. **52**(6), 1547 (2007)
12. Wachinger, C., Yigitsoy, M., Navab, N.: Manifold learning for image-based breathing gating with application to 4D ultrasound. In: Jiang, T., Navab, N., Pluim, J.P.W., Viergever, M.A. (eds.) Medical Image Computing and Computer-Assisted Intervention – MICCAI 2010. Lecture Notes in Computer Science, vol. 6362, pp. 26–33. Springer, Heidelberg (2010)
13. Wein, W., Cheng, J.Z., Khamene, A.: Ultrasound based respiratory motion compensation in the abdomen. In: MICCAI Worshop on Image Guidance and Computer Assistance for Soft-tissue Interventions (2008)

Whole-Heart Single Breath-Hold Cardiac Cine: A Robust Motion-Compensated Compressed Sensing Reconstruction Method

Javier Royuela-del-Val[1(✉)], Muhammad Usman[2], Lucilio Cordero-Grande[2],
Marcos Martin-Fernandez[1], Federico Simmross-Wattenberg[1],
Claudia Prieto[2], and Carlos Alberola-López[1]

[1] Laboratorio de Procesado de Imagen, Universidad de Valladolid, Valladolid, Spain
{jroyval,marcma,fedsim,carlos}@lpi.tel.uva.es
[2] Division of Imaging Sciences and Biomedical Engineering,
King's College London, London, UK
{muhammad.usman,lucilio.cordero_grande,claudia.prieto}@kcl.ac.uk

Abstract. In this paper we propose a methodology to achieve single breath-hold whole-heart cine MRI with a temporal resolution of $\sim$46 ms and a spatial resolution of $2 \times 2\,\text{mm}^2$ out of a previously described method (JW-tTV) for single slice reconstruction. Its feasibility is tested by itself and in comparison with another state-of-the-art reconstruction method (MASTeR); both methods are adapted to Golden Radial k-space trajectories. From a formal viewpoint, we make use of a realistic numerical phantom to have a ground truth of deformation fields so that the methods performances against noise can be quantified and the sparsity regularization parameter involved in the reconstructions can be fixed according to the signal to noise ratio. Phantom results show that the adapted JW-tTV method is more robust against noise and provides more precise motion estimations and better reconstructions than MASTeR. Both methods are then applied to the reconstruction of 12–14 short axis slices covering the whole heart on eight volunteers. Finer details are better preserved with JW-tTV. Ventricle volumes and ejection fractions were computed from the volunteers data and preliminary results show agreement with conventional multiple breath-hold Cartesian acquisitions.

1 Introduction

Cine MRI has become the preferred technique for the noninvasive study of the ventricular volumes and cardiac function [4], where a stack of short axis slices covering the ventricles are acquired during several breath-holds (BH), typically one per slice, to avoid respiratory motion artifacts. This approach leads to long scan durations, misalignments between the slices acquired at slightly different BH positions and requires patient cooperation, a need that may be hindered by the patient pathology degree. The development of a technique able to cover the whole heart in a single BH would significantly palliate these shortcomings.

© Springer International Publishing AG 2017
M.A. Zuluaga et al. (Eds.): RAMBO 2016/HVSMR 2016, LNCS 10129, pp. 58–69, 2017.
DOI: 10.1007/978-3-319-52280-7_6

However, such a technique would involve the application of very high acceleration factors given the short time available for data acquisition.

Compressed sensing (CS) [7] based reconstruction methods have been developed and successfully applied to multi-slice 2D SSFP sequences. In [8], a free-breathing approach is presented in which a pseudorandom, eight-fold undersampling acquisition pattern in the Cartesian k-t space is applied. In [14] a closely related approach is applied to acquire four short axis and three long axis views of the heart in a single BH. Shape model is fitted to estimate the volume of the left ventricle (LV).

In the mentioned methods, the application of a Cartesian acquisition scheme leads to limited spatio-temporal resolution and, in some cases, aliasing problems along the phase-encoding direction [14]. Moreover, the targeted temporal resolution must be strictly defined before the examination, as it would determine the acquisition pattern (roughly speaking, the temporal resolution will determine how often the center of the k-space is sampled). These limitations can be overcome by the application of a Golden radial (GR) trajectory in k-space [16]. Since no phase-encoding is used, there is no interference from objects outside the field of view and the wisely selected golden-angle step allows to continuously acquire data regardless of the final temporal resolution of the reconstructed images, resulting in a more versatile and simpler procedure.

Recently, motion estimation (ME) and motion compensation (MC) techniques have been introduced in CS methods in order to minimize the degradation of CS reconstructions due to inter frame motion [1,9,12]. In CS with ME/MC, motion is jointly estimated from the reconstructed images themselves which, in turn, will be affected by both remaining undersampling artifacts and noise. The degree to which these errors in the images affect the estimated motion will determine the final quality of the reconstructions. Therefore, the application of a robust ME method turns out crucial [13]. However, the lack of a noise-free ground-truth for the images and the deformation fields hinders the performance analysis of the ME techniques and the CS reconstruction methods against noise in real situations. Signal to noise ratio (SNR) is also determinant in the choice of the regularization parameters involved in CS reconstruction [6,8]. A common procedure is to sweep the parameter space and select those parameters that provide the best reconstruction according to an expert criterion. This approach has clear limitations in real-world applications.

In this work we achieve higher acceleration factors with respect to recently published methods so whole-heart multi-slice cine single BH coverage is achieved. This is done by extending the Jacobian weighted temporal total variation (JW-tTV) [12] method, originally applied to the reconstruction of single-slice Cartesian acquired data, to use a GR acquisition scheme. This allows us to reach a $\times 16$ acceleration factor (with respect to a fully sampled Cartesian acquisition) that had remained unachieved so far. This proposal is compared with MASTeR [1], a related method which differs mainly in the ME technique used and which we have also extended to use GR. We show that quantitative cardiac function indicators, namely end diastolic (ED), end systolic (ES) and ejection fraction (EF) values calculated from the images reconstructed with the proposed method are in accordance with those obtained from a gold standard multi-BH Cartesian acquisition.

In addition, and as a preliminary step, we analyze the effect of noise on the acquired data in two aspects. First, in the selection of the optimal value for the regularization parameter involved in the CS reconstruction in order to obtain a empirical rule to select it. Second, in the errors induced in the estimated motion fields and in the quality of the final images. To this end, we use the numerical phantom XCAT [11, 17] to generate realistic ground truth deformation fields and synthetic k-space data affected by different levels of noise. The resulting extensions of both compared methods (JW-tTV-GR and MASTeR-GR) are tested.

2 Methods

CS Reconstruction of Undersampled Dynamic MRI with ME/MC

In CS with ME/MC, the reconstruction of an MRI image $\mathbf{m}$ from the acquired undersampled k-space data $\mathbf{y}$ can be formulated as [13]

$$\underset{\mathbf{m}}{\text{minimize}} \ \frac{1}{2} \parallel \mathbf{y} - \mathbf{Em} \parallel_{\ell_2}^2 + \lambda \parallel \boldsymbol{\Phi} \mathcal{T}_\Theta \mathbf{m} \parallel_{\ell_1} \tag{1}$$

where $\mathbf{E}$ is the encoding operator that models the acquisition process. In Cartesian acquisitions, $\mathbf{E}$ comprises the multiplication of the image $\mathbf{m}$ by the coils sensitivity profiles and the application of the regular fast Fourier transform (FFT) followed by the undersampling of the data with the used sampling pattern. In cine cardiac MRI, the sparsifying transform $\boldsymbol{\Phi}$ is typically chosen to be the temporal Fourier transform or the temporal total variation, in order to exploit the temporal redundancy between different cardiac phases. However, inter-frame motion will affect the redundancy of the signal along time reducing, reducing its sparsity level. The MC operator $\mathcal{T}_\Theta$ comprises a set of spatial deformations, governed by the set of parameters Θ, that deform each temporal instant in the dynamic image $\mathbf{m}$ to a common reference motion state. This way, the sparsity of the resulting motion compensated sequence along the temporal dimension is restored and the quality of the reconstruction improved, consequently. The parameter λ, referred to as regularization parameter in the introduction section, establishes a trade off between data consistency and the sparsity of the solution.

Since the motion in $\mathbf{m}$ is not known beforehand, a regular CS reconstruction is performed as a first step, which is equivalent to solve Eq. (1), with $\mathcal{T}_\Theta$ set to the identity. Then, a ME step follows and $\mathcal{T}_\Theta$ is estimated. The ME technique consists on a groupwise registration method based on a B-spline deformation model [10], controlled by the set of control points Θ, and a simple groupwise registration metric based on the variance of the intensity along time. Those control points that minimize the value of the registration metric are found by solving the following optimization problem:

$$\underset{\Theta}{\text{minimize}} \left\Vert \sum_{n=1}^{N} \left(\mathcal{T}_{\Theta,n} \mathbf{m}_n - \frac{1}{N} \sum_{k=1}^{N} \mathcal{T}_{\Theta,k} \mathbf{m}_k \right) \right\Vert^2 + R(\Theta) \tag{2}$$

where $R(\Theta)$ stands for an additional regularization term given by the second spatio-temporal derivatives of the motion fields that encourages smoothness of the estimated spatial deformations [13]. Equation (2) is solved by means of a non linear conjugate gradient algorithm. Once T_Θ has been obtained, CS with ME/MC is performed by solving Eq. (1). The NESTA optimization algorithm [3] is used to this end. Once Eq. (1) has been solved, and iterative procedure can be followed by alternating the ME/MC and the image reconstruction steps to obtain successively refined motion fields and images. In this work, the number of ME iterations has been set to three.

Finally, in JW-tTV a modification is introduced in the computation of the sparsity regularization term. The ℓ_1 term in Eq. (1) is substituted by a motion-based sparsity promoting metric given by

$$\|m\|_{T_\Theta} = \left\| \sum_{n=1}^{N} |T_{\Theta,n+1}\mathbf{m}_{n+1} - T_{\Theta,n}\mathbf{m}_n| \, \mathcal{J}_{n+1/2} \right\|_{\ell_1} \tag{3}$$

where $\mathcal{J}_{n+1/2}$ stands for the Jacobian of the deformation, averaged between instants n and $n+1$. The Jacobian is introduced in order to weigh the contributions of the temporal differences in Eq. (3) according to their corresponding spatial extent in the original sequence (before MC), instead of in the motion compensated one. Therefore, the following reconstruction problem results:

$$\underset{\mathbf{m}}{\text{minimize}} \; \frac{1}{2} \left\| \mathbf{y} - \mathbf{Em} \right\|_{\ell_2}^2 + \lambda \left\| \mathbf{m} \right\|_{T_\Theta} \tag{4}$$

Adaptation to Golden Radial acquisition

As stated in the introduction, in this work we have adapted the previously proposed JW-tTV method to work with GR trajectories in k-space in order to overcome the limitations derived from Cartesian acquisitions. In the GR scheme [16], radial profiles are continuously acquired with an angular separation given y the golden angle ($\sim 111.24°$).

In order to work with non Cartesian k-space data, the encoding operator in Eq. (4) is modified by substituting the regular FFT and the undersampling pattern by the calculation of a non-uniform FFT (NUFFT). To implement the NUFFT, we resort to the well established gridding algorithm [2]. In this algorithm, the k-space data is convolved with a finite kernel, sampled onto a Cartesian grid, converted to image domain performing a regular FFT and multiplied by a deapodization function to compensate for the effect of the convolution kernel in the frequency domain.

Even if efficient implementations exist, given the need of gridding operations the computational cost of the NUFFT is significantly higher than the Cartesian FFT. However, the benefits resumed in the introduction justify its application. In order to briefly compare the results obtained with the proposed GR method and the equivalent Cartesian counterpart, in Fig. 1 the reconstruction of a single SA view of the heart of one volunteer is shown. The GR pattern covers the

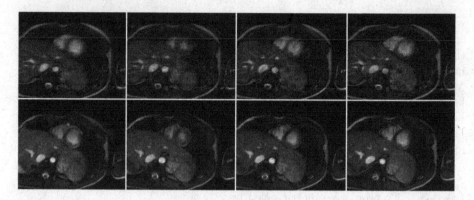

Fig. 1. Comparison of a Cartesian (top) and GR (bottom) reconstruction of a medial SA slice of the heart for an equivalent acceleration factor of 16 at different cardiac phases (left to right).

k-space more efficiently leading to better reconstructions, specially for the high acceleration factors involved in the single BH application.

Comparison with MASTeR

The proposed method is compared in the results section with MASTeR [1] which mainly differs from JW-tTV in the method used to estimate the motion in the image. In MASTeR, motion is estimated sequentially between each pair of consecutive frames to define a set of operators that predict each frame $\mathbf{m}_i$ out of its leading and trailing frames:

$$
\begin{aligned}
\mathbf{m}_i &= \mathcal{F}_{i-1}\mathbf{m}_{i-1} + \mathbf{f}_i \\
\mathbf{m}_i &= \mathcal{B}_{i+1}\mathbf{m}_{i+1} + \mathbf{b}_i
\end{aligned}
\tag{5}
$$

where $\mathcal{F}_{i-1}$ and $\mathcal{B}_{i+1}$ denote the forward and backward MC operators. Residuals $\mathbf{f}_i$ and $\mathbf{b}_i$ are assumed to be sparse and are used as sparsity term:

$$
\underset{\mathbf{m}}{\text{minimize}} \; \frac{1}{2} \parallel \mathbf{y} - \mathbf{Em} \parallel_{\ell_2}^2 + \alpha \parallel \mathbf{f} \parallel_{\ell_1} + \beta \parallel \mathbf{b} \parallel_{\ell_1}
\tag{6}
$$

where $\mathbf{f}$ and $\mathbf{b}$ are the concatenation of the residuals for all the cardiac phases. In our implementation, we choose $\alpha = \beta = 0.5\lambda$, since there is no apparent reason to favor any of the two terms. A method based on complex wavelets is used for estimating inter-frame motion.

Numerical Phantom for Heart Motion and MR Images Simulation

XCAT [11] was used to obtain a ground truth both for reconstructed images and tor the motion deformation fields. We modified MRXCAT [17] to simulate the k-space data with a desired SNR of a medial short axis slice with the following main parameters: b-SSFP sequence, TR/TE/flip angle = 3 ms/1.5 ms/60°, in-plane resolution of $1 \times 1\,mm^2$, field of view $= 256 \times 256\,mm^2$. 320 radial profiles were acquired and grouped into 20 cardiac phases (16 profiles per phase). 8 virtual coils were simulated. MASTeR-GR and JW-tTV-GR were used for reconstruction and the motion fields estimated by each of those methods were stored for posterior analysis. A dense sweep on the regularization parameter λ was performed for each SNR in order to find its optimal value in order to get both the maximum signal to error ratio (SER) and the best structure similarity index (SSIM) [15], calculated using the noise-free phantom image as the reference.

In-Vivo Experiments: Single BH Whole-Heart Acquisitions

Eight healthy volunteers were scanned with a 32-element cardiac coil in two 1.5T Philips scanners (four each). Relevant scan parameters include: b-SSFP sequence, TR/TE/flip angle $= 2.9\,ms/1.44\,ms/60°$, field of view $= 320 \times 320\,mm^2$, spatial resolution $= 2 \times 2\,mm^2$, slice thickness $= 8\,mm$ with no gap between slices. For each slice (12 to 14 were acquired, depending on volunteers heart size) between 216 and 272 radial profiles with 320 frequency encoding samples were acquired during a single cardiac cycle with ECG triggering. 13–16 cardiac phases were retrospectively reconstructed with a fixed temporal resolution of 46.4 ms (16 profiles per frame). A fully sampled, Cartesian, multi BH scan was performed with similar parameters for comparison. Breath-hold duration ranged 9 to 15 s. Sensitivity maps were estimated from a separate scan.

All the reconstructions were run off line on a server with two Intel Xeon E5-2695 v3 CPUs @ 2.30 GHz and 64 GB of RAM using MATLAB (R2015a, The MathWorks, Natick, MA). At the current implementation, both methods are applied to each slice independently from the others, what makes parallelization of the reconstruction straight forward.

3 Results

Figure 2 shows the SER and SSIM values for the JW-tTV reconstruction of the phantom data for a range of SNR and λ values. As the SNR diminishes, the optimal value of λ increases steadily. Therefore, higher level of sparse regularization results in better reconstructed images, as predicted by CS theory [7]. Only small differences in optimal λ appear depending on the quality metric used. These results were used as a reference to select λ in the reconstruction of in vivo data, where the SNR was estimated from the fully sampled, Cartesian images taking a background region as a reference for noise level. After revision by an experienced observer, the final values of λ were increased in order to maximize the subjective quality perception.

The reconstructions obtained for a selection of the SNR values simulated with the numerical phantom are summarized in Fig. 3. Sharper edges are recovered with JW-tTV than with MASTeR, specially for lower SNR values. More interestingly, MASTeR reconstructions show an erratic motion in the temporal profiles than can be appreciated even for high SNR values. The presence of

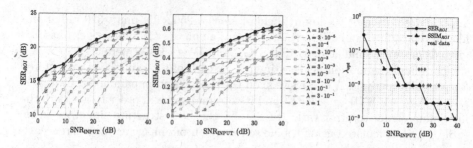

Fig. 2. SER (left) and SSIM index (center) obtained for each combination of λ in Eq. (4) and SNR value are plotted –dashed lines–. The envelope –continuous line– marks the optimal value of λ according to each metric for each SNR value and is plotted separately (right). The value of λ used to reconstruct the real data from volunteers is indicated in blue. (Color figure online)

erratic motion grows as the SNR decreases. These results agree with the motion fields obtained with both ME/MC CS based methods, analyzed in Fig. 4. For the whole range of SNR values simulated, the groupwise ME/MC technique employed in JW-tTV results in more precise estimations. The differences with the phantom ground-truth, measured as the root mean squared error on a mask over the myocardium, remain almost constant even for the lowest SNR values, while higher errors and faster degradation can be observed for MASTeR.

Figure 5 shows the results obtained from in-vivo data for two of the eight volunteers acquired. Sharper edges and finer details are better preserved with JW-tTV, while contrast between myocardium and blood pool is preserved. For each volunteer, ventricular volumes at end systole (ESV), end diastole (EDV) and ejection fraction (EF) were computed from the short axis slices using Simpson's rule and manual segmentation on a dedicated software for the three reconstructions. Functional parameters computed from fully sampled Cartesian reconstructions were used as reference values. Bland-Altman plots of the results are shown in Fig. 6. The mean and standard deviation of the differences between the functional parameters computed with each method and the reference scan are summarized in Table 1. JW-tTV results in lower mean ESV, EDV and EF differences and lower standard deviation for ESV and EF than MASTeR reconstructions.

4   Discussion and Conclusion

In this paper we have proposed a new reconstruction method based on the adaptation of a previously described ME/MC CS based method to comply with Golden Radial, multi-slice acquisitions. We have achieved an undersampling factor that allows us to cover the whole-heart (12–14 slices) with a temporal resolution of 46.4 ms, 13–16 cardiac phases with 16 profiles per frame, in a single BH of 10–13 s.

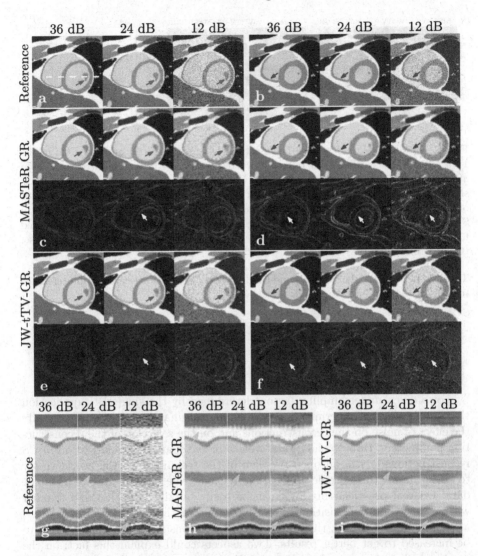

Fig. 3. Phantom reconstructions for different SNR values. Reference noisy images reconstructed from fully sampled Cartesian data (a, b) and from Golden Radial undersampled data (16 spokes per frame) with MASTeR-GR (c, d) and JW-tTV-GR (e, f) at systole and diastole, respectively. Error images are shown scaled by a factor of 2. Temporal evolution of the dashed line in (a) for the corresponding reconstructions (g, h, i). In JW-tTV-GR reconstructions thin details such as borders of the papillary muscle (red arrows) or the wall of the right ventricle are better preserved and present sharper edges than MASTeR-GR. Errors in MASTeR-GR are mainly concentrated in the edges of the structures, due to edge blurring and motion errors (white arrows), while JW-tTV-GR presents noisy errors due to low SNR. In the temporal evolutions yellow arrows indicate areas where MASTeR-GR presents some erratic motion in the heart even for high SNR values, while in JW-tTV-GR this effect is much less present. (Color figure online)

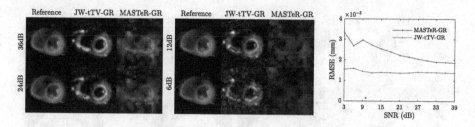

Fig. 4. Absolute value of motion fields estimated with MASTeR and JW-tTV in the 14th phase of the cardiac cycle out of 20, corresponding with large inter frame motion after end-systole for different SNR values (left and center). Phantom ground truth is shown at the left of each image. Red mask represents left and right myocardium. Plot of the RMSE of the motion fields calculated over the myocardium mask for a range of SNR values (right). Larger errors and faster degradation for low SNR can be observed for MASTeR, while JW-tTV shows to be almost immune to the presence of noise. (Color figure online)

Table 1. Left ventricular volumes and EF differences between accelerated and reference scan. Mean ± standard deviations are shown.

Method	ESV difference (ml)	EDV difference (ml)	EF difference (%)
MASTeR-GR	1.65 ± 3.62	−4.23 ± 2.62	−2.63 ± 2.61
JW-tTV-GR	−0.28 ± 3.06	−2.98 ± 5.00	−0.73 ± 2.19

For a given undersampling factor, determined by the single BH application that we pursue, the experiments on the numerical phantom allowed us to study the effect of noise on the reconstructions and on the selection of the reconstruction parameters. How to choose the weight of the sparsity regularization in CS reconstructions is still an open problem of the technique. In this work we try to establish, for this specific application, a choice rule based on the SNR of the data. On real practice, this SNR can be easily obtained by the MRI scanner with a short noise acquisition at the beginning of the examination. However, after visual examination, the final value of the reconstruction parameter had to be increased to get better results. Two aspects could explain this fact: on the one hand, the metrics used (SER and SSIM) are known to be limited when used to quantify image quality perception; on the other, different systematic errors in the real data reconstruction that are absent on the simulated data could affect the results (e.g. errors in the sensitivity maps and in the k-space trajectories). Consequently, a higher regularization term could partially mitigate the effect of the systematic errors mentioned.

Simulated and in vivo results show that better ME and more detailed reconstructions are obtained with the adapted JW-tTV than with MASTeR. For the latter, some erratic motion is observed in the reconstructions that could be explained by the lower performance of the ME procedure in the whole range of SNR considered. These results illustrate how ME errors can propagate to the final solution and the importance of using a robust ME technique.

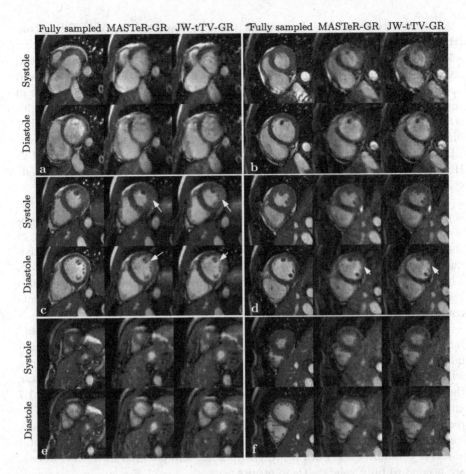

Fig. 5. Cartesian fully sampled, MASTeR and JW-tTV reconstructions of the data from two of the volunteers acquired. Basal (a, b), medial (c, d) and apical (e, f) short axis views are shown both at systole and diastole. White arrows indicate areas where thinner details are recovered with JW-tTV therefore permitting better delineation of the papillary muscles at systole.

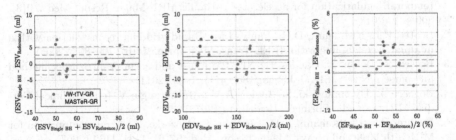

Fig. 6. Bland-Altman plots of the ESV (left), EDV (center) and EF (right) calculated from the fully sampled data (reference values) and from the accelerated single BH acquisition with MASTeR and JW-tTV.

Accordingly with this observation, the erratic motion in MASTeR reconstructions seems to affect the LV functional parameters calculated, introducing a larger mean difference in ESV, EDV and EF, since it can introduce artificial volume variations in the images and makes more difficult to identify systolic and diastolic cardiac phases. It is worth mentioning the higher standard deviation in the calculation of the EDV with JW-tTW. As Fig. 6 shows, in MASTeR reconstructions EDV values are systematically underestimated. With JW-tTV that bias does not occur, but underestimation takes place in volunteers with larger EDV. This fact increases the standard deviation of EDV differences in JW-tTV. However, the mean difference remains lower (in absolute value) than the one calculated from MASTeR reconstructions.

For the current MATLAB implementation, the reconstruction times for the single BH acquisitions lasted 12.5 min per slice with all the slices being reconstructed in parallel independently, what clearly limits the practical application of the proposed method. However, an initial reconstruction is provided in approximately 2 min that can be useful to check the correct planning of the acquisition. The introduction of coil compression techniques [5] and the development of a high performance implementation of the algorithm on graphics processing units could significantly reduce these reconstruction times.

Although the number of volunteers is reduced, reconstructed images and functional values computed from the highly accelerated data show preliminary evidence of the feasibility of the extended JW-tTV method to realize a whole heart cine examination in a single BH of short duration. For comparison, the acquisition time in the conventional Cartesian acquisition was between 1.7 and 2.2 min, without considering resting intervals between breath holds. This reduction in scan time could drastically impact on patient comfort and medical resources exploitation. However, further studies including intra and inter observer variability and both healthy volunteers and patients with heart disease are needed to fully validate these results.

References

1. Asif, M., Hamilton, L., Brummer, M., Romberg, J.: Motion-adaptive spatio-temporal regularization for accelerated dynamic MRI. Magn. Reson. Med. **70**(3), 800–812 (2013)
2. Beatty, P.J., Nishimura, D.G., Pauly, J.M.: Rapid gridding reconstruction with a minimal oversampling ratio. IEEE Trans. Med. Imag. **24**(6), 799–808 (2005)
3. Becker, S., Bobin, J., Candès, E.: NESTA: a fast and accurate first-order method for sparse recovery. SIAM J. Imag. Sci. **4**(1), 1–39 (2011)
4. Bogaert, J., Dymarkowski, S., Taylor, A.M., Muthurangu, V. (eds.): Clinical Cardiac MRI, 2nd edn. Springer, Heidelberg (2012)
5. Buehrer, M., Pruessmann, K.P., Boesiger, P., Kozerke, S.: Array compression for MRI with large coil arrays. Magn. Reson. Med. **57**(6), 1131–1139 (2007)
6. Doneva, M., Nielsen, T., Boernert, P.: Parameter-free compressed sensing reconstruction using statistical non-local self-similarity filtering. In: Proceedings of the 20th Annual Meeting of ISMRM, Melbourne, Australia (2012)

7. Donoho, D.: Compressed sensing. IEEE Trans. Inf. Theory **52**(4), 1289–1306 (2006)
8. Feng, L., Srichai, M.B., Lim, R.P., Harrison, A., King, W., Adluru, G., Dibella, E.V.R., Sodickson, D.K., Otazo, R., Kim, D.: Highly accelerated real-time cardiac cine MRI using kt SPARSE-SENSE. Magn. Reson. Med. **70**(1), 64–74 (2013)
9. Lingala, S., DiBella, E., Jacob, M.: Deformation corrected compressed sensing (DC-CS): a novel framework for accelerated dynamic MRI. IEEE Trans. Med. Imag. **34**(1), 1–23 (2015)
10. Rueckert, D., Sonoda, L., Hayes, C., Hill, D., Leach, M., Hawkes, D.: Nonrigid registration using free-form deformations: application to breast MR images. IEEE Trans. Med. Imag. **18**(8), 712–721 (1999)
11. Segars, W.P., Sturgeon, G., Mendonca, S., Grimes, J., Tsui, B.M.W.: 4D XCAT phantom for multimodality imaging research. Med. Phys. **37**(9), 4902–4915 (2010)
12. Royuela-del Val, J., Cordero-Grande, L., Simmross-Wattenberg, F., Martín-Fernández, M., Alberola-López, C.: Jacobian weighted temporal total variation for motion compensated compressed sensing reconstruction of dynamic MRI. Magn. Reson. Med. (2016). doi:10.1002/mrm.26198
13. Royuela-del Val, J., Cordero-Grande, L., Simmross-Wattenberg, F., Martín-Fernández, M., Alberola-López, C.: Nonrigid groupwise registration for motion estimation and compensation in compressed sensing reconstruction of breath-hold cardiac cine MRI. Magn. Reson. Med. **75**(4), 1525–1536 (2016)
14. Vincenti, G., Monney, P., Chaptinel, J., Rutz, T., Coppo, S., Zenge, M.O., Schmidt, M., Nadar, M.S., Piccini, D., Chèvre, P., Stuber, M., Schwitter, J.: Compressed sensing single breath-hold CMR for fast quantification of LV function, volumes, and mass. JACC Cardiovasc. Imag. **7**(9), 882–892 (2014)
15. Wang, Z., Bovik, A.C., Sheikh, H.R., Simoncelli, E.P.: Image quality assessment: from error visibility to structural similarity. IEEE Trans. Imag. Proc. **13**(4), 600–612 (2004)
16. Winkelmann, S., Schaeffter, T., Koehler, T., Eggers, H., Doessel, O.: An optimal radial profile order based on the golden ratio for time-resolved MRI. IEEE Trans. Med. Imag. **26**(1), 68–76 (2007)
17. Wissmann, L., Santelli, C., Segars, W.P., Kozerke, S.: MRXCAT: realistic numerical phantoms for cardiovascular magnetic resonance. J. Cardiov. Magn. Reson. **16**(1), 63 (2014)

Motion Estimated-Compensated Reconstruction with Preserved-Features in Free-Breathing Cardiac MRI

Aurélien Bustin[1,2,3]($\boxtimes$), Anne Menini[1], Martin A. Janich[1],
Darius Burschka[2], Jacques Felblinger[3,4,5], Anja C.S. Brau[6],
and Freddy Odille[3,4,5]

[1] GE Global Research Center, Munich, Germany
aurelien.bustin@tum.de
[2] Computer Science, Technische Universität München, Munich, Germany
[3] U947, INSERM, Nancy, France
[4] IADI, Université de Lorraine, Nancy, France
[5] CIC-IT 1433, INSERM, Nancy, France
[6] GE Healthcare, MR Applications and Workflow, Menlo Park, CA, USA

Abstract. To develop an efficient motion-compensated reconstruction technique for free-breathing cardiac magnetic resonance imaging (MRI) that allows high-quality images to be reconstructed from multiple undersampled single-shot acquisitions. The proposed method is a joint image reconstruction and motion correction method consisting of several steps, including a non-rigid motion extraction and a motion-compensated reconstruction. The reconstruction includes a denoising with the Beltrami regularization, which offers an ideal compromise between feature preservation and staircasing reduction. Results were assessed in simulation, phantom and volunteer experiments. The proposed joint image reconstruction and motion correction method exhibits visible quality improvement over previous methods while reconstructing sharper edges. Moreover, when the acceleration factor increases, standard methods show blurry results while the proposed method preserves image quality. The method was applied to free-breathing single-shot cardiac MRI, successfully achieving high image quality and higher spatial resolution than conventional segmented methods, with the potential to offer high-quality delayed enhancement scans in challenging patients.

Keywords: Magnetic resonance imaging · Free-breathing · Motion correction · Single-shot · Late gadolinium enhancement · Non-rigid registration

1 Introduction

Cardiac magnetic resonance imaging is a valuable tool for myocardial structure, function, and tissue assessment, providing essential information for clinical diagnosis and treatment decisions in cardiovascular disease. Using standard segmented sequences in which data acquisition is segmented over multiple heart beats, good image quality can be obtained in patients with regular cardiac rhythm and good breath-holding

© Springer International Publishing AG 2017
M.A. Zuluaga et al. (Eds.): RAMBO 2016/HVSMR 2016, LNCS 10129, pp. 70–80, 2017.
DOI: 10.1007/978-3-319-52280-7_7

ability; however, image quality can be degraded by motion artifacts when scanning patients with arrhythmia or poor breath-hold compliance.

In comparison to segmented acquisitions, single-shot techniques can be applied for rapid image acquisition of a whole slice within a single shot, greatly reducing the scan time. Due to the short acquisition duration of single-shot techniques (typically < 200 ms), artifacts from intra-shot motion are negligible, therefore such methods tend to be robust against cardiac and breathing motion. However, this motion robustness comes at the expense of lower spatial resolution and signal to noise ratio (SNR). An example of the benefit of single-shot over segmented Late Gadolinium Enhanced (LGE) imaging in a patient who could not breath-hold is shown in Fig. 1.

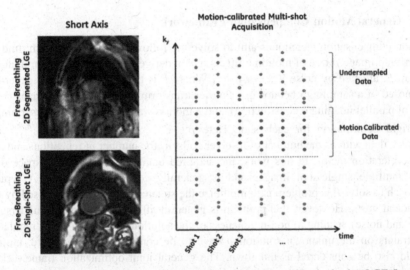

Fig. 1. (Left) Comparison between 2D segmented LGE (top) and 2D single-shot LGE (bottom) on a 77-year-old patient with breath-holding difficulties. The segmented LGE has higher resolution than the single-shot LGE but shows severe motion artefacts. (Right) Proposed hybrid k-space acquisition scheme including motion-calibration data (fully sampled center) and undersampled periphery, aimed to combine the resolution of segmented LGE with the motion-robustness of single-shot LGE.

Recent techniques proposed to enhance the SNR of single-shot methods by motion correcting and then averaging multiple single-shot images acquired in free-breathing [1]. While this technique shows good results with low acceleration factors, it may not provide optimal image quality for higher undersampling, introducing blurring and undersampling artifacts, mainly due to higher weight given to the regularization. Batchelor et al. [2] proposed a first generalized reconstruction framework for motion compensation. The method allows arbitrary motion to be compensated by solving a general matrix inversion problem. This technique, however, requires an adequate knowledge of the displacement fields. The recent GRICS method [3] extended this work by jointly estimating the motion and the recovered image, however, it relied on a motion model provided by external sensors (e.g. ECG, respiratory belt).

In this work, we sought to develop an efficient motion correction implementation suitable for reconstructing a high-resolution, high-SNR image from multiple accelerated single-shot images. The proposed method combines the benefits of using a hybrid self-navigated sampling scheme (see Fig. 1) with a joint reconstruction framework. In the image reconstruction step, a highly efficient feature-preserving regularization scheme (Beltrami) is proposed for recovering sharp details. We show that the proposed method is robust to high acceleration factors and yields results with efficient noise reduction and better overall image quality at a low computational cost.

2 Theory

2.1 General Motion Compensation Framework

Motion compensation techniques aim to solve the following inverse problem: find an underlying image ρ free of motion artifacts, given derived measurements s through the system E, affected by noise v: $s = E\rho + v$. Where E is the encoding matrix, generally composed of a sampling operator ξ, a Fourier transform F, coil sensitivity maps σ (in case of parallel imaging reconstruction), and a motion warping operator W describing a non-rigid deformation for each shot. Here $\rho \in \mathbb{C}^{n_x \times n_y}$ and $s \in \mathbb{C}^{n_x \times n_y/acc \times n_r \times n_c}$ are complex data with n_c the number of receiver coils, n_r the number of repetitions and acc the acceleration factor. In this work, the acquired data s represents the k-space data from multiple single-shot images and is generally corrupted by noise. A typical approach to solve this problem is to minimize the squared difference as assessed by the Euclidean norm. However, this problem is generally ill-posed (e.g. due to undersampling and noise), leading to non-uniqueness of the solution, if it exists. Thus, regularity constraints on the unknown solution ρ have to be considered. Furthermore, motion should also be considered as unknown. The general joint optimization framework is then defined as

$$\rho = \operatorname{argmin}_{(\rho,\vec{u})} \left\{ \|s - E(\vec{u})\rho\|_2^2 + \lambda \Phi(\rho) \right\} \text{ where } E(\vec{u}) = \xi F \sigma W(\vec{u}) \qquad (1)$$

Here $\vec{u}$ represents the displacement fields, Φ is the chosen regularization function and $\lambda > 0$ is the corresponding regularization parameter. The optimization problem in Eq. 1 is solved in four steps: (i) we first use the k-space center of the single-shot images to extract a self-navigation signal and to cluster the raw data into a reduced number of respiratory bins [4]; (ii) we reconstruct the images from each bin independently using a Beltrami-regularized SENSE (B-SENSE) reconstruction; (iii) then an estimate of the motion is obtained using a non-rigid registration (minimization of Eq. 1 with regards to $\vec{u}$ [5]) and (iv) a high resolution/SNR image is generated using the proposed motion-compensated reconstruction process (minimization with regards to ρ). A general description of the method is shown in Fig. 2.

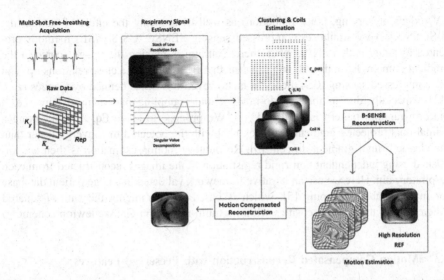

Fig. 2. Schematic illustration of the proposed reconstruction, including the non-rigid motion extraction. Acquisition is performed using complementary trajectories, leading to uniform samplings in the phase encoding direction, which allows for an optimal combination of the k-spaces according to their positions in the breathing signal. The motion model, initialized by registering the images from each respiratory bin, is incorporated into the reconstruction process.

2.2 Beltrami-Regularized SENSE

In our framework, a respiratory signal is extracted from the motion calibration data itself. This pre-processing step is achieved by stacking the low resolution images along the time dimension. Singular value decomposition is then applied to the stack and the first left-singular vector is used as a good approximation of the true respiratory signal. A specific respiratory phase is then assigned to each acquired shot, as explained in [4]. This binning strategy would split the data into fewer motion states $n_b(<n_r)$ with negligible respiration motion and lower undersampling in each of them. Images from each respiratory bin $(\rho_i)_{i=1...n_b}$ are then individually reconstructed by solving

$$\rho_i = \underset{\rho}{\operatorname{argmin}}\left\{\|s_i - E_i\rho\|_2^2 + \lambda\sqrt{1 + \beta^2|\nabla\rho|^2}\right\} \qquad (2)$$

The first term in Eq. 2 is a data fidelity term that aims to minimize the difference between the reconstructed image and the acquired data. The Beltrami regularization $\sqrt{1 + \beta^2|\nabla\rho|^2}$ has been introduced in the field of string theory for physics and has shown high potential in several imaging problems, including image denoising and enhancement [6] and super-resolution reconstruction [7]. In particular, the metric can be chosen such that the Beltrami energy corresponds to an arbitrary interpolation between Gaussian diffusion $\beta \to 0$ and total variation (TV) [8] regularization $\beta \gg 1$. In [9], the authors showed that Beltrami regularization is able to maintain the advantage of

TV (edges preserving, noise reduction) as well as reducing the effect of staircasing. B-SENSE is very similar to compressed sensing SENSE (CS-SENSE) methods presented by other authors [10], where here Beltrami is making the image sparse in the gradient domain. Even though this suggests that B-SENSE has a close relationship with the compressed sensing (CS) theory, it is, however, not CS as defined by Candès *et al.* [11], especially due to the pseudo-random undersampling pattern used here (i.e. a uniform random pattern is used in [11]). We propose to solve Eq. 2 by adopting a primal-dual projected gradient approach [12] with the potential to converge faster than the classic primal gradient-descent [9]. Respiratory motion estimation is then accomplished using independent non-rigid registration of the images reconstructed from each respiratory bin. Here we use an iterative framework validated in a large patient database for myocardial T_2 mapping [5], which is based on minimizing the sum-of-squared differences of the pixel intensities within a multi-resolution Gauss-Newton scheme.

2.3   Motion Compensated Reconstruction with Preserved-Features

This section presents the final step for solving the motion compensated problem in Eq. 1. The aim of the method is to reconstruct the high resolution, high SNR image ρ from the acquired raw data $s = (s_i)_{i=1...n_b}$. For the motion compensated reconstruction, we solve the following optimization problem, with the acquisition model now including the estimated motion fields:

$$\rho = \underset{\rho}{\mathrm{argmin}}\left\{ \|s - E(\vec{u})\rho\|_2^2 + \lambda\sqrt{1 + \beta^2|\nabla\rho|^2} \right\} \tag{3}$$

As in the previous section, we use a primal-dual projected gradient approach, employing the Beltrami energy as regularity prior [9]. Note that regularization is always preferred in motion compensated reconstruction due to the ill-conditioning induced by the motion operators, as shown in [13].

3   Materials and Methods

The proposed reconstruction algorithm was applied and validated with different experiments using Matlab (The MathWorks, Natick, MA) on a PC with Intel Xeon 3.3 GHz CPU and 64 GB RAM. The experiments were performed on 3T MR750w and 1.5T MR450w systems (GE Healthcare, WI, USA).

3.1   Offline Simulation on Synthetic Data

In order to perform a realistic simulation, we first created a synthetic dataset based on actual LGE patient images. In one patient with suspected cardiovascular disease, 4 repetitions of a cardiac-gated, inversion recovery prepared, single-shot LGE scan were acquired in free-breathing 10 min after Gadolinium injection. Cardiac images were obtained with a spoiled fast gradient echo sequence and the following parameters: matrix size 192 × 256, in-plane spatial resolution 1.52 mm × 1.52 mm in short axis with slice thickness = 8 mm, readout flip angle = 20°, echo time (TE) = 2.02 ms, mid-diastolic trigger delay, pulse repetition time (TR) = 4.43 ms and SENSE factor = 2 with partial Fourier. Synthetic k-space data were created by the application of synthetic coil sensitivity maps (with Gaussian profiles) to the LGE images, Fourier transformation and undersampling in the phase encoding direction. A full sampling of the central k-space area (17 lines) was used and the peripheral area was undersampled with a Golden Step Cartesian trajectory [14] with an acceleration factor R = 3.3. Spacing between samples was proportional to the Golden ratio (p = 0.618). This trajectory enables an irregular but almost uniform distribution of the acquired data for any arbitrary number of repetitions, leading to incoherent aliasing (Fig. 1, right). The motion-free image was reconstructed using our reconstruction and compared to a motion correction method similar to that proposed by Kellman et al. [1], where the motion-free image is recovered by averaging the registered images obtained after the B-SENSE reconstruction step. We call this prior method reconstruction-registration-average (RRA).

3.2 Phantom Imaging

Single-shot pulse sequences were used to acquire phantom images with a 26-channel cardiac coil. The sequence was modified to take into account the same Golden ratio sampling as in our offline simulation experiment. The protocol was applied to acquire phantom images with a resolution of 1.48 mm × 1.48 mm. A translational motion was imposed to the table to mimic respiratory motion.

3.3 In Vivo Validation Experiment with Self-navigation

In vivo cardiac datasets from two healthy adult volunteers were acquired on a 1.5T scanner using a 32-channel cardiac coil. A multi-shot slice (15 shots) of a free-breathing, cardiac-gated, spoiled fast gradient echo sequence (without inversion-recovery preparation) was collected with the following parameters: TE = 2.10 ms, TR = 4.52 ms, 8 mm slice thickness, FOV = 253 mm × 338 mm, matrix size 192 × 256 and 1.32 mm × 1.32 mm in-plane resolution, diastolic trigger delay. A fully sampled reference was acquired additionally in breath-hold for visual comparison. Each shot consists of 60 k-space lines: the central k-space was fully sampled with 17 lines and the periphery (43 lines) was undersampled, leading to a global acceleration factor of 3.2. An estimate of the respiratory signal was extracted using the proposed self-navigated technique, and was subsequently used to separate the acquired data into 5 respiratory bins. An overview of the parameters used in this study is given in Table 1.

Table 1. Parameters used for the different experiments. The acquisition matrix size was 192×256.

	#repetition n_r	#calib lines	#periphery lines	acc peri	acc shot pre-bin	acc shot post-bin	NEX sequence
Simulation 1	4	32	48	3.3	2.4	–	1.67
Simulation 2	4	32	32	5	3	–	1.33
Phantom	6	32	48	3.3	2.4	–	2.5
In vivo	15	17	43	4.1	3.2	1.1 (5 bins)	4.7

4   Results

The time needed to run the motion-compensated reconstruction for 15 shots of matrix size equal to 192×256 with 32-channel cardiac coils was about 1 min 35 s, including the time to compute the motion between shots.

4.1   Offline Simulation on Synthetic Data

Example reconstruction results on the simulated data generated from a patient with nonischemic cardiomyopathy are shown in Fig. 3. One can see a spatially blurred result with a standard reconstruction-registration-average (RRA) method. The proposed reconstruction exhibits significant quality improvements over each method with an acceleration factor r = 3.3 while reconstructing sharper edges (arrows) and small structures. For higher acceleration factors the performance of our method is much better compared to RRA, both in terms of reconstruction accuracy and image quality.

4.2   Phantom Imaging

Similar results can be observed in phantom experiments (Fig. 4). Comparisons with a classic Tikhonov reconstruction are shown in Fig. 4. The results present the recon-structed phantom motion experiments where here the motion has been applied with the table. The sum-of-squares reconstruction (Fig. 4, left) clearly exhibits the effect of motion. As in the previous experiment, the RRA method exhibits blurry results (due to the undersampling), although providing a motion-corrected denoised image. A visual improvement can be noticed when applying a motion compensated reconstruction with Tikhonov regularization. The latter method performs well but is, however, unable to recover sharp edges and some residual artifacts can still be seen on the recovered image. The use of a fast primal-dual algorithm combined with Beltrami regularization makes the proposed reconstruction robust with better performance in terms of image quality, reduced artifacts and sharpness (Fig. 4, Bel).

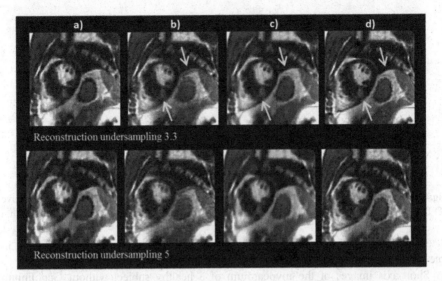

Fig. 3. Cardiac short-axis reconstruction of a synthetic dataset generated from 4 single-shot LGE acquisitions in free-breathing on a 37-year old patient with acceleration factors r = 3.3 and r = 5. (a) One reconstruction using a classic SENSE (192 × 256), (b) Sum-of-Squares (all repetitions), (c) Reconstruction-Registration-Average, (d) proposed reconstruction.

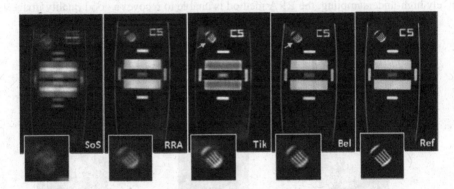

Fig. 4. Reconstructions on a phantom using two different regularization methods with acceleration factor 3.3. 6 single-shot repetitions have been acquired. From left to right: Sum-of-Squares (SoS), Reconstruction-Registration-Average (RRA), Tikhonov, Beltrami, Reference.

4.3 In Vivo Validation Experiment with Self-navigation

Figure 5 shows an example of the proposed fast and automatic self-navigated binning method on 150 consecutive slices of liver SPGR acquisition. The temporal rate was 400 ms, corresponding to a total acquisition duration of 1 min. The extracted respiratory signal (red) shows good agreement with the respiratory belt placed on the subject's thorax (blue), with a coefficient of determination $R^2 = 0.76$. Raw data acquired in similar motion states can be clustered into a reduced number of motion

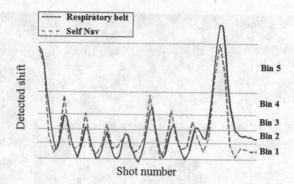

Fig. 5. Data binning step of the proposed self-navigated signal obtained from 150 consecutive 2D fast spoiled gradient echo acquisitions in free-breathing liver imaging. (Color figure online)

states, thereby improving the quality of images from which to extract motion in free-breathing without the need for navigators or external sensors.

Short-axis images of the myocardium of a healthy subject without Gadolinium injection and without inversion recovery preparation are shown in Fig. 6. Both cardiac structures (myocardium wall, papillary muscles) and non-cardiac structures (blood vessels) are very well recovered with our reconstruction. The method yields significant sharpening of the myocardium wall and papillary muscles. However, due to the relatively high-undersampling, the RRA method is unable to recover a good quality image,

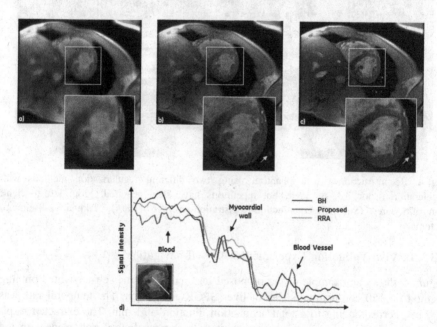

Fig. 6. Cardiac single-shot spoiled fast gradient echo images from a breath-held acquisition (c) and from a free-breathing acquisition with a naïve reconstruction (a) and with the proposed reconstruction (b). A profile of the reconstructed short axis image is shown (d).

exhibiting blurry structures and losing some of the details in the image such as blood vessels (arrows). This particularity is also seen in Fig. 6d where a specific intensity profile is plotted. The sharpness of the edges on our motion-corrected reconstruction is confirmed as well as the fidelity to the breath-hold acquisition.

5   Discussion and Conclusion

We introduced a new free-breathing single-shot LGE pipeline, including an optimized sampling and the associated joint reconstruction and motion correction algorithm designed for fast and robust cardiac imaging. By incorporating the estimated motion into the reconstruction process, we increased the robustness of the model and exhibited good quality images.

In this study, we used a fast and automatic self-navigated binning strategy that aims to cluster the acquired raw data into similar motion states. While preliminary results have shown improved image quality and better motion estimation, additional optimization of number of bins and number of repetitions is still required to maintain an optimal tradeoff between reconstruction quality, reconstruction time and accuracy of motion estimates.

The motion corrected images show better visual quality than classic reconstructions but appear less sharp than corresponding breath-held acquisitions, especially for high accelerations. Possible explanations are the inaccuracies in motion estimates or other effects related to MR physics, such as spin history or changes in B_0 and B_1 inhomogeneities induced by breathing.

One interesting application of the proposed motion correction model is for high-resolution 3D isotropic LGE single-shot imaging of the heart, such as the one proposed recently in [15] for myocardial scar assessment. This will allow for the reconstruction of 3D isotropic motion corrected volumes by keeping the advantages of a 2D acquisition (high tissue and vessel contrast, short acquisition time), e.g. using super-resolution techniques [7]. Other applications, such as abdominal imaging [16] and coronary vessel imaging [17], are being investigated.

A limitation to the method is that potential through-plane motion cannot be corrected, although it remains small compared to the slice thickness. To overcome this problem, one could consider weighting the images according to the motion amplitude compared to the target image or acquiring 3D slab instead of 2D slice data and applying motion compensation. The preliminary results presented in this work should be confirmed with further patient studies.

The feasibility of the proposed reconstruction has been evaluated in simulation, phantom and volunteer experiments. The method has been shown to allow non-rigid motion correction while efficiently recovering features, thanks to the Beltrami regularization scheme. The conventional segmented LGE acquisition is limited by the maximum breath-hold time, which limits the signal-to-noise ratio and/or spatial resolution. This limitation is overcome by the presented free breathing approach. Ultimately, this method could enable accurate motion corrected reconstruction of single-shot images with higher spatial resolution and a higher signal-to-noise ratio compared to conventional segmented methods, with the potential to offer high-quality LGE imaging in challenging patients.

Acknowledgement. The authors thank Mayo Clinic (Rochester, MN), Advanced Cardiovascular Imaging (New York, NY) and Morriston Hospital (Swansea, UK) for providing some of the imaging data. This publication was supported by the European Commission, through Grant Number 605162. The content is solely the responsibility of the authors and does not necessarily represent the official views of the EU.

References

1. Kellman, P., et al.: Motion-corrected free-breathing delayed enhancement imaging of myocardial infarction. Magn. Reson. Med. **53**(1), 194–200 (2005)
2. Batchelor, P.G., et al.: Matrix description of general motion correction applied to multishot images. Magn. Reson. Med. **54**(5), 1273–1280 (2005)
3. Odille, F., et al.: Generalized reconstruction by inversion of coupled systems (GRICS) applied to free-breathing MRI. Magn. Reson. Med. **60**(1), 146–157 (2008)
4. Usman, M., et al.: Motion corrected compressed sensing for free-breathing dynamic cardiac MRI. Magn. Reson. Med. **70**(2), 504–516 (2013)
5. Odille, F., et al.: Nonrigid registration improves MRI T2 quantification in heart transplant patient follow-up. J. Magn. Reson. Imaging **42**(1), 168–174 (2015)
6. Polyakov, A.M.: Quantum geometry of bosonic strings. Phys. Lett. B **103**(3), 207–210 (1981)
7. Odille, F., Bustin, A., Chen, B., Vuissoz, P.-A., Felblinger, J.: Motion-corrected, super-resolution reconstruction for high-resolution 3D cardiac cine MRI. In: Navab, N., Hornegger, J., Wells, W.M., Frangi, A.F. (eds.) MICCAI 2015. LNCS, vol. 9351, pp. 435–442. Springer, Heidelberg (2015). doi:10.1007/978-3-319-24574-4_52
8. Rudin, L., Osher, S., Fatemi, E.: Nonlinear total variation based noise removal algorithms. Phys. D **60**, 259–268 (1992)
9. Zosso, D., Bustin, A.: A primal-dual projected gradient algorithm for efficient beltrami regularization. Cam Report (2014)
10. Liang, D., Liu, B., Ying, L.: Accelerating sensitivity encoding using compressed sensing. In: IEEE Engineering in Medicine and Biology Society, Conference, vol. 2008(3), pp. 1667–1670 (2008)
11. Candes, E., et al.: Robust uncertainty principles: exact signal reconstruction from highly incomplete frequency information. IEEE Trans. Inform. Theor. **52**(2), 489–509 (2006)
12. Chan, T.F., Golub, G.H., Mulet, P.: A nonlinear primal-dual method for total variation-based image restoration. SIAM J. Sci. Comput. **20**(6), 1964–1977 (1999)
13. Atkinson, D., Hill, D.L.G.: Reconstruction after rotational motion. Magn. Reson. Med. **49**(1), 183–187 (2003)
14. Derbyshire, A.J., et al.: Golden-step phase encoding for flexible realtime Cardiac MRI. J. Cardiovasc. Magn. Reson. **13**(Suppl 1), P23 (2011)
15. Dzyubachyk, O., et al.: Super-resolution reconstruction of late gadolinium-enhanced MRI for improved myocardial scar assessment. J. Magn. Reson. Imaging **42**(1), 160–170 (2015)
16. Buerger, C., Prieto, C., Schaeffter, T.: Highly efficient 3D motion-compensated abdomen MRI from undersampled golden-RPE acquisitions. Magma **26**, 419–429 (2013)
17. Cruz, G., et al.: Highly efficient nonrigid motion-corrected 3D whole-heart coronary vessel wall imaging. Magn. Reson. Med. Early View (2016)

RAMBO and HVSMR: Deep Learning for Heart Segmentation

Recurrent Fully Convolutional Neural Networks for Multi-slice MRI Cardiac Segmentation

Rudra P.K. Poudel, Pablo Lamata, and Giovanni Montana[✉]

Department of Biomedical Engineering,
King's College London, London SE1 7EH, UK
giovanni.montana@kcl.ac.uk

Abstract. In cardiac magnetic resonance imaging, fully-automatic segmentation of the heart enables precise structural and functional measurements to be taken, e.g. from short-axis MR images of the left-ventricle. In this work we propose a recurrent fully-convolutional network (RFCN) that learns image representations from the full stack of 2D slices and has the ability to leverage inter-slice spatial dependences through internal memory units. RFCN combines anatomical detection and segmentation into a single architecture that is trained end-to-end thus significantly reducing computational time, simplifying the segmentation pipeline, and potentially enabling real-time applications. We report on an investigation of RFCN using two datasets, including the publicly available MICCAI 2009 Challenge dataset. Comparisons have been carried out between fully convolutional networks and deep restricted Boltzmann machines, including a recurrent version that leverages inter-slice spatial correlation. Our studies suggest that RFCN produces state-of-the-art results and can substantially improve the delineation of contours near the apex of the heart.

Keywords: Recurrent fully convolutional networks · Recurrent restricted Boltzmann machine · Left ventricle segmentation

1 Introduction

Cardiovascular disease is one of the major causes of death in the world. Physicians use imaging technologies such as magnetic resonance imaging (MRI) to estimate structural (e.g. volume) and functional (e.g. ejection fraction) cardiac parameters for both diagnosis and disease management. Fully-automated estimation of such parameters can facilitate early diagnosis of the disease and has the potential to remove the more mechanistic aspects of a radiologist's assessment. As such, lately there has been increasing interest in machine learning algorithms for fully automatic left-ventricle (LV) segmentation [1,8,10,12,17]. This is a challenging task due to the variability of LV shape across slices, cardiac phases, patients and scanning machines as well as weak boundaries of LV due to the presence of blood flow, papillary muscles and trabeculations. A review of LV segmentation methods in short-axis cardiac MR images can be found in [20].

© Springer International Publishing AG 2017
M.A. Zuluaga et al. (Eds.): RAMBO 2016/HVSMR 2016, LNCS 10129, pp. 83–94, 2017.
DOI: 10.1007/978-3-319-52280-7_8

The main image analysis approaches to LV segmentation can be grouped into three broad categories: active contour models, machine learning models, and hybrid versions that combine elements of the two approaches. Active contour models with either explicit [13] or implicit [15] contour representations minimize an energy function composed of internal and external constraints. The internal constraints represent continuity and smoothness of the contour and external constraints represent appearance and shape of the target object. However, designing appropriate energy functions that can handle all sources of variability is challenging. Also, the quality of the segmentations produced by these methods typically depends on the region-of-interest (ROI) used to initialise the algorithms. Machine learning approaches have been proposed to circumvent some of these issues [1,9,17,18] at the expense of collecting large training datasets with a sufficient number of examples. Investigating hybrid methods that combine some elements of both approaches is an active research area [4]. Current state-of-the-art LV segmentation approaches rely on deep artificial neural networks [1,17,18]. Typically, these solutions consists of three distinct stages carried out sequentially. Initially, the LV is localised within each two-dimensional slice; then the LV is segmented, and finally the segmentation is further refined to improve its quality. For instance, a pipeline consisting of Deep Belief Networks (DBNs) for both localisation and segmentation, followed by a level-set methodology, has shown to generate high-quality segmentations [17]. In more recent work, a different pipeline has been proposed that consists of convolutional neural networks for initial LV detection, followed by a segmentation step deploying stacked autoencoders, and a fine-tuning strategy also based on level-sets methodology [1]. The latter approach has been proved to produce state-of-the-art results on the MICCAI 2009 LV segmentation challenge [21]. Both approaches share a number of common features. First, the segmentation is carried out using two-dimensional patches that are independently extracted from each MRI slice. Second, they use a separate architecture for the two tasks, localization and segmentation. Third, different neural network architectures are trained for cardiac MR slices containing the base and apex of the heart, due to the observed heterogeneity in local shape variability.

In this work we investigate a neural network architecture, trained end-to-end, that learns to detect and segment the LV jointly from the entire stack of short-axis images rather than operating on individual slices. Recently, fully convolutional networks (FCN) have been proposed for the segmentation of 2D images [16]. They take arbitrarily sized input images, and use feature pooling coupled with an upsampling step to produce same size outputs delivering the segmentation. Compared to more traditional sliding-window approaches, FCNs are more efficient. They have received increasing interest lately as they unify object localization and segmentation in a single process by extracting both global and local context effectively [16,22]. Applications of FCNs to medical imaging segmentation problems have also started to appear, for instance for the identification of neuronal structures in electron microscopic recordings [22]. In independent work, Valipour et al. [25] have recently adapted recurrent fully convolutional networks for video segmentation.

Here we propose an extension of FCNs, called Recurrent Fully-Convolutional Networks (RFCN), to directly address the segmentation problem in multi-slice MR images. We are motivated by the desire to exploit the spatial dependences that are observed across adjacent slices and learn image features that capture the global anatomical structure of the heart from the full image stack. We investigate whether exploiting this information is beneficial for accurate anatomical segmentation, especially for cardiac regions with weak boundaries, e.g. poor structural contrast due to the presence of blood flow, papillary muscles and trabeculations.

2   Datasets

Our experiments are based on two independent datasets consisting of short-axis cardiac MR images for which the endocardium has been manually segmented by expert radiologists in each axial slice. Further details are provided below.

2.1   MICCAI Dataset

The MICCAI 2009 LV Segmentation Challenge [21] dataset was made publicly available by the Sunnybrook Health Sciences Center (Canada) and has been extensively used to compare a number of LV segmentation algorithms [1,8,10,12, 17,18]. It consists of 45 CINE MRI images from a number of different pathologies. The individual exams have been pre-grouped into training, validation and online testing subsets. Each subset contains 15 cases of which 4 heart failure with infarction (HF-I), 4 heart failure without infarction (HF), 4 LV hypertrophy (HYP) and 3 healthy subjects. However, the clinical information has not been used by any of the algorithms discussed here and in our experiments. All the images were obtained during breath-hold sessions lasting 10–15 s with a temporal resolution of 20 cardiac phases over the heart cycle. A typical phase, end diastole (ED) or end systole (ES), contains 6–12 short-axis slices obtained from the base to apex. In all the images, the slice thickness is 8 mm, the inter-slice gap is 8 mm, the field of view is 320 mm × 320 mm and the pixel size is 256 ×256. In all 45 samples, LV endocardial contours were drawn by an experienced cardiologist by taking 2D slices at both the end-systolic and end-diastolic phases, and then independently confirmed by a second reader. The manual segmentations were used as ground truth for the evaluation of the proposed models. Each set consists of 30 sequences (15 samples for each one of the two cardiac phases) with an average sequence length 8.94 slices.

2.2   PRETERM Dataset

A second and larger dataset was used for an independent evaluation of all the cardiac segmentation algorithms. The dataset consists of 234 subjects used to study perinatal factors modifying the left ventricular parameter [14]. All the individuals are between 20 to 39 years of age. Of these, 102 were followed prospectively since preterm birth, and are characterised by an average gestational age of 30.3 ± 2.5

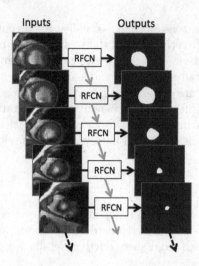

Fig. 1. A stack of short-axis cardiac MR slices (left) with corresponding left-ventricular binary masks (right) for a cardiac phase. The proposed RFCN leverages the spatial correlations that can be observed moving from the base of the heart to the apex.

weeks and a birth weight of 1.3 ± 0.3 kg. The remaining 132 subjects were born at term to uncomplicated pregnancies. Short-axis CINE MRI stacks were acquired with a 1.5-T Siemens Sonata scanner. All images have a 7 mm slice thickness and 3 mm inter-slice gap, the in-plane resolution is 1.43 ± 0.29 mm (min. 0.57, max. 2.17). All cardiovascular MRI was prospectively ECG gated and acquired during end-expiration breath holding. LV slices and endocardial masks were resampled into a homogeneous in-plane resolution of 2 mm, which yield slice pixel size of 212×212. Left ventricular short-axis endocardial borders were manually contoured by an expert reader at ES and ED using Siemens analytic software (Argus, Siemens Medical Solutions, Germany). The dataset was randomly divided into training, validation and testing sets of sizes 194, 20 and 20, respectively.

3 Recurrent Fully-Convolutional Networks

The proposed recurrent fully-convolutional network (RFCN) is an extension of the architecture originally introduced in [16] for predicting pixel-wise, dense outputs from arbitrarily-sized inputs. The main idea underlying FCNs is to extend a contracting path, in which a sequence of pooling operators progressively reduces the size of the network, by adding successive layers where pooling operators are replaced by upsampling operators. In this respect, our architecture is similar to U-net [22] where the expanding path is characterised by a large number of feature channels allowing the network to propagate context information to higher resolution layers.

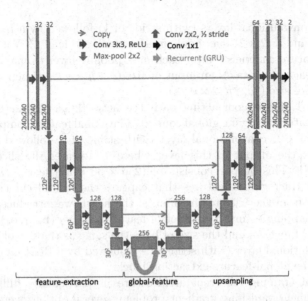

Fig. 2. Overview of the RFCN architecture. Blue boxes represent feature maps and white boxes represent copied feature maps. The number of feature maps and their dimensions are displayed above each box and on the left-side, respectively. Arrows represent network operations: gray arrows indicate copy operations, blue arrows indicate convolutional operations, red arrows indicate max-pooling operations, green arrows indicate convolutional operations with 1/2 stride, black arrow indicates 1 × 1 convolutional operation and orange arrow indicates a recurrent connection to handle inter-slice dependences learned through GRU. (Color figure online)

Our purpose is to model the full stack of short-axis images extracted from cardiac MRI and improve the segmentation of the left ventricle in each slice by leveraging inter-slice spatial dependences. The input is the entire sequence of $\acute{S}$ slices obtained at a particular cardiac phase (ED or ES) and the output is the sequence of corresponding (manually produced) left-ventricular masks. Each input and output image is assumed to have equal size. A schematic illustration is given in Fig. 1. As can be seen there, slices around the base of the heart (at the top) cover larger LV regions and show relatively clear boundaries whereas slices around the apex (at the bottom) cover smaller LV regions and present more blurred boundaries. Learning the typical shape deformations that are observed as we move from the base towards the apex is expected to improve the overall quality of the segmentation in challenging regions around the apex.

Three main building blocks characterise the proposed RFCN as illustrated in Fig. 2: a feature-extraction (contracting) path, a global-feature component and an upsampling (expanding) path. The feature-extraction component, which is independently applied to each image in the stack, deploys successive convolution and max-pooling operations to learn higher level features and remove local redundancy. In our architecture, this component consists of a repeated block of two (3×3) convolutional layers (with stride of 1) followed by a rectified linear unit (ReLU) and a (2×2) max pooling layer (with stride of 2). We doubled the number of feature channels c after each max pooling layer to maintain enough context, i.e. each block takes an input of size $(c \times h \times w)$ and generates output feature maps of size $(2c \times h/2 \times w/2)$.

At the end of this contracting path the network has extracted the most compressed features carrying global context. The global feature component starts here with a (3×3) convolutional layer (with stride of 1) followed by a ReLU. We denote $\mathbf{e}_s$ the output of this layer where s indicates the slice index, i.e. $s \in \{1, \ldots, S\}$. This output consists of $(256 \times 30 \times 30)$ feature maps. In an attempt to extract global features that capture the spatial changes observed when moving from the base to the apex of the heart, we introduce a recurrent mechanism mapping $\mathbf{e}_s$ into a new set of features, $\mathbf{h}_s = \phi(\mathbf{h}_{s-1}, \mathbf{e}_s)$, where $\phi(\cdot)$ is a non-linear function, and the size of $\mathbf{h}_s$ is the same as the size of $\mathbf{e}_s$. Another (3×3) convolutional layer (with stride of 1) followed by a ReLU is then applied to complete the global-feature extraction block.

Given that training recurrent architectures is particularly difficult due to the well-document vanishing gradient problem, several options were considered for the implementation of recurrent function ϕ, including a Long Short-Term Memory (LSTM) [7] and Gated Recurrent Units (GRUs) module [2]. GRUs in particular have been shown to achieve a performance comparable to LSTM on a number of tasks involving sequential data whilst requiring fewer parameters and less memory [3]. Here we have chosen to use a convolutional variant of GRU so that the local correlation of the input images are preserved whilst achieving a notable reduction in the number of parameters compared to its non-convolutional counter part.

For every slice, the dense feature maps that have been learned by the convolutional GRU module are then upsampled to compensate for the input size reduction caused by the max-pooling operations. The upsampled features are concatenated with a high resolution parallel layer aligned to the feature-extraction component, similarly to the U-net architecture [22]. Our upsampling component consists of a repeated block of a convolutional layer (with a fractional stride of $1/2$), a feature map concatenation module and two 3×3 convolutional layers (with stride of 1) followed by ReLU. The feature map concatenation module combines the outputs of the upsample layer and parallel feature-extraction block. Each block of the upsampling component takes a three-dimensional input $c \times h \times w$ and output $c/2 \times 2h \times 2w$ dimensional tensor. A convolutional operation with fractional stride is employed to compensate the reduction in input size due to the max pooling operation. Even though the upsampling procedure smooths out the boundaries of the object to be segmented, the concatenation of up-sampled feature maps with high-resolution feature maps helps mitigate this smoothing problem by providing better local and boundary information. The final segmentation is obtained by using a 1×1 convolutional layer, which maps the output of the upsampling component onto the two classes, i.e. LV and background. The probability for each class is given by a softmax function across all pixel locations.

4 Other Architectures and Model Training

Recently, deep belief networks (DBNs) have been proposed for automatic LV detection and segmentation using short-axis MR images [17,18]. A DBN was first used to detect the region of interest containing the LV. Anatomical segmentation was then carried out using distance-regularised level sets, which were modified to leverage prior shape information inferred by a separate DBN. In these models, as in FCNs, each slice in the short-axis stack is segmented independently of all the others. The main building block of a DBN model is a restricted Boltzmann machine (RBM), typically trained using the contrast divergence algorithm [5]. In some of our experiments, we have assessed the performance of DBNs for LV segmentation comparably to FCNs and the proposed RFCNs.

In order to further investigate whether modelling the dependence across slices typically yields improved performance, and motivated by the existing body of work on DBNs, we have also assessed the performance of a recurrent version of restricted Boltzmann machines (RRBM), originally proposed to learn human body motion [23], but never used for LV segmentation. RRBMs are stacked together to form what we call a recurrent deep belief network (RDBN). Similarly to the proposed RFCN, RDBN takes the entire sequence of short-axis slices as input and leverages the spatial correlations through additional bias units. For further information, we refer the reader to the original work [23].

The two convolutional architectures, FCN and RFCN, were trained by minimizing the cross-entropy objective function. FCN was trained using a stochastic gradient descent algorithm with momentum whereas RFCN was trained using a stochastic gradient descent algorithm with RMSProp [24]. Back-propagation was used to compute the gradient of the cross-entropy objective function with respect to all parameters of the model, including the GRU component in the case of RFCN. We also learned h_0 as required by the first slice of the sequence. In each block, batch normalization [11] was added after each convolutional layer, i.e. just before the max-pooling and upsampling layers. All reported results refer to the best out of 5 experiments in which the models were initialised with random parameters. RFCN was initialised using weights obtained from FCN, which reduces the training time and provided the good initial weights. Both the DBN and RDBN architectures were trained using the contrast divergence algorithm [5]. Dropout [6] was found to improve their overall performance. For all these models, best results were achieved using a learning rate of 0.01 with constant decay of 3% after each epoch, a momentum of 0.9 and weight decay of 0.00005. At the training phase, both the MICCAI and PRETERM datasets were augmented by generating additional artificial training images to prevent model overfitting. During training, we performed translation (± 16 pixels) and rotation ($\pm 40°$) data augmentation, which was found to yield better performance.

5   Experimental Results

This section presents an empirical evaluation of several LV endocardium segmentation algorithms using three performance metrics: good contours (GC) [1], Dice index, and average perpendicular distance (APD) between manually drawn and predicted contours [21]. In order to make our experimental results comparable with published studies on MICCAI dataset, all models were validated using the online set, and we report on results obtained on the validation set. Table 1 summarises the experimental results. On the MICCAI dataset, the DBN-based results presented in [17] include a Dice index of 0.88, a GC of 95.71% and an APD of 2.34 mm whereas the pipeline described in [1] results in a Dice index of 0.90, a GC of 90% and an APD of 2.84 mm (before further post-processing). A comparable Dice index is obtained by both FCN and RFCN, which yield higher GC and smaller ADP. Here RFCN outperforms FCN with a substantially improved ADP of 2.05 mm.

The PRETERM dataset was modelled using the same architectures, without further customisation. The results of this application are also summarised in Table 1. For this dataset, we compared the performance of four different architectures: FCN, RFCN, DBN and RDBN. The latter two models were given as input a region of interest containing the LV thus conferring them an advantage compared to FCN and RFCN. On this dataset we were not able to test the recently proposed pipeline described in [1], which relies on multiple stages. As in the MICCAI dataset, the fully convolutional architectures have achieved superior performance. RFCN has outperformed all other architectures in terms of Dice index and APD, which was found to be as small as 1.56 mm. In comparison, DBN with known LV location yields an APD of 2.05 mm. RDBN yields higher GC and lower APD compared to DBN thus providing additional evidence that performance gains can be obtained by modelling intra-slice dependences.

In order to shed insights into the regional improvements introduced by RFCN, the Dice index was computed separately for different local regions of the LV, and the results are summarised in Table 2. Here, Base-1, Base-2 and Base-3 indicates that 1, 2 and 3 slices were taken starting from the base of the heart and moving towards the middle, and analogously for the apex. All the remaining slices contributed towards the Central class. In all cases, the Dice index is calculated using all the samples at once to reflect overall pixels accuracy. In both datasets, RFCN outperforms FCN around the central slices and around the apex, as expected. However, in the MICCAI dataset, FCN yields better performance around the base of the heart. On the PRETERM dataset, both DBN

Table 1. Performance assessment on MICCAI and PRETERM datasets. For the MICCAI dataset, for completeness we also report on published results after a post-processing stage based on level-sets. The DBN and RDBN models only performed endocardium segmentation, not detection, i.e. they were applied to focused regions of interest centered around the left-ventricle. All other architectures performed LV detection and endocardium segmentation from full short-axis slices.

Dataset	Model	GC	Dice	APD
MICCAI with level-sets	[17]	95.91 (5.28)	0.880 (0.03)	2.34 (0.46)
	[1]	97.80 (4.70)	0.94 (0.02)	1.70 (0.37)
	[19]	95.91 (5.28)	0.880 (0.03)	2.34 (0.46)
MICCAI without level-sets	[17]	**95.71 (6.96)**	0.880 (0.03)	2.34 (0.45)
	[1]	90.00 (10.00)	0.900 (0.10)	2.84 (0.29)
	[19]	90.29 (12.73)	0.880 (0.03)	2.42 (0.36)
	FCN	94.78 (06.27)	**0.902 (0.04)**	2.14 (0.38)
	RFCN	95.34 (07.20)	0.900 (0.04)	**2.05 (0.29)**
PRETERM	DBN	92.01 (8.36)	0.913 (0.02)	2.05 (0.38)
	RDBN	97.50 (6.77)	0.909 (0.02)	1.94 (0.23)
	FCN	**97.59 (4.82)**	0.916 (0.03)	1.80 (0.41)
	RFCN	95.37 (5.69)	**0.935 (0.03)**	**1.56 (0.31)**

Table 2. Breakdown of the Dice index by LV regions on both MICCAI and PRETERM datasets. Base-X and Apex-X represent number of slice(s) included starting from the base and apex of the left ventricle, respectively. The index is calculated using all slices from the all samples at once hence measuring overall pixels accuracy. DBN and RDBN performed the segmentation task using a pre-defined region of interest containing the LV region.

Dataset	Model	Base-1	Base-2	Base-3	Central	Apex-3	Apex-2	Apex-1
MICCAI	FCN	**0.9313**	**0.9314**	**0.9342**	0.9367	0.8751	0.8441	0.7581
	RFCN	0.9040	0.9178	0.9268	**0.9433**	**0.9112**	**0.8917**	**0.8468**
PRETERM	DBN	0.9285	0.9374	0.9413	0.9385	0.8465	0.7809	0.6139
	RDBN	0.9319	0.9379	0.9420	0.9433	0.8856	0.8409	0.7542
	FCN	0.9486	0.9536	0.9559	0.9610	0.9051	0.8686	0.7468
	RFCN	**0.9576**	**0.9621**	**0.9631**	**0.9625**	**0.9178**	**0.8800**	**0.7571**

and RDBN gave the worst performance, compared to FCN and RFCN, despite using focused region of interests instead of full-sized images. Here again it can be observed that RDBN improves upon DBN across all cardiac locations.

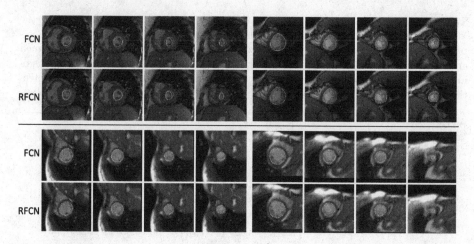

Fig. 3. Example of segmented left ventricle using RFCN and FCN architectures from MICCAI dataset (top two rows) [21] and PRETERM dataset (bottom two rows). Green contours represent the ground truth and red contours are the predicted contours. RFCN is often able to better delineate the left-ventricle contours with weaker boundaries compared to FCN. (Color figure online)

6   Conclusions

In this paper we have investigated whether a single neural network architecture, trained end-to-end, can deliver a fully-automated and accurate segmentation of the left ventricle using a stack of MR short-axis images. The proposed architecture, RFCN, learns image features that are important for the localisation of the LV in a sequential manner, going from the base to the apex of the heart, through a recurrent modification of fully convolutional networks.

Experimental findings obtained from two independent applications demonstrate that propagating information from adjacent slices can help extract improved context information with positive effect on the resulting segmentation quality. The hypothetical value of the large inter-slice correlation has been further tested by introducing a recurrent version of deep belief networks, and verified with our results showing that RDBNs generally outperform DBNs on the segmentation task, assuming the LV has already been localised. As expected, notable improvements can be seen in the delineation of cardiac contours around the apex, which are notoriously more difficult to identify.

One surprising finding was to note that performance of RFCN in apical slices was better for MICCAI than for PRETERM cohort (0.85 vs. 0.76 Dice index in the most apical slice, see Table 2), when one could expect the opposite: a regular and homogeneous cohort, PRETERM, should lead to a better performance when leveraging the inter-slice spatial dependence. This aspect will warrant further investigations.

Compared to other models, RFCN has the advantage of carrying out both LV detection and segmentation in a single architecture with clear computational benefits and the potential for real-time application. In future work, we are planning to investigate alternatives operations that can capture inter-slice correlations, such as 3D convolutions, and further extend RFCN by incorporating a bi-directional mechanism for the inclusion of an inverse path (from the apex to the base of the heart) as well as a temporal extension to handle all cardiac phases at once.

Acknowledgements. The authors would like to thank Paul Leeson and Adam Lewandowski from Oxford University for their assistance with the PRETERM dataset.

References

1. Avendi, M.R., Kheradvar, A., Jafarkhani, H.: A combined deep-learning and deformable-model approach to fully automatic segmentation of the left ventricle in cardiac MRI. Med. Image Anal. **30**, 108–119 (2016)
2. Cho, K., van Merrienboer, B., Gulcehre, C., Bahdanau, D., Bougares, F., Schwenk, H., Bengio, Y.: Learning Phrase Representations using RNN Encoder-Decoder for Statistical Machine Translation. arXiv:1406.1078 (2014)
3. Chung, J., Gulcehre, C., Cho, K., Bengio, Y.: Empirical Evaluation of Gated Recurrent Neural Networks on Sequence Modeling. arXiv:1412.3555 (2014)
4. Georgescu, B., Zhou, X.S., Comaniciu, D., Gupta, A.: Database-guided segmentation of anatomical structures with complex appearance. In: CVPR, vol. 2, pp. 429–436 (2005)
5. Hinton, G.E., Salakhutdinov, R.R.: Reducing the dimensionality of data with neural networks. Science **313**(5786), 504–507 (2006)
6. Hinton, G.E., Srivastava, N., Krizhevsky, A., Sutskever, I., Salakhutdinov, R.R.: Improving neural networks by preventing co-adaptation of feature detectors. arXiv:1207.0580 [cs] (2012)
7. Hochreiter, S., Schmidhuber, J.: Long short-term memory. Neural Comput. **9**(8), 1735–1780 (1997)
8. Hu, H., Liu, H., Gao, Z., Huang, L.: Hybrid segmentation of left ventricle in cardiac MRI using Gaussian-mixture model and region restricted dynamic programming. Magn. Reson. Imaging **31**(4), 575–584 (2013)
9. Huang, R., Pavlovic, V., Metaxas, D.N.: A graphical model framework for coupling MRFs and deformable models, vol. 2, pp. 739–746 (2004)
10. Huang, S., Liu, J., Lee, L.C., Venkatesh, S.K., Teo, L.L.S., Au, C., Nowinski, W.L.: An image-based comprehensive approach for automatic segmentation of left ventricle from cardiac short axis cine MR images. J. Digit. Imaging **24**(4), 598–608 (2011)
11. Ioffe, S., Szegedy, C.: Batch Normalization: Accelerating Deep Network Training by Reducing Internal Covariate Shift. arXiv:1502.03167 [cs], February 2015
12. Jolly, M.: Fully automatic left ventricle segmentation in cardiac cine MR images using registration and minimum surfaces. MIDAS J. **49** (2009)
13. Kass, M., Witkin, A., Terzopoulos, D.: Snakes: active contour models. Int. J. Comput. Vision **1**(4), 321–331 (1988)

14. Lewandowski, A.J., Augustine, D., Lamata, P., Davis, E.F., Lazdam, M., Francis, J., McCormick, K., Wilkinson, A.R., Singhal, A., Lucas, A., Smith, N.P., Neubauer, S., Leeson, P.: Preterm heart in adult life: cardiovascular magnetic resonance reveals distinct differences in left ventricular mass, geometry, and function. Circulation **127**(2), 197–206 (2013)
15. Li, C., Xu, C., Gui, C., Fox, M.: Distance regularized level set evolution and its application to image segmentation. IEEE Trans. Image Process. **19**(12), 3243–3254 (2010)
16. Long, J., Shelhamer, E., Darrell, T.: Fully convolutional networks for semantic segmentation. In: CVPR (2015)
17. Ngo, T.A., Carneiro, G.: Fully automated non-rigid segmentation with distance regularized level set evolution initialized and constrained by deep-structured inference. In: CVPR, pp. 3118–3125 (2014)
18. Ngo, T.A., Carneiro, G.: Left ventricle segmentation from cardiac MRI combining level set methods with deep belief networks. In: ICIP, pp. 695–699 (2013)
19. Ngo, T.A., Lu, Z., Carneiro, G.: Combining deep learning and level set for the automated segmentation of the left ventricle of the heart from cardiac cine magnetic resonance. Med. Image Anal. **35**, 159–171 (2017)
20. Petitjean, C., Dacher, J.N.: A review of segmentation methods in short axis cardiac MR images. Med. Image Anal. **15**(2), 169–184 (2011)
21. Radau, P., Lu, Y., Connelly, K., Paul, G., Dick, A.J., Wright, G.A.: Evaluation framework for algorithms segmenting short axis cardiac MRI. MIDAS J. Card. MR Left Ventricle Segmentation Challenge (2009)
22. Ronneberger, O., Fischer, P., Brox, T.: U-Net: convolutional networks for biomedical image segmentation. In: MICCAI (2015)
23. Sutskever, I., Hinton, G.E., Taylor, G.W.: The recurrent temporal restricted Boltzmann machine. In: NIPS, pp. 1601–1608 (2009)
24. Tieleman, T., Hinton, G.: Lecture 6.5-rmsprop: Divide the gradient by a running average of its recent magnitude. In: COURSERA: Neural Networks for Machine Learning, vol. 4 (2012)
25. Valipour, S., Siam, M., Jagersand, M., Ray, N.: Recurrent Fully Convolutional Networks for Video Segmentation. arXiv:1606.00487 [cs] (2016)

Dilated Convolutional Neural Networks for Cardiovascular MR Segmentation in Congenital Heart Disease

Jelmer M. Wolterink[1]($\boxtimes$), Tim Leiner[2], Max A. Viergever[1], and Ivana Išgum[1]

[1] Image Sciences Institute,
University Medical Center Utrecht, Utrecht, The Netherlands
j.m.wolterink@umcutrecht.nl
[2] Department of Radiology,
University Medical Center Utrecht, Utrecht, The Netherlands

Abstract. We propose an automatic method using dilated convolutional neural networks (CNNs) for segmentation of the myocardium and blood pool in cardiovascular MR (CMR) of patients with congenital heart disease (CHD).

Ten training and ten test CMR scans cropped to an ROI around the heart were provided in the MICCAI 2016 HVSMR challenge. A dilated CNN with a receptive field of 131×131 voxels was trained for myocardium and blood pool segmentation in axial, sagittal and coronal image slices. Performance was evaluated within the HVSMR challenge.

Automatic segmentation of the test scans resulted in Dice indices of 0.80 ± 0.06 and 0.93 ± 0.02, average distances to boundaries of 0.96 ± 0.31 and 0.89 ± 0.24 mm, and Hausdorff distances of 6.13 ± 3.76 and 7.07 ± 3.01 mm for the myocardium and blood pool, respectively. Segmentation took 41.5 ± 14.7 s per scan.

In conclusion, dilated CNNs trained on a small set of CMR images of CHD patients showing large anatomical variability provide accurate myocardium and blood pool segmentations.

Keywords: Deep learning · Dilated convolutional neural networks · Medical image segmentation · Cardiovascular MR · Congenital heart disease

1 Introduction

Congenital heart diseases (CHD) are a type of congenital defect affecting almost 1% of live births [2]. Patients with severe congenital heart disease often require surgery in their childhood. It has been shown that the use of patient-specific 3D models is helpful for preoperative planning [9]. Such models are typically based on a segmentation of the patient's anatomy in cardiovascular MR (CMR). However, segmentation of cardiac structures in CMR requires several hours of manual annotations [11]. Hence, there is a need for semi-automatic or fully automatic

© Springer International Publishing AG 2017
M.A. Zuluaga et al. (Eds.): RAMBO 2016/HVSMR 2016, LNCS 10129, pp. 95–102, 2017.
DOI: 10.1007/978-3-319-52280-7_9

segmentation methods to speed up this time-consuming process and reduce the workload for clinicians.

The large anatomical variability among patients poses a major challenge for (semi)automatic segmentation of CMR in CHD patients (Fig. 1). Methods relying on multi-atlas based segmentation would require a highly diverse training set representing the various manifestations of CHD. Hence, local analysis based on intensity and texture might be advantageous. Pace et al. proposed a patch-based semi-automatic segmentation method that produces highly accurate segmentations, requiring one hour of manual interaction and one hour of offline processing per scan [7]. The label of each voxel in an image is determined based on patch similarity to manually segmented sections in the image. To eliminate any user interaction, we propose a fully automatic patch-based voxel classification method. Voxel labels are determined based on similarities to voxels in training images using a convolutional neural network (CNN).

CNNs have been widely adopted in medical image analysis for segmentation of e.g. tissue classes [6] and tumors [3] in brain MR, neuronal structures in electron-miscroscopy [8] and coronary artery calcium in cardiac CT angiography [12]. A CNN labels each voxel in an image based on one or multiple patches surrounding that voxel. An effective voxel classification method should combine both local structure information and global context information. To this end, Moeskops et al. proposed a multi-scale approach using differently-sized patches extracted for every voxel [6], and Ronneberger et al. used a CNN which merges information at different scales by skipping layers [8]. However, patch extraction at every voxel is time-consuming and downsampling layers affect the output resolution and translational equivariance, meaning that the exact output may depend on the positioning of the input.

Recently, stacks of dilated convolutions have been proposed for image segmentation [13]. Such stacks aggregate features at multiple scales through convolutional layers with very few parameters, thereby avoiding problems such as overfitting, while generating high resolution output images with translation equivariance. The promise of a large receptive field with few trainable parameters is particularly interesting in medical imaging, where data sets are often small. In this work, we use CNNs with dilated convolutions to automatically segment CMR images of CHD patients.

2   Data

The method was developed and evaluated within the framework of the MICCAI Workshop on Whole-Heart and Great Vessel Segmentation from 3D Cardiovascular MRI in Congenital Heart Disease (HVSMR 2016)[1]. Ten training and ten test CMR scans were provided by the workshop organizers. The scans were acquired at Boston Children's Hospital with a 1.5T Philips Achieva scanner (TR = 3.4 ms, TE = 1.7 ms, $\alpha = 60°$). Three images were provided for each patient: a complete axial CMR image, the same image cropped around the heart

---

[1] http://segchd.csail.mit.edu.

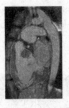
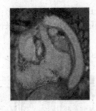

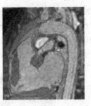

Fig. 1. Example cardiovascular MR data of four patients with congenital heart disease. The examples illustrate the high variability in the structure and appearance of the blood pool and myocardium. Reference annotations for the blood pool and myocardium are shown in blue and green, respectively. (Color figure online)

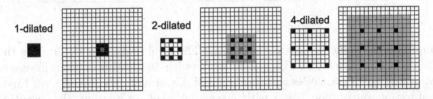

Fig. 2. Convolution with a standard 1-dilated 3×3 kernel, followed by convolution with a 2-dilated and a 4-dilated kernel (kernels shown in black). The receptive field (shown in gray) increases from 3×3 after the first convolution, to 7×7 after the second convolution and 15×15 after the third convolution. All convolutions only use $3 \times 3 = 9$ trainable parameters.

and thoracic aorta, and a cropped short axis reconstruction. In the current work, we use the cropped image around the heart and thoracic aorta. Reconstructed in-plane resolution of the images ranged from 0.73 mm to 1.15 mm, while slice spacing ranged from 0.65 mm to 1.15 mm.

Reference segmentations of the blood pool and myocardium were provided for the training scans, but not for the test scans. These segmentations were made by a trained observer and validated by two clinical experts. The blood pool class contained both atria and ventricles, the aorta, pulmonary veins, and superior and inferior vena cava. The myocardium class contained the thick muscle around the two ventricles and their separating septum. Example reference segmentations are shown in Fig. 1.

3   Methods

We trained a purely convolutional CNN to assign a class label to each voxel in a CMR volume based on classification of three orthogonal patches centered at the voxel. The CNN uses dilated convolutions allowing large receptive fields with few trainable parameters.

CNNs consist of a sequence of convolution layers, which convolve an image F_l at layer l with a kernel k to obtain image F_{l+1} at layer $l+1$. Dilated convolutions are extensions of these convolutions, that add spacing between the elements of the kernel k so that neighboring voxels at larger intervals are considered when

Table 1. The convolutional neural network architecture used in this study. For each layer, the convolution kernel size, the level of dilation, the receptive field, the number of output channels and the number of trainable parameters are listed. Figures in the top row illustrate the receptive field at each layer shown in red.

Layer	1	2	3	4	5	6	7	8	9	10
Convolution	3×3	3×3	3×3	3×3	3×3	3×3	3×3	3×3	1×1	1×1
Dilation	1	1	2	4	8	16	32	1	1	1
Field	3×3	5×5	9×9	17×17	33×33	65×65	129×129	131×131	131×131	131×131
Channels	32	32	32	32	32	32	32	32	192	3
Parameters	320	9248	9248	9248	9248	9248	9248	9344	6912	579

computing the value for a voxel x in F_{l+1}. The level of dilation determines the stride between kernel elements (Fig. 2). CNNs with dilated convolutions have several advantages over CNNs with non-dilated, i.e. standard, convolutions. First, by stacking convolution layers with increasing levels of dilation, the receptive field for every voxel can be substantially extended at the cost of only few additional trainable parameters. Second, dilated convolution operations are translationally equivalent: the same multi-scale feature aggregation pyramid is applied at each location in the image. Hence, translating the image results in a translated version of the original output. Third, no downsampling layers are required to obtain large receptive fields and hence, high resolution label maps can be directly predicted by the network.

Table 1 lists the CNN architecture used in this study. We adapt the dilated convolution context module proposed by Yu et al. [13] and extend the receptive field from 67×67 voxels to 131×131 voxels by inserting layer 7, with 32-dilated kernels. Layers 1 to 8 serve as feature extraction layers, while layers 9 and 10 are fully connected classification layers, implemented as 1×1 convolutional layers for increased efficiency. In each feature extraction layer, 32 kernels are used. The dilation level is increased between layers 2 and 7. This allows the receptive field to grow exponentially, while the number of trainable parameters grows linearly; the same number of parameters is used in each layer. The figures in the top row illustrate the receptive field in each layer. Layers 1 to 9 are each followed by an exponential linear unit (ELU) activation function [1], while layer 10 is followed by a softmax function. Batch normalization and dropout are applied to the fully connected layers 8 and 9 [4,10]. Classification is performed in a wider layer with 192 channels and a final layer with 3 output channels, i.e. for the myocardium, blood pool and background. In total, the network contains 72,643 trainable parameters.

To correct for differences in intensity signals between CMR images, each image was normalized to have zero mean and unit variance. Furthermore, to correct for potential differences in orientation of patients, copies of the images rotated 90, 180 and 270° along each axis were added to the training set. Finally, to guarantee that structures appear at similar scales in different images and along different axes, all images were resampled to an isotropic resolution of

Table 2. Results for the training and test set as provided by the HVSMR challenge. For both the myocardium and the blood pool, the Dice index, the average distance to boundaries (ADB) and the Hausdorff distance (Hausdorff) are listed.

		Myocardium			Blood pool		
		Dice	ADB	Hausdorff	Dice	ADB	Hausdorff
Training	Average	0.80 ± 0.06	1.01 ± 0.43	6.70 ± 3.52	0.92 ± 0.03	0.81 ± 0.28	5.86 ± 3.36
Test	Patient 10	0.72	1.34	10.75	0.94	0.74	5.23
	Patient 11	0.81	0.68	2.50	0.93	0.94	9.17
	Patient 12	0.87	0.60	3.94	0.93	0.83	9.74
	Patient 13	0.88	1.03	10.19	0.94	0.94	10.62
	Patient 14	0.71	1.33	8.69	0.90	1.07	4.21
	Patient 15	0.76	1.07	3.97	0.89	1.44	11.78
	Patient 16	0.76	0.80	3.14	0.91	0.77	6.12
	Patient 17	0.87	0.70	4.14	0.95	0.61	4.27
	Patient 18	0.85	0.61	2.19	0.94	0.64	3.29
	Patient 19	0.79	1.41	11.76	0.93	0.87	6.28
	Average	0.80 ± 0.06	0.96 ± 0.32	6.13 ± 3.76	0.93 ± 0.02	0.89 ± 0.24	7.07 ± 3.01

$0.65 \times 0.65 \times 0.65$ mm per voxel, the smallest voxel dimension present in the data set. These isotropic volumes were used for voxel classification. A single CNN was trained to segment axial, sagittal and coronal image slices. During testing, full slices with 65-voxel zero-padding were processed so that for each viewing direction, 3D probabilistic maps were obtained for the myocardium, blood pool and background classes. These maps were averaged per segmentation class and resampled to the original input dimensions using trilinear interpolation. Finally, each voxel was assigned the segmentation class label with the highest posterior probability. Hence, the final probability for the myocardium, blood pool or background for each voxel depends on three 131×131 patches centered at that voxel. To guarantee contiguous myocardium and blood pool segmentations, only the largest component for each class was included in the final segmentation.

Evaluation was performed through an online system provided by the HVSMR challenge. The overlap between reference and automatically obtained segmentations was computed using the Dice index. Furthermore, the difference between reference and automatically obtained boundaries was computed using the average distance to boundaries (ADB) and the Hausdorff distance.

4   Experiments and Results

We performed a five-fold cross-validation experiment on the training set, where each fold contained two CMR scans. Furthermore, to segment the test set, we trained a single CNN using all training images. Network parameters were optimized with Adam [5] using categorical cross-entropy as the cost function. Each CNN was trained with 10,000 training steps, which required 12 hours using a state-of-the-art GPU. In each training step a mini-batch containing 128 randomly selected 201×201 subimages from the training set was provided. Hence, in each training step the network optimized parameters for $71 \times 71 \times 128 = 645,248$ training voxels.

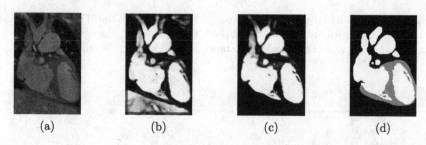

(a)   (b)   (c)   (d)

Fig. 3. (a) Example CMR image slice. Probabilistic blood pool maps obtained using (b) a CNN without dilation (17 × 17 voxel receptive field) showing oversegmentation in the liver and (c) a CNN with dilation (131 × 131 voxel receptive field) showing no response in the liver. (d) reference annotation with the blood pool shown in white. Both networks have 72,643 trainable parameters.

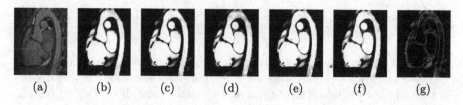

(a)   (b)   (c)   (d)   (e)   (f)   (g)

Fig. 4. (a) CMR image slice, Patient 18. (b)–(f) Probabilistic blood pool maps obtained using CNNs trained on five different folds during cross-validation. (g) Standard deviation of probabilities predicted by CNNs.

Table 2 lists the Dice index, the average distance to boundary (ADB), and the Hausdorff distance for automatic myocardium and blood pool segmentation in each of the ten test scans provided by the HVSMR challenge, as well as average scores for the training and test sets. Automatic segmentation of the *training* scans resulted in Dice indices of 0.80 ± 0.06 and 0.92 ± 0.03, average distances to boundaries of 1.01 ± 0.43 and 0.81 ± 0.28 mm, and Hausdorff distances of 6.70 ± 3.52 and 5.86 ± 3.36 mm for the myocardium and blood pool, respectively. Automatic segmentation of the *test* scans resulted in Dice indices of 0.80 ± 0.06 and 0.93 ± 0.02, average distances to boundaries of 0.96 ± 0.31 and 0.89 ± 0.24 mm, and Hausdorff distances of 6.13 ± 3.76 and 7.07 ± 3.01 mm for the myocardium and blood pool, respectively. The Dice index for myocardium was in all cases lower than the Dice index for blood pool segmentation. In several cases, Dice indices for the blood pool were affected by the (partial) identification of vessels that were not included in the reference standard, as shown in Fig. 3c. Segmentation of a CMR image took between 12.9 and 64.0 s, depending on image size, with an average of 41.5 ± 14.7 s.

To compare the performance of a CNN with dilated convolutions and a CNN without dilated convolutions, segmentations were performed using an otherwise identical CNN architecture containing 72,643 trainable parameters. Figure 3 shows the obtained results. By omitting dilation, the receptive field for each voxel was reduced. While local information was used in classification by the

CNN without dilation, long-range information was not, and hence the network was much less specific than the network with dilation.

To investigate whether overfitting may have occurred in the five CNNs trained during cross-validation, we compared predictions made by these CNNs on an unseen image from the test set. Figure 4 shows this image and probabilistic blood pool maps obtained by the CNNs. Even though each CNN was trained with only eight training images, the variance among the five predictions (Fig. 4g) was generally low, with higher values at the edges of the blood pool. Hence, it is unlikely that overfitting to the training data in each fold occurred.

5   Discussion and Conclusion

We have presented a method for automatic segmentation of cardiovascular MR images in congenital heart disease using dilated convolutional neural networks. The method was able to accurately segment the myocardium and the blood pool without any expert intervention.

The current study showed that dilated convolution layers allow the combination of local structure and global context information with very few trainable parameters. Visual inspection of feature maps suggested that shallow layers enhanced local image features such as edges, and deeper layers distinguished between locally similar but globally different areas. Our network used only 76,423 parameters, while comparable networks for medical image segmentation typically use more than 500,000 parameters [3]. This substantially reduces the risk of overfitting on the training data, which is particularly likely when training with very few scans as done in this study. In future work, we will investigate if the number of parameters can be further reduced without affecting performance, e.g. by reducing the number of output channels in each layer. The CNN was applied to full image slices to produce high-resolution output images, without downsampling of input or internal representations. We found that the method on average required only 41.5 s per scan, compared to 12.58 min in a recently published method for whole heart segmentation in cardiac MRI [14].

The method occasionally identified structures that were not included in the reference standard, but that are part of the blood pool, such as the distal sections of the descending aorta. It is unlikely that this will be problematic for the clinical purpose of segmentation of CMR in CHD patients. Dice indices for automatically obtained segmentations of the blood pool were in all patients higher than those of the myocardium. This is likely due to the lower image contrast between the myocardium and surrounding tissue, the more irregular shape of the myocardium and the difference in size between the myocardium and blood pool.

For each voxel, the final label depended on three orthogonal patches centered at that voxel. The information in these patches was combined in a late stage, by averaging of the three probabilities provided by the CNN. In future work, the features extracted from the three orthogonal patches may be fused before classification. In addition, we will investigate dilated convolutions in 3D, which might allow us to fully leverage the volumetric information present in the image.

However, hardware limitations currently force a trade-off between dimensionality and receptive field size, i.e. it would be infeasible to train a 3D dilated CNN with $131 \times 131 \times 131$ receptive fields. Therefore, we have here chosen to use a larger receptive field at the cost of reduced volumetric information.

Acknowledgments. We gratefully acknowledge the support of NVIDIA Corporation with the donation of the Tesla K40 GPU used for this research.

References

1. Clevert, D.A., Unterthiner, T., Hochreiter, S.: Fast and accurate deep network learning by exponential linear units (ELUs). In: ICLR (2016)
2. Gilboa, S.M., Devine, O.J., Kucik, J.E., Oster, M.E., Riehle-Colarusso, T., Nembhard, W.N., Xu, P., Correa, A., Jenkins, K., Marelli, A.J.: Congenital heart defects in the United States: Estimating the magnitude of the affected population in 2010. Circulation **134**(2), 101–109 (2016)
3. Havaei, M., Davy, A., Warde-Farley, D., Biard, A., Courville, A., Bengio, Y., Pal, C., Jodoin, P.M., Larochelle, H.: Brain tumor segmentation with deep neural networks. Med. Imag. Anal. **35**, 18–31 (2017)
4. Ioffe, S., Szegedy, C.: Batch normalization: accelerating deep network training by reducing internal covariate shift. In: ICML (2015)
5. Kingma, D., Ba, J.: Adam: a method for stochastic optimization. In: ICLR (2015)
6. Moeskops, P., Viergever, M.A., Mendrik, A.M., de Vries, L.S., Benders, M.J., Išgum, I.: Automatic segmentation of MR brain images with a convolutional neural network. IEEE Trans. Med. Imag. **35**(5), 1252–1261 (2016)
7. Pace, D.F., Dalca, A.V., Geva, T., Powell, A.J., Moghari, M.H., Golland, P.: Interactive whole-heart segmentation in congenital heart disease. In: Navab, N., Hornegger, J., Wells, W.M., Frangi, A.F. (eds.) MICCAI 2015. LNCS, vol. 9351, pp. 80–88. Springer, Heidelberg (2015). doi:10.1007/978-3-319-24574-4_10
8. Ronneberger, O., Fischer, P., Brox, T.: U-net: convolutional networks for biomedical image segmentation. In: Navab, N., Hornegger, J., Wells, W.M., Frangi, A.F. (eds.) MICCAI 2015. LNCS, vol. 9351, pp. 234–241. Springer, Heidelberg (2015). doi:10.1007/978-3-319-24574-4_28
9. Schmauss, D., Haeberle, S., Hagl, C., Sodian, R.: Three-dimensional printing in cardiac surgery and interventional cardiology: a single-centre experience. Eur. J. Cardiothorac. Surg. **47**(6), 1044–1052 (2015)
10. Srivastava, N., Hinton, G., Krizhevsky, A., Sutskever, I., Salakhutdinov, R.: Dropout: a simple way to prevent neural networks from overfitting. J. Mach. Learn. Res. **15**(1), 1929–1958 (2014)
11. Valverde, I., Gomez, G., Gonzalez, A., Suarez-Mejias, C., Adsuar, A., Coserria, J.F., Uribe, S., Gomez-Cia, T., Hosseinpour, A.R.: Three-dimensional patient-specific cardiac model for surgical planning in Nikaidoh procedure. Cardiol. Young **25**(04), 698–704 (2015)
12. Wolterink, J.M., Leiner, T., de Vos, B.D., van Hamersvelt, R.W., Viergever, M.A., Išgum, I.: Automatic coronary artery calcium scoring in cardiac CT angiography using paired convolutional neural networks. Med. Imag. Anal. **34**, 123–136 (2016)
13. Yu, F., Koltun, V.: Multi-scale context aggregation by dilated convolutions. In: ICLR (2016)
14. Zhuang, X., Shen, J.: Multi-scale patch and multi-modality atlases for whole heart segmentation of MRI. Med. Imag. Anal. **31**, 77–87 (2016)

3D FractalNet: Dense Volumetric Segmentation for Cardiovascular MRI Volumes

Lequan Yu[1(✉)], Xin Yang[1], Jing Qin[2], and Pheng-Ann Heng[1]

[1] Department of Computer Science and Engineering,
The Chinese University of Hong Kong, Sha Tin, Hong Kong
lqyu@cse.cuhk.edu.hk
[2] Centre for Smart Health, School of Nursing,
The Hong Kong Polytechnic University, Kowloon, Hong Kong

Abstract. Cardiac image segmentation plays a crucial role in various medical applications. However, differentiating branchy structures and slicing fuzzy boundaries from cardiovascular MRI volumes remain very challenging tasks. In this paper, we propose a novel deeply-supervised 3D fractal network for efficient automated whole heart and great vessel segmentation in MRI volumes. The proposed 3D fractal network takes advantage of fully convolutional architecture to perform efficient, precise and volume-to-volume prediction. Notably, by recursively applying a single expansion rule, we construct our network in a novel self-similar fractal scheme and thus promote it in combining hierarchical clues for accurate segmentation. More importantly, we employ deep supervision mechanism to alleviate the vanishing gradients problem and improve the training efficiency of our network on small medical image dataset. We evaluated our method on the HVSMR 2016 Challenge dataset. Extensive experimental results demonstrated the superior performance of our method, ranking top in both two phases.

1 Introduction

Noninvasive cardiac imaging is an invaluable tool for the diagnosis and treatment of cardiovascular disease. Accurate cardiac image segmentation is a prerequisite for various applications, such as quantification of volume, surgical planning for complex congenital heart disease and radio-frequency ablation. However, facing with the explosive growth of volume data, manual delineation is severely inhibited and tends to be tedious, time-consuming, and prone to inter- and intra-observer variability. Subjecting to the low tissue contrast of the myocardium against surroundings, patient variability and spatial inhomogeneities, it is very challenging to develop automatic solutions for efficient whole heart segmentation. Based on hand-crafted features, previous automatic methods typically exploited deformable models [11], non-rigid registration [16] and expert emendation involved interactive segmentation [10]. Relighted by their powerful feature learning capability, Convolutional Neural Networks (CNNs) have been utilized

© Springer International Publishing AG 2017
M.A. Zuluaga et al. (Eds.): RAMBO 2016/HVSMR 2016, LNCS 10129, pp. 103–110, 2017.
DOI: 10.1007/978-3-319-52280-7_10

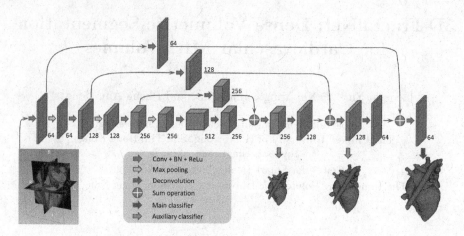

Fig. 1. Illustration of our proposed deeply-supervised 3D FractalNet architecture. Numbers represent the number of feature volumes in each layer.

in a 2D context for biomedical image segmentation [12] and ventricle segmentation [14]. However, leveraging the effectiveness of CNNs in capturing 3D spatial contextual information to segment the whole heart and great vessel from MRI volumes has not been well studied. Recently, dense volumetric labeling has attracted attention in medical image computing community [1,2,9]. How to construct a more effective network and train it efficiently, and how to distill hierarchical features to better performance are emerging as important concerns.

In this paper, we propose a deeply-supervised 3D fractal network (3D FractalNet) for whole heart and great vessel segmentation in MRI volumes. Based on fully convolutional architecture [8], our 3D FractalNet can map a whole volumetric data to its volume-wise label directly. Notably, multi-paths with different receptive fields in our network are organized in a self-similar fractal scheme to capture the hierarchical features of myocardium and vessels. Additionally, we utilize the deep supervision to alleviate the vanishing gradients problem of training process. Deep supervision also greatly boosts the training efficiency on small medical dataset as it functions as a strong regularization [7]. We evaluated our method on the datasets of HVSMR 2016 Challenge in conjunction with MIC-CAI 2016 [10]. Experimental results corroborated that our method can achieve superior performance on the cardiovascular segmentation task.

2   Method

Figure 1 demonstrates the architecture of our proposed deeply-supervised 3D FractalNet for dense volumetric whole heart and great vessel segmentation. It employs a 3D fully convolutional architecture and is organized in a self-similar fractal scheme. In this section, we first elaborate the technical details of fractal networks, and then we will present the details of our proposed 3D FractalNet. Finally, we will introduce the deep supervision scheme used to tackle potential optimization difficulties in training the 3D FractalNet.

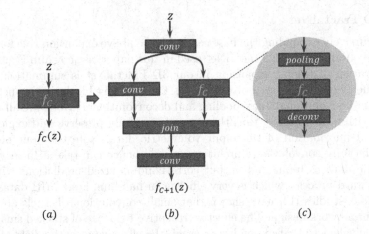

Fig. 2. An illustration of the expansion rule in our fractal architecture. We add downsampling and upsampling operations in the expansion rule to utilize multi-scale features.

2.1 Fractal Networks

Fractal networks are constructed by repeatedly applying an expansion rule from a base case [6]. Let C denotes the index of a truncated fractal $f_C(\cdot)$ (i.e., a few stacked layers) and the base case of a truncated fractal (Fig. 2(a)) is a single convolution:

$$f_1(z) = \text{conv}(z). \tag{1}$$

Then the successive fractals (Fig. 2(b)) can be defined recursively according to the expansion rule:

$$z' = \text{conv}(z),$$
$$f_{C+1}(z) = \text{conv}[\text{conv}(z') \oplus f_C(z')] \tag{2}$$

where $\oplus$ is a join operation and $\text{conv}(\cdot)$ is a convolution operator. The join operation $\oplus$ merges two blobs. As these two blobs contain features from different visual levels, joining them can enhance the discrimination capability of our network. Generally, the join operation can be summation, maximization and concatenation. We employ summation in our experiments, which achieved the best performance via cross-validation on training dataset.

In order to enlarge the receptive field and enclose more contextual information, we add downsampling and upsampling operation in the above expansion rule, as shown in Fig. 2(c). Specifically, we add a max-pooling with stride of 2 and a deconvolution also with stride of 2. The receptive field of a fractal thus becomes broader after the downsample operation. When combining different receptive fields through the join operation, the network can harness multi-scale visual cues and promote itself in discriminating.

2.2   3D FractalNet

After recursively expanding the base case with the above expansion rule for three times, we obtained the 3D FractalNet used in this paper, as shown in Fig. 1. The join operation of fractal expansion in our 3D FractalNet is summation, computing the element-wise sum of two blobs. The building blocks of our network, such as the convolutional, max-pooling and deconvolutional layers, are all implemented with a 3D manner, thus the network can fully preserve and exploit the 3D spatial information of the input volumetric data. Note that our network adopts the fully convolutional architecture, and hence can take arbitrary-sized volumetric data as input and output corresponding sized predictions within a single forward process, which is very efficient in handling large MRI dataset.

Previous studies [13] have shown that small convolutional kernels are more efficient in network design. The effective receptive field size of stacked small kernels is equivalent to that of one large kernel (the effective receptive field of three $3 \times 3 \times 3$ kernels is same as one $7 \times 7 \times 7$ kernel), while giving lower computation cost. Therefore, we adopt small convolution kernels with size of $3 \times 3 \times 3$ in convolutional layers. Each convolutional layer is followed by a rectified linear unit (ReLU) as the activation function. Note that we also employ batch normalization layer (BN) before each ReLU layer to accelerate the training process. At the end of the network, we add a $1 \times 1 \times 1$ convolutional layer as a main classifier to generate the segmentation results and further get the segmentation probability map after passing the softmax layer.

2.3   Deeply-Supervised 3D FractalNet

Directly training such a deep 3D fractal network is challenging due to the issue of vanishing gradients [4], which makes the back-propagation ineffective in early layers. Following previous studies on training deep neural networks with deep supervision [3,15], we proposed the deeply-supervised 3D FractalNet by injecting direct supervision into the hidden layers of the network. Specifically, we added M auxiliary classifiers (convolutional layers with size of $1 \times 1 \times 1$) following some hidden layers of the network and employed deconvolutional layers to upsample the auxiliary classifiers' output. This scheme can effectively alleviate the vanishing gradients problem and assist the training process with direct supervision on the hidden layers.

Specifically, let W be the weights of main network and $w = (w^1, w^2, .., w^M)$ be the weights of auxiliary classifiers. Then the cross-entropy loss function of the main classifier is

$$\mathcal{L}(\mathcal{X}; W) = \sum_{x_i \in \mathcal{X}} -\log p(y_i = \ell(x_i)|x_i; W), \qquad (3)$$

where $\mathcal{X}$ represents the training samples and $p(y_i = \ell(x_i)|x_i; W)$ is the probability of target class label $\ell(x_i)$ corresponding to sample $x_i \in \mathcal{X}$. Similarly, the loss function of the mth auxiliary classifier is

$$\mathcal{L}_m(\mathcal{X}; W, w^m) = \sum_{x_i \in \mathcal{X}} -\log p(y_i = \ell(x_i)|x_i; W, w^m). \qquad (4)$$

Therefore, the total loss function of our deeply-supervised 3D FractalNet is:

$$\mathcal{L}(\mathcal{X}; W, w) = \mathcal{L}(\mathcal{X}; W) + \sum_{m=1}^{M} \alpha_m \mathcal{L}_m(\mathcal{X}; W, w^m) + \lambda \psi(W), \qquad (5)$$

where the first two terms are the classifier loss and the last part is the regularization term (L_2 norm in our experiments); α_m is the weight of different auxiliary classifiers.

3   Experiments and Results

3.1   Dataset and Pre-processing

We evaluated our network on two phases: cropped axial images (phase 2) and cropped short-axial images (phase 3) of HVSMR 2016 Challenge dataset. The dataset consists of 20 cardiovascular magnetic resonance (CMR) images (10 training and 10 testing). Note that the ground truth of testing dataset is held out by the organizer for independent evaluation. Before training networks, we pre-process the training dataset by normalizing them as zero mean and unit variance. In order to tackle the insufficiency of training data and avoid overfitting, we also utilize the data augmentation to enlarge the training dataset. The augmentation operators include rotation (90, 180 and 270°) and flip in the axial plane and we totally use 80 examples to train our network.

3.2   Implementation Details

The proposed method was implemented with C++ and Matlab under the open source deep learning library of Caffe [5], using a standard PC with a 2.60 GHz Intel(R) Xeon(R) E5-2650 CPU and a NVIDIA TITAN X GPU. The weights of networks were initialized from the Gaussian distribution ($\mu = 0, \sigma = 0.01$) and updated using stochastic gradient descend (SGD) method (batch size $= 4$, momentum $= 0.9$, weight decay $= 0.0005$). The learning rate was set as 0.002 initially and divided by 10 every 3000 iterations. The network were trained for up to 10000 iterations. We added two auxiliary classifiers and the weights α_m are 0.33 and 0.67, respectively. We randomly cropped a $64 \times 64 \times 64$ sub-volume from each sample in every iteration for the input when training our network, and therefore we totally extracted 40000 patches in training. We used an overlap-tiling strategy to generate the whole volume probability map by stitching sub-volume predictions. We also employed some morphology operations including removing small isolated components and filling holes to process the prediction. Generally, it took about 12 s to process one volume with size of $200 \times 140 \times 120$ using above configuration.

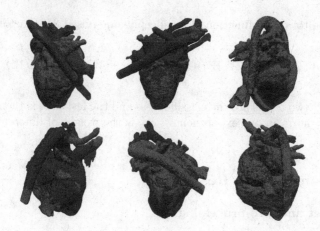

Fig. 3. Explicit surface-to-surface comparison of our segmentation results (blue) with ground truth (red) of different hearts in training dataset. (Color figure online)

3.3 Qualitative Results

To explicitly visualize the difference between our segmentation results and the ground truth, we illustrate 6 surface-to-surface comparison examples of training dataset using cross validation in Fig. 3. We can observe that our segmentation results coincide well with ground truth. Benefiting from the multi-scale features, our network can tackle the large variation of blood pool and myocardium and effectively separate the touching boundaries of vessel. Also, the proposed method can even present more complete vessel segmentation comparing to the ground truth.

Table 1. Quantitative evaluation results on testing dataset

Sample	Phase 2						Phase 3					
	Adb1	Adb2	Dice1	Dice2	Hdb1	Hdb2	Adb1	Adb2	Dice1	Dice2	Hdb1	Hdb2
Volume 10	1.120	0.843	0.727	0.939	7.640	6.508	1.228	0.643	0.671	0.948	5.820	3.713
Volume 11	1.010	1.137	0.831	0.921	8.842	8.553	2.518	1.040	0.719	0.929	30.204	13.579
Volume 12	0.784	0.682	0.848	0.940	5.701	7.318	0.590	0.810	0.862	0.940	2.840	9.245
Volume 13	0.971	0.980	0.836	0.936	6.467	10.860	0.949	0.854	0.824	0.940	4.275	8.677
Volume 14	0.872	0.916	0.762	0.926	3.951	3.877	1.043	0.983	0.690	0.920	5.372	4.292
Volume 15	1.705	0.842	0.648	0.915	9.675	4.229	1.111	1.022	0.664	0.896	6.563	6.399
Volume 16	0.639	1.224	0.796	0.899	3.877	12.903	0.746	0.731	0.717	0.913	3.622	7.230
Volume 17	0.950	0.555	0.803	0.954	6.528	3.408	0.847	0.697	0.789	0.948	4.516	7.874
Volume 18	0.504	0.588	0.851	0.948	2.032	3.771	0.513	0.695	0.819	0.937	2.089	4.100
Volume 19	1.410	0.914	0.762	0.935	9.474	8.703	1.296	0.814	0.700	0.939	8.064	5.141
Average	0.997	0.868	0.786	0.931	6.419	7.013	1.084	0.829	0.746	0.931	7.336	7.025

Note: class 1: myocardium; class 2: blood pool

Table 2. Quantitative evaluation results of cross-validation on training dataset

Sample	Phase 2						Phase 3					
	Adb1	Adb2	Dice1	Dice2	Hdb1	Hdb2	Adb1	Adb2	Dice1	Dice2	Hdb1	Hdb2
Volume 0	0.420	0.641	0.888	0.950	1.982	2.938	0.353	0.502	0.898	0.952	1.536	1.255
Volume 1	0.681	0.636	0.868	0.943	5.388	4.324	0.992	0.555	0.858	0.947	8.577	4.314
Volume 2	0.758	0.725	0.825	0.940	3.198	4.162	0.695	0.642	0.844	0.944	2.813	4.058
Volume 3	0.669	0.650	0.849	0.940	2.570	4.297	0.600	0.531	0.857	0.942	3.625	2.562
Volume 4	0.399	0.682	0.898	0.909	1.979	5.002	0.697	0.749	0.838	0.900	4.717	5.015
Volume 5	0.485	0.544	0.876	0.921	3.053	4.016	0.304	0.729	0.920	0.903	1.674	6.544
Volume 6	0.938	0.927	0.762	0.902	4.559	6.266	0.849	0.740	0.790	0.915	3.969	5.977
Volume 7	1.331	0.418	0.818	0.954	13.752	1.635	0.734	0.397	0.822	0.954	5.942	2.312
Volume 8	0.317	0.847	0.888	0.926	1.536	6.271	0.485	0.651	0.852	0.941	2.662	5.681
Volume 9	0.748	0.866	0.844	0.917	4.776	7.515	0.549	0.651	0.861	0.934	3.192	4.609
Average	0.675	0.694	0.852	0.930	4.279	4.643	0.626	0.615	0.854	0.933	3.871	4.233

3.4 Quantitative Results

The main evaluation criteria in the Challenge include Dice coefficient (Dice), Hausdorff Distance of Boundaries (Hdb[mm]) and Average Distance of Boundaries (Adb[mm]). Auxiliary metrics, such as Jaccard index, Cohen's Kappa, Sensitivity and Specificity are also considered. For distance related metrics, lower values indicates better performance. We report two types of result: testing dataset result and leave-one-out cross-validation result of training dataset on phase 2 and 3. On the Challenge website, these results are reported from our teams CUMED2 (cross-validation) and CUMED1 (testing).[1] Tables 1 and 2 illustrate the automated segmentation results under the main metrics on testing dataset and cross-validation of training dataset, respectively.

4 Conclusion

In this paper, we propose a novel deeply-supervised 3D FractalNet for automated whole heart and great vessel segmentation from cardiovascular magnetic resonance (CMR) images. By adopting 3D fully convolutional neural networks, our network can perform accurate, efficient and volume-to-volume prediction. Under a recursive fractal scheme, our network can fuse interacting subpaths of different convolution lengths and thus utilize multi-scale features to enhance its discrimination capacity. In addition, to facilitate the training process of this network on small medical dataset, deep supervision is injected to alleviate the vanishing gradients problem. Experimental results on MICCAI 2016 HVSMR Challenge dataset demonstrated the superior performance of our proposed method in handling large shape variation and delineating branchy structures. Our proposed network is general and promising to be extended to other medical volumetric segmentation applications.

---

[1] See: https://challenge.kitware.com/#challenge/56f421d6cad3a53ead8b1b7e.

Acknowledgments. The work described in this paper was supported by a grant from the Research Grants Council of the Hong Kong Special Administrative Region (Project no. CUHK 412513).

References

1. Chen, H., Dou, Q., Yu, L., Heng, P.A.: Voxresnet: deep voxelwise residual networks for volumetric brain segmentation. arXiv preprint arXiv:1608.05895 (2016)
2. Çiçek, Ö., Abdulkadir, A., Lienkamp, S.S., Brox, T., Ronneberger, O.: 3d u-net: learning dense volumetric segmentation from sparse annotation. arXiv preprint arXiv:1606.06650 (2016)
3. Dou, Q., Chen, H., Jin, Y., Yu, L., Qin, J., Heng, P.A.: 3d deeply supervised network for automatic liver segmentation from CT volumes. arXiv preprint arXiv:1607.00582 (2016)
4. Glorot, X., Bengio, Y.: Understanding the difficulty of training deep feedforward neural networks. Aistats **9**, 249–256 (2010)
5. Jia, Y., Shelhamer, E., Donahue, J., Karayev, S., Long, J., Girshick, R., Guadarrama, S., Darrell, T.: Caffe: convolutional architecture for fast feature embedding. arXiv preprint arXiv:1408.5093 (2014)
6. Larsson, G., Maire, M., Shakhnarovich, G.: Fractalnet: ultra-deep neural networks without residuals. arXiv preprint arXiv:1605.07648 (2016)
7. Lee, C.Y., Xie, S., Gallagher, P., Zhang, Z., Tu, Z.: Deeply-supervised nets (2015)
8. Long, J., Shelhamer, E., Darrell, T.: Fully convolutional networks for semantic segmentation. In: Proceedings of the IEEE Conference on Computer Vision and Pattern Recognition, pp. 3431–3440 (2015)
9. Merkow, J., Kriegman, D., Marsden, A., Tu, Z.: Dense volume-to-volume vascular boundary detection. arXiv preprint arXiv:1605.08401 (2016)
10. Pace, D.F., Dalca, A.V., Geva, T., Powell, A.J., Moghari, M.H., Golland, P.: Interactive whole-heart segmentation in congenital heart disease. In: Navab, N., Hornegger, J., Wells, W.M., Frangi, A.F. (eds.) MICCAI 2015. LNCS, vol. 9351, pp. 80–88. Springer, Heidelberg (2015). doi:10.1007/978-3-319-24574-4_10
11. Peters, J., Ecabert, O., Meyer, C., Schramm, H., Kneser, R., Groth, A., Weese, J.: Automatic whole heart segmentation in static magnetic resonance image volumes. In: Ayache, N., Ourselin, S., Maeder, A. (eds.) MICCAI 2007. LNCS, vol. 4792, pp. 402–410. Springer, Heidelberg (2007). doi:10.1007/978-3-540-75759-7_49
12. Ronneberger, O., Fischer, P., Brox, T.: U-net: convolutional networks for biomedical image segmentation. In: Navab, N., Hornegger, J., Wells, W.M., Frangi, A.F. (eds.) MICCAI 2015. LNCS, vol. 9351, pp. 234–241. Springer, Heidelberg (2015). doi:10.1007/978-3-319-24574-4_28
13. Simonyan, K., Zisserman, A.: Very deep convolutional networks for large-scale image recognition. arXiv preprint arXiv:1409.1556 (2014)
14. Tran, P.V.: A fully convolutional neural network for cardiac segmentation in short-axis MRI. arXiv preprint arXiv:1604.00494 (2016)
15. Xie, S., Tu, Z.: Holistically-nested edge detection. In: Proceedings of the IEEE International Conference on Computer Vision, pp. 1395–1403 (2015)
16. Zhuang, X., Rhode, K.S., Razavi, R.S., Hawkes, D.J., Ourselin, S.: A registration-based propagation framework for automatic whole heart segmentation of cardiac MRI. IEEE Trans. Med. Imag. **29**(9), 1612–1625 (2010)

Automatic Whole-Heart Segmentation in Congenital Heart Disease Using Deeply-Supervised 3D FCN

Jinpeng Li[1], Rongzhao Zhang[2], Lin Shi[2,3], and Defeng Wang[1,4(✉)]

[1] Department of Imaging and Interventional Radiology,
The Chinese University of Hong Kong, Shenzhen, China
dfwang@cuhk.edu.hk
[2] Department of Medicine and Therapeutics,
The Chinese University of Hong Kong, Shenzhen, China
[3] Chow Yuk Ho Technology Centre for Innovative Medicine,
The Chinese University of Hong Kong, Shenzhen, China
[4] Shenzhen Research Institute,
The Chinese University of Hong Kong, Shenzhen, China

Abstract. Accurate whole-heart segmentation plays an important role in the surgical planning for heart defects such as congenital heart disease (CHD). In this work, we propose a deep learning method for automatic whole-heart segmentation in cardiac magnetic resonance (CMR) images with CHD. First, we start with a 3D fully convolutional network (3D FCN) in order to ensure an efficient voxel-wise labeling. Then we introduce dilated convolutional layers (3D-HOL layers) into the baseline model to expand its receptive field, so as to make better use of the spatial information. Last, we employ deeply-supervised pathways to accelerate training and exploit multi-scale information. We evaluate the proposed method on 3D CMR images from the dataset of the HVSMR 2016 Challenge. The results of controlled experiments demonstrate the efficacy of the proposed 3D-HOL layers and deeply-supervised pathways. We achieve an average Dice score of 80.1% in training (5-fold cross-validation) and 69.5% in testing.

1 Introduction

Congenital heart disease (CHD) is characterized by the defects of the heart structure presented at birth. During the surgical planning for CHD, a patient-specific 3D model is essential for surgeons to analyze the condition of heart defects and evaluate the prognosis.

Accurate whole-heart segmentation is a prerequisite for generating patient-specific 3D heart models. Since the manual annotation is tedious, laborious and error prone, fully automatic whole-heart segmentation algorithms have become a research focus [9] and achieved reasonable performance in recent works

---

J. Li and R. Zhang—Joint first authors.

M.A. Zuluaga et al. (Eds.): RAMBO 2016/HVSMR 2016, LNCS 10129, pp. 111–118, 2017.
DOI: 10.1007/978-3-319-52280-7_11

(an overall Dice score of 89.9 in [10]). However, similar performance seems irreproducible in CHD. This is because these model-based algorithms are prone to the various malformations in CHD particularly with limited data. In Pace et al. [8], an efficient interactive segmentation method was proposed for the whole-heart segmentation in CHD. With this method, only a small set of annotated slice regions are needed to delineate the whole volume, thus the workload can be significantly reduced (from 4 to 8 h to less than an hour). Nevertheless, the interactive segmentation still needs manual annotation, and its application in clinical practices remains limited.

In this work, we tackle the challenge of CHD whole-heart segmentation under a 3D-FCN [7] framework with deep supervision [6]. Specifically, first, we extend the 2D-FCN to 3D volumetric data to ensure an efficient volume-to-volume inference. Second, dilated convolutional layers, i.e., 3D-HOL layers, are proposed to enlarge the receptive field of our model. Thus, the network could make full use of the spatial information. Third, deeply-supervised (DS) pathways are exploited, in order to force intermediate layers to learn more discriminate features and improve convergence speed [6]. And the output of DS pathways are fused with the original network's output to maintain the fine-grained information. We demonstrated the efficacy of the proposed method by extensive experiments on the dataset of the HVSMR 2016 Challenge.

2   Method

We propose an end-to-end trainable 3D fully convolutional network (FCN) with broad receptive fields (RFs) and deeply-supervised pathways to deal with the voxel-wise whole-heart segmentation on 3D cardiac magnetic resonance (CMR) images. And the 3D fully connected Conditional Random Field (CRF) [5] is exploited as a post-processing step to refine the segmentation result.

2.1   3D Fully Convolutional Network

Generally, a convolutional neural network (CNN) is composed of alternate convolutional (C) and max-pooling (M) layers, as well as fully connected (FC) layers on the top of the network. The FCN [7] is a variant of the CNN, which removes the abundant computation of overlapped patches thus becomes much more efficient for semantic segmentation. Structurally, the FCN introduces deconvolutional (DC) layers to up-sample the feature maps to the input dimension, and converts FC layers into a convolutional fashion to adapt to arbitrarily sized input. In this section, we formulate FCNs in the context of 3D volumetric image segmentation [2].

3D Convolutional Layers. In convolutional layers, the input, i.e. the output of the preceding layer, is, successively, convolved with convolution kernels, plus a bias term, and applied non-linearity. The result is called feature volumes. Let h_i^l denotes the i-th feature volume of the l-th layer (a convolutional layer) and

h_j^{l-1} the j-th feature volume of the preceding layer, the convolution operation is performed in a 3D manner:

$$u_{ki}^l(x,y,z) = \sum_{m,n,t} h_k^{l-1}(x-m, y-n, z-t)W_{ki}^l(m,n,t), \qquad (1)$$

where u_{ki}^l is the convolution result of 3D kernel $\mathbf{W}_{ki}^l$ and feature volume h_k^{l-1}. $u_{ki}^l(x,y,z)$ denotes the element of u_{ki}^l at position (x,y,z), $\mathbf{W}_{ki}^l$ and h_k^{l-1} similarly. Then the operation of a 3D convolutional layer is given by

$$h_i^l = \sigma\left(\sum_k u_{ki}^l + b_i^l\right). \qquad (2)$$

3D FCN Construction. A 3D FCN is constructed by stacking C, M, FC and DC layers, all in 3D fashions. The 3D max pooling is performed by subsampling feature volumes in a cubic neighborhood. FC layers are implemented with 1^3 kernels.

2.2   Receptive Fields Control Using 3D-HOL Layer

In CMR images, it is difficult to do high-quality voxel-wise segmentation solely based on the small neighborhood of each voxel, since contextual information also plays an important role in the task. In this regard, we employ a new type of convolutional layer called 3D-HOL layer to expand the network's receptive field to the whole image without adding computational complexity.

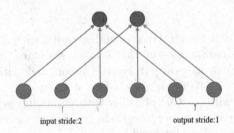

Fig. 1. Illustration of 1-D hole algorithm with input stride 2 and output stride 1. In convolution, the output stride s_O is the stride length by which kernels sweep over the original signal.

3D-HOL Layer. The 3D-HOL layer is a type of convolutional layer, in which the convolution operation is modified by hole algorithm [1]. Given a signal $s[n]$ and a convolution kernel $k[n]$, 1-D hole algorithm (Fig. 1) can be formulated as

$$s[n]\hat{*}k[n] = \sum_{i=0}^{K-1} s\left[n \cdot s_O - i \cdot s_I\right] \cdot k[i] \qquad (3)$$

where K denotes the kernel size, $\hat{*}$ is the modified convolution, and s_I the input stride and s_O the output stride. All indices start from 0. Note that by setting s_I to 1 the 3D-HOL layer degenerates into a traditional 3D convolutional layer with output stride s_O. This algorithm is implemented by downsampling the input signal by a factor of s_I and then applying ordinary convolution operation.

Receptive Fields Expand. For a 3D-HOL layer with kernel size $K = (K_x, K_y, K_z)$ and input stride $s_I = (s_x, s_y, s_z)$, it has the same RF size as a traditional convolutional layer with kernel size $K' = (K_x s_x - s_x + 1, K_y s_y - s_y + 1, K_z s_z - s_z + 1)$. And from (3), the computational complexity only depends on the kernel size K. Therefore, with 3D-HOL layers, the network's RF can be expanded by increasing the input stride, while its computational complexity remains unchanged. Specifically, the RF size (with zero-padding) of our proposed 3D FCN (see Fig. 2) reaches 250^3, compared to 74^3 with only traditional convolutional layers.

2.3 Deeply-Supervised Pathways

Deeply-supervised pathways refer to the pathway from a hidden layer to its corresponding "companion loss", which generally includes FC and DC layers. This idea comes from a recently proposed framework called deeply-supervised network (DSN) [6]. DSNs use additional "companion loss" to directly supervise hidden layers, which helps hidden layers learn more discriminate features and speeds up the network's convergence [6]. In this work, we employ DS pathways on selected hidden layers, and integrate the outputs of different pathways for multi-scale processing.

Formulation. Assuming an L-layer neural network with M side-output layers, we denote the parameters of the L-layer standard network by $\mathbf{W} = (\mathbf{W}^{(1)}, \ldots, \mathbf{W}^{(L)})$. Each side-output layer is associated with a classifier, and the weights of these classifiers are denoted by $\mathbf{w} = (\mathbf{w}^{(1)}, \ldots, \mathbf{w}^{(M)})$. The final output is associated with another classifier with parameter $\mathbf{w}^{(out)}$, by which the outputs of different pathways are integrated to generate a more reliable result. Then the total loss function is defined as:

$$\mathcal{L}_{\text{total}}(\mathbf{W}, \mathbf{w}, \mathbf{w}^{(out)}) = \mathcal{L}_{\text{final}}(\mathbf{W}, \mathbf{w}, \mathbf{w}^{(out)}) + \sum_{m=1}^{M} \ell_{\text{side}}^{(m)}(\mathbf{W}, \mathbf{w}^{(m)}) \quad (4)$$

where $\mathcal{L}_{\text{final}}$ measures the deviation of the network's final output from the ground truth, and $\ell_{\text{side}}^{(m)}$ is the m-th companion loss, which is associated with the output of the m-th side-output hidden layer.

Network Setup. As shown in Fig. 2, we add a DS pathway after the first max-pooling layer, and fuse the outputs of the two paths (associated with Loss1 and

Loss2, respectively) by stacking[1] the feature volumes together and adding an FC layer to retrieve the final output (associated with Loss3). The network uses PReLU nonlinearity [3]. Batch Normalization [4] is applied before the nonlinear activations. All the DC layers are fixed to tri-linear upsample of factor 2.

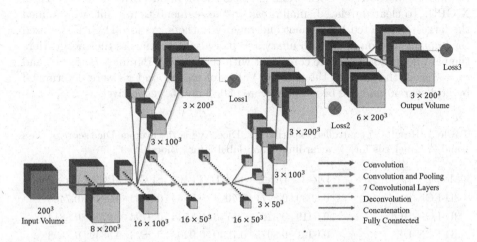

Fig. 2. The architecture of the proposed Deeply-Supervised 3D FCN. Feature volumes are represented as blue cubes. Operations, such as convolution, max-pooling, concatenation etc., are denoted by arrows in different colors. The first two convolutions use 3^3 kernels with input stride $s_I = 1$, the third one (denoted by the second blue arrow) uses 3^3 kernels with input stride $s_I = 2$, and other 7 convolutional layers (denoted by the grey dashed arrow) use 3^3 kernels with input stride $s_I = 4$ and with a Dropout rate of 30%. Output strides s_O are set to 1 for all convolutional layers. (Color figure online)

3   Experimentation and Results

Data. We trained and tested our model on the HVSMR 2016 Challenge dataset of cropped and short-axis images, containing 10 and 10 3D CMR images for training and testing, respectively. Each image consists of two foreground object classes (i.e., blood pool and ventricular myocardium) and one background class. The 3D CMR images were acquired during clinical practice at Boston Childrens Hospital, Boston, MA, USA. Cases include a variety of congenital heart defects. Detailed data specification and segmentation criteria can be found at the HVSMR 2016's website[2]. Data augmentation was carried out on the training set by uniformly rotating each 3D image by 8 angles along its vertical axis. For convenience, all images were resampled to a dimension of $200 \times 200 \times 200$.

---

[1] Other combination operators such as summation or max fusion need more memory to store the new volumes, whereas by concatenation we can directly do the processing on the existed volumes.

[2] http://segchd.csail.mit.edu/data.html.

Implementation Details. The network was trained by SGD on the cross-entropy loss function. The mini-batch size was set to 1 due to memory limit. We used an initial learning rate of 0.01, dividing it by 3 after 2000 iterations. The weight decay was 0.005 and momentum was 0.9. We initialized kernel weights by the MSRA method [3]. Each training session took about 10 h on a GTX Titan X GPU. To clear unrelated small areas on the segmentation result, we retained the largest connected component and removed others. As for 3D CRF, we used the implementation in [5] with unary and pairwise potentials as the energy. Here the parameter notations are consistent with those in [1]. Parameters $w_2 = 3$ and $\sigma_\gamma = 3$ were the same as the default. Values of w_1, σ_α and σ_β were determined by grid search, and the best values were 650, 2 and 5, respectively.

Table 1. Results of controlled experiments. Dice_Avg is the average Dice score of class 1 and 2. Label 1 is for "Myocardium", and label 2 for "Blood Pool".

Model	Dice1	Dice2	TPR1	TPR2	SPC1	SPC2	Dice_Avg
3D-FCN	0.6039	0.8771	0.7004	0.8869	0.9803	0.9844	0.7405
3D-FCN-HOL	0.5419	0.8207	0.5753	0.8544	0.9794	0.9753	0.6814
3D-FCN-DS	0.6421	0.8975	0.7240	0.9203	0.9823	0.9849	0.7698
3D-FCN-DS-HOL	0.6966	0.8857	0.7183	0.9045	0.9864	0.9845	**0.7912**
3D-FCN-DS-HOL-CRF	0.7115	0.8975	0.6830	0.8805	0.9900	0.9910	**0.8045**

Evaluation on Training Set. We split the training set into two groups, sample-6 and sample-7 for validation and others for training. The evaluation metrics include Dice score, sensitivity (TPR) and specificity (SPC) of each non-background classes. We tested the efficacy of the 3D-HOL layer and the deeply-supervised structure by controlled experiments. All the models were trained for the same number of epochs (43 in this work) for fairness. As shown in Table 1, incorporating the 3D-HOL layer and deep supervision (DS) to the baseline model yields considerable improvement (average Dice score from 0.7405 to 0.7912, CRF provides a slight improvement from 0.7912 to 0.8045), evidencing the advantage of the proposed method. Specifically, we note that the performance of 3D-FCN-HOL is worse than the baseline model's while the 3D-FCN-DS-HOL outperforms the 3D-FCN-DS. It can be interpreted as the network with 3D-HOL layers is more difficult to train[3], but deep supervision compensates for this, so the combination of 3D-HOL layers and deep supervision achieves the best performance. In addition, 5-fold cross-validation was carried out on the training dataset to evaluate the generalization performance of our model. The accuracy metrics were automatically computed by the online evaluation system of the HVSMR

---

[3] During the training phase, we noticed that the time point at which the loss of the 3D-FCN-HOL network started to decrease was later than the baseline's, and the descent speed was also lower, which indicates that the network with 3D-HOL layers is more difficult to train.

2016 Challenge, as shown in Table 2. An example of the segmentation result is shown in Fig. 3.

Table 2. Results on training set (cross-validation) and testing set.

Type	Dice1	Dice2	TPR1	TPR2	SPC1	SPC2	Dice_Avg
Training	0.7260	0.8760	0.7290	0.8840	0.9880	0.9800	0.8010
Testing	0.5170	0.8730	0.4660	0.8140	0.9870	0.9920	0.6950

Evaluation on Testing Set. To clear unbiased errors and get better performance, we formed an ensemble of the five networks trained in the 5-fold cross-validation by averaging their outputs. We applied the ensemble model to the testing dataset. The segmentation accuracy was evaluated by the online system of the HVSMR 2016 Challenge, as shown in Table 2.

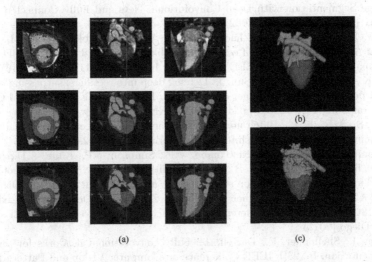

Fig. 3. An example of our segmentation results. In (a), from top to bottom, the rows demonstrate the original image, ground truth and our segmentation in axial, sagittal and frontal planes. (b) and (c) show the reconstructed 3D models of the ground truth annotation and our result, respectively.

4 Conclusion

In this paper, we proposed a 3D fully convolutional network for whole-heart segmentation in CHD. The model employs deep supervision to speed up the network's convergence, and exploits 3D-HOL layers to incorporate spatial information into the network. By experimentation, we demonstrated that our proposed method was capable of the fine segmentation of defective heart structures.

Furthermore, our model inherited the efficiency of FCNs [7]. The inference time of a typical short-axis and cropped 3D CMR image is 5.8 s (without CRF) and 2.5 min (with CRF) on a modern GPU. These advantages make our model highly applicable in clinical practices.

Acknowledgements. The work described in this paper was partially supported by a grant from the Science, Technology and Innovation Commission of Shenzhen Municipality (No.: CXZZ20140606164105361), a grant from Technology and Business Development Fund (No.: TBF15MED004), a grant from the Innovation and Technology Commission (No.: ITS/293/14FP), and grants from the Research Grants Council of the Hong Kong Special Administrative Region, China (No.: CUHK 416712, and CUHK 14113214), and a grant from the National Natural Science Foundation of China (No.: 81271653).

References

1. Chen, L.C., Papandreou, G., Kokkinos, I., Murphy, K., Yuille, A.L.: Semantic Image Segmentation with Deep Convolutional Nets and Fully Connected CRFs. arXiv preprint arXiv:1412.7062 (2014)
2. Dou, Q., Chen, H., Yu, L., Zhao, L., Qin, J., Wang, D., Mok, V.C., Shi, L., Heng, P.A.: Automatic detection of cerebral microbleeds from MR images via 3D convolutional neural networks. IEEE Trans. Med. Imaging **35**, 1182–1195 (2016)
3. He, K., Zhang, X., Ren, S., Sun, J.: Delving deep into rectifiers: surpassing human-level performance on imagenet classification. In: 28th IEEE International Conference on Computer Vision, pp. 1026–1034. IEEE Press, New York (2015)
4. Ioffe, S., Szegedy, C.: Batch normalization: accelerating deep network training by reducing internal covariate shift. arXiv preprint arXiv:1502.03167 (2015)
5. Kamnitsas, K., Ledig, C., Newcombe, V.F., Simpson, J.P., Kane, A.D., Menon, D.K., Rueckert, D., Glocker, B.: Efficient multi-scale 3D CNN with fully connected CRF for accurate brain lesion segmentation. arXiv preprint arXiv:1603.05959
6. Lee, C.Y., Xie, S., Gallagher, P., Zhang, Z., Tu, Z.: Deeply-supervised nets. In: 18th International Conference on Artificial Intelligence and Statistics, p. 6, San Diego (2015)
7. Long, J., Shelhamer, E., Darrell, T.: Fully convolutional networks for semantic segmentation. In: 28th IEEE Conference on Computer Vision and Pattern Recognition, pp. 3431–3440. IEEE Press, New York (2015)
8. Pace, D.F., Dalca, A.V., Geva, T., Powell, A.J., Moghari, M.H., Golland, P.: Interactive whole-heart segmentation in congenital heart disease. In: Navab, N., Hornegger, J., Wells, W.M., Frangi, A.F. (eds.) MICCAI 2015. LNCS, vol. 9351, pp. 80–88. Springer, Heidelberg (2015). doi:10.1007/978-3-319-24574-4_10
9. Zhuang, X.: Challenges and methodologies of fully automatic whole heart segmentation: a review. J. Healthc. Eng. **4**, 371–408 (2013)
10. Zhuang, X., Shen, J.: Multi-scale patch and multi-modality atlases for whole heart segmentation of MRI. Med. Image Anal. **31**, 77–87 (2016)

RAMBO and HVSMR: Discrete Optimization and Probabilistic Intensity Modeling

A GPU Based Diffusion Method
for Whole-Heart and Great Vessel Segmentation

Philipp Lösel[(✉)] and Vincent Heuveline

Engineering Mathematics and Computing Lab (EMCL),
Interdisciplinary Center for Scientific Computing (IWR),
Heidelberg University, Heidelberg, Germany
{philipp.loesel,vincent.heuveline}@uni-heidelberg.de
https://biomedisa.de

Abstract. Segmenting the blood pool and myocardium from a 3D cardiovascular magnetic resonance (CMR) image allows to create a patient-specific heart model for surgical planning in children with complex congenital heart disease (CHD). Implementation of semi-automatic or automatic segmentation algorithms is challenging because of a high anatomical variability of the heart defects, low contrast, and intensity variations in the images. Therefore, manual segmentation is the gold standard but it is labor-intensive. In this paper we report the set-up and results of a highly scalable semi-automatic diffusion algorithm for image segmentation. The method extrapolates the information from a small number of expert manually labeled reference slices to the remaining volume. While results of most semi-automatic algorithms strongly depend on well-chosen but usually unknown parameters this approach is parameter-free. Validation is performed on twenty 3D CMR images.

Keywords: Segmentation · Diffusion · Random walks · Interactive segmentation · Semi-automatic segmentation · Multi-GPU

1 Introduction

Physicians highly benefit from 3D models, and particularly from 3D printings, for their surgical planing in childrens with congenital heart defects. They give a detailed understanding of the cardiovascular anatomy and allow to simulate surgical procedures and interventions [5]. But whole-heart segmentation in pediatric cardiac magnetic resonance imaging (MRI) is challenging due to high variability of the heart's topology and the congenital heart defects. In addition an automatic segmentation is complicated by intensity inhomogeneities, low contrast, and thin heart walls. Therefore, the standard method is manual segmentation, which lasts several hours for 100–200 slices [3,4], and makes it difficult to use 3D models for clinical application.

The MICCAI workshop HVSMR 2016 on whole-heart and great vessel segmentation from 3D cardiovascular MRI in congenital heart disease was combined with a challenge. In the first phase of the challenge participants were called to

© Springer International Publishing AG 2017
M.A. Zuluaga et al. (Eds.): RAMBO 2016/HVSMR 2016, LNCS 10129, pp. 121–128, 2017.
DOI: 10.1007/978-3-319-52280-7_12

train their algorithms on ten provided training images where an expert manual segmentation was given. In the second phase the participants tested their algorithms on ten testing images without a given segmentation. In both cases the results were uploaded and evaluated online by means of their Dice scores. The Dice coefficient is a statistic function used for comparing the similarity between the expert manual segmentation and the participants' results. Finally, the results were ranked based on their average Dice score.

As mentioned in [3] an interactive segmentation fits well into clinical workflows, since physicians must validate the accuracy of the segmentation and correct eventual errors before using a segmentation for surgical planing and decision making. But to enable a feasible interactive segmentation it is absolutely necessary to achieve a sufficiently high computational speed and to reduce the manual process to a minimum without losing accuracy.

We therefore chose a parameter-free and hardware-aware diffusion method [2] to approach the whole-heart and great vessel segmentation challenge. Most semi-automatic segmentation methods require the definition of usually unknown parameters. For example, in gradient based approaches a parameter determines whether an edge will be detected or not [1]. But finding such a parameter is time consuming, especially if the algorithm lasts several minutes or hours, and sometimes it is not possible to find a proper parameter which fits well for the complete volume due to high inhomogeneities in the image.

The diffusion method presented in this paper bases on several weighted random walks which start in a small set of manually labeled reference slices (Fig. 1). Due to the definition of the weights this approach is parameter-free. The idea of the diffusion method is that an unlabeled voxel will be hit by several random walks over time, where each voxel can be hit by random walks starting in the background, myocardium or blood pool label. By counting the number of hits, one can determine the probability that a voxel can be assigned to one specific segment. For example, if a voxel is hit by 1000 random walks starting in the background and only by 20 random walks starting in the myocardium and by 10 random walks starting in the blood pool label, then the voxel most likely belongs to the background. This approach takes the variability of human hearts and heart defects into account, since the random walks have the ability to adapt to shapes of unknown topology.

Besides the absence of parameters the advantage of this method lies in the independence of the random walks. This allows a fully exploited use of graphics processing units (GPUs) by computing all random walks in parallel and therefore allowing the processing time to be minimized.

2   Description of the Model

In this section we describe the semi-automatic diffusion method [2]. We show that the underlying random walks are highly scalable and that the result does not depend on a manually chosen parameter. First, we define the weights of the random walks which describe how likely a random walk move from one voxel to

Fig. 1. Weighted random walk starting from a reference slice with manually labeled area.

an adjacent voxel. Second, due to the complexity of segmenting the myocardium, we describe a model-based optimization.

We follow the definition of the weights by Lösel [2]. A graph is a couple (V, E) where V is a set of vertices in $\mathbb{R}^n$ and E is a set of edges, that is, E consists of some couples (x, y) where $x, y \in V$. We write $x \sim y$ if x is adjacent to y, i.e. $(x, y) \in E$. A weighted graph is a couple $((V, E), P)$ where P is a non-negative function on $V \times V$. It represents the weight of the edge between two nodes x and y. Let $I(x)$ be the image data, i.e. I maps x to a gray-value (e.g. for unsigned 16-bit images $I\colon \mathbb{R}^n \to \{0, 1, 2, 3, \ldots, 65535\}$). Further, let x_0 be the starting point of a random walk and σ_{x_0} the standard deviation from x_0 in a local area A (Fig. 2), then we set

$$\mu_{x_0}(y) = \frac{1}{\sqrt{2\pi\sigma_{x_0}^2}}\exp\left(-\frac{(I(x_0) - I(y))^2}{2\sigma_{x_0}^2}\right) \quad \text{for all } y \in V, \tag{1}$$

and

$$\mu(x) = \sum_{y \in V, y \sim x} \mu_{x_0}(y) \quad \text{for all } x \in V. \tag{2}$$

The function μ induces a Markov kernel

$$P_{x_0}(y, x) = \begin{cases} \frac{\mu_{x_0}(y)}{\mu(x)} & \text{if } y \sim x \\ 0 & \text{else,} \end{cases} \tag{3}$$

where $P_{x_0}(y, x)$ is the conditional probability of a random walk moving from x to y given its position x. Due to the definition of $P_{x_0}(y, x)$, the random walks tend to stay in an area which is similar to the starting area A. All variables in (1), (2) and (3) are well-defined, therefore it is not necessary to manually set the value of any parameter. Furthermore, since the random walks are independent from each other, their computation can be easily parallelized. Hence, the diffusion method is highly scalable and predestinated to be computed on any number of GPUs.

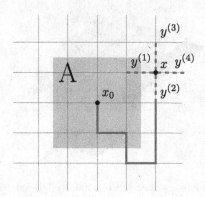

Fig. 2. Random walk after seven steps starting at an initial seed point x_0 with local area A. Dashed lines: determining the conditional probabilities $P_{x_0}(y^{(i)}, x)$ for the next step.

Starting several random walks in each pixel of the reference slices, a voxel will be hit by several random walks over time. The number of hits by random walks starting in the same segment implies the probability that the voxel belongs to this segment. Thus, the image can be segmented by assigning each voxel to the segment where the most random walks which hit the voxel started from. If a voxel is never hit, it will be assigned to the background.

Since it is difficult to distinguish the myocardium from its surrounding tissue and since we expect the myocardium in an area around the blood pool, we introduce a penalty term based on the distance between a voxel and the blood pool to reduce the risk of a false positive segmentation of the myocardium far away from the blood pool.

Its value goes to 0 as the distance increases. Therefore, we segment the image, multiply the number of hits caused by random walks starting in the myocardium by the penalty score, and finally recalculate the segmentation based on the updated probabilities.

3   Experimental Results

As described above, the architecture of the algorithm allows the use of any number of GPUs. We assigned the computation of random walks belonging to one reference slice to one GPU and calculated several slices in parallel on various GPUs, that means, in case of three reference slices we used three GPUs, for eight reference slices we used eight GPUs, and so on. Further, we used the parallel architecture of each GPU and computed several random walks belonging to one reference slice simultaneously where one random walk was assigned to one thread. For all images we started 10 random walks in each labeled pixel and performed 4000 steps respectively. The algorithm was implemented in Python 2.7 using PyCUDA 2015 with CUDA 7.5 and up to 10 GPUs[1]. If the amount of reference slices exceeded the number of GPUs, the random walks of several slices were assigned to one GPU. As in [3], we validated the algorithm for 3, 8 and 14 uniformly distributed reference slices (Fig. 1).

---

[1] 4 Nvidia Tesla K40, 4 Nvidia Tesla K20, 1 Nvidia Grid K2, 1 Nvidia GeForce GTX 770.

Table 1. *Training Data*: Results for cropped images using 3, 8 and 14 uniformly distributed reference slices. Dic1 is the Dice score for the myocardium. Dic2 is the Dice score for the blood pool.

Image	3 reference slices			8 reference slices			14 reference slices		
	Dic1	Dic2	Time (s)	Dic1	Dic2	Time (s)	Dic1	Dic2	Time (s)
Average	0.824	0.929	20	0.862	0.950	25	0.869	0.952	32
pat0	0.846	0.938	21	0.882	0.955	26	0.893	0.956	34
pat1	0.834	0.923	20	0.864	0.955	26	0.877	0.958	32
pat2	0.788	0.941	25	0.837	0.956	34	0.833	0.956	40
pat3	0.770	0.922	19	0.843	0.943	24	0.844	0.945	32
pat4	0.843	0.915	10	0.858	0.926	13	0.869	0.927	20
pat5	0.818	0.901	13	0.870	0.938	17	0.880	0.938	25
pat6	0.823	0.932	18	0.866	0.954	22	0.874	0.954	28
pat7	0.863	0.959	33	0.888	0.970	42	0.898	0.973	48
pat8	0.802	0.933	18	0.836	0.952	21	0.837	0.956	28
pat9	0.857	0.923	22	0.876	0.955	27	0.883	0.959	35

3.1   Training Data

We evaluated the segmentation method by means of the provided datasets. In the training phase, the algorithm were tested on cropped images (Table 1) as well as on full-volume images (Table 2). The average sizes of the cropped and full-volume images were $124 \times 179 \times 149$ and $387 \times 387 \times 165$ respectively. The reference slices were extracted from the provided manual segmentations. These expert

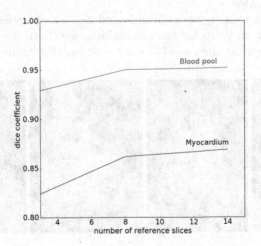

Fig. 3. Average accuracy of the diffusion segmentation as a function of the number of uniformly distributed reference slices (cropped images).

Table 2. *Training Data*: Results for full-volume images using 8 uniformly distributed reference slices. Dic1 is the Dice score for the myocardium. Dic2 is the Dice score for the blood pool.

Image	Full-volume		
	Dic1	Dic2	Time (s)
Average	0.870	0.948	103
pat0	0.884	0.955	88
pat1	0.879	0.955	91
pat2	0.837	0.956	118
pat3	0.843	0.942	96
pat4	0.903	0.915	42
pat5	0.878	0.933	55
pat6	0.869	0.947	152
pat7	0.887	0.969	204
Pat8	0.842	0.952	81
pat9	0.883	0.954	105

manually labeled segmentations were also used to determine the Dice score of the segmentation results. Figure 3 shows that increasing the number of reference slices increases the accuracy measured by Dice's coefficient. Since we spread an increasing number of reference slices over an increasing number of GPUs, the computing time mainly increased due to a higher amount of communication. For cropped images with 8 reference slices, the Dice score was in average 0.862 for the myocardium and 0.950 for the blood pool. Figure 4 shows segmentation results for patient 0 and 7 as well as the corresponding false positive and false negative segmentation.

For full-volume images, we only considered the case of 8 reference slices. Here we scored in average 0.870 for the myocardium and 0.948 for the blood pool. The average computing time was 103 s. As expected, the results are comparable

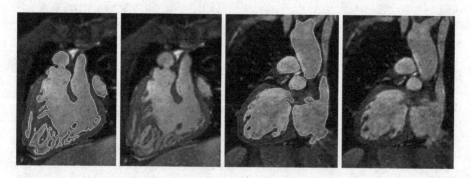

Fig. 4. Results for pat0 and pat7. Red = myocardium, yellow = blood pool. Additionally, false positive and false negative segmentation. (Color figure online)

Table 3. *Testing Data*: Results for cropped images using 8 reference slices. Comparing results using expert and non-expert manually labeled reference slices. Dic1 is the Dice score for the myocardium. Dic2 is the Dice score for the blood pool.

Image	Non-expert		Expert		
	Dic1	Dic2	Dic1	Dic2	Time (s)
average	0.739	0.903	0.832	0.957	49
pat10	0.720	0.922	0.779	0.963	54
pat11	0.762	0.905	0.806	0.966	48
pat12	0.769	0.913	0.866	0.952	50
pat13	0.785	0.913	0.864	0.959	58
pat14	0.665	0.877	0.805	0.948	36
pat15	0.683	0.898	0.835	0.955	62
pat16	0.769	0.901	0.816	0.951	31
pat17	0.791	0.924	0.844	0.954	58
pat18	0.721	0.895	0.854	0.958	55
pat19	0.723	0.877	0.847	0.963	40

to the cropped images, since the diffusion method does not depend on alignment or cropping. The computation time increased due to a larger background area. Therefore, more random walks starting in the background label have been computed. Since 8 reference slices achieve a high accuracy and seem to be an acceptable amount of manual labeling, we chose 8 reference slices to participate in the HVSMR 2016 challenge. Based on the fast computation, we recommend to start with a small number of labeled reference slices and only add further slices wherever it is necessary.

3.2   Testing Data

In the testing phase, no labeled reference slices were available. Therefore, the manual segmentation for the reference slices were done by the authors of this paper. Following the challenge, 8 uniformly distributed expert labeled reference slices were provided. Table 3 compares the results for the cropped images of the testing dataset using expert and non-expert manually labeled reference slices. The average Dice score is almost 10 Dice points higher for the myocardium and 5.4 Dice points higher for the blood pool when expert labeled slices were used. Similar results were scored for the full-volume images. Here the Dice scores for the myocardium and blood pool using expert labled slices were 0.828 and 0.946, and 0.734 and 0.902 when using non-expert labeled slices. The computation time for the full-volume images was in average 157 s. The average sizes of the cropped and full-volume images were $189 \times 252 \times 184$ and $470 \times 470 \times 194$ respectively, thus, they were significantly larger than in the training phase. Consequently, the computation time increased in average by 24 s. for the cropped and by 54 s. for the full-volume images.

4   Conclusions

In this paper, we reported the set-up and results of a semi-automatic diffusion algorithm for segmenting the blood pool and myocardium from a 3D cardio-vascular magnetic resonance image. We showed that increasing the number of reference slices increases the accuracy of the results. A high segmentation accu-racy combined with a small amount of manual labeling can be achieved for 8 reference slices. Due to its independence of manually chosen parameters, the short computing time as well as an easy and fast adaptation of the results by adding further reference slices, the algorithm supports the daily use of 3D heart models for surgical planning. The algorithm was implemented as part of the soft-ware service Biomedisa (Biomedical image segmentation app). As an universal application, Biomedisa can be used in addition to any segmentation tool like Amira, ImageJ or MITK.

Acknowledgements. This work was carried out with the support of the Federal Min-istry of Education and Research (BMBF), Germany, within the collaboration center ASTOR (Arthropod Structure revealed by ultra-fast Tomography and Online Recon-struction) and NOVA (Network for Online Visualization and synergistic Analysis of Tomographic Data).

References

1. Grady, L.: Random walks for image segmentation. IEEE Trans. Pattern Anal. Mach. Intell. **28**, 1768–1783 (2006)
2. Lösel, P., Heuveline, V.: Enhancing a diffusion algorithm for 4D image segmentation using local information. In: Proceedings of SPIE 9784, Medical Imaging 2016: Image Processing, 97842L (2016). doi:10.1117/12.2216202
3. Pace, D.F., Dalca, A.V., Geva, T., Powell, A.J., Moghari, M.H., Golland, P.: Interactive whole-heart segmentation in congenital heart disease. In: Navab, N., Hornegger, J., Wells, W.M., Frangi, A.F. (eds.) MICCAI 2015. LNCS, vol. 9351, pp. 80–88. Springer, Heidelberg (2015). doi:10.1007/978-3-319-24574-4_10
4. Schmauss, D., Haeberle, S., Hagl, C., Sodian, R.: Three-dimensional printing in cardiac surgery and interventional cardiology: a single-centre experience. Eur. J. Cardio.-Thorac. Surg. **47**, 1044–1052 (2014)
5. Valverde, I., Gomez, G., Gonzalez, A., Suarez-Mejias, C., Adsuar, A., Coserria, J.F., Uribe, S., Gomez-Cia, T., Hosseinpour, A.R.: Three-dimensional patient-specific cardiac model for surgical planning in Nikaidoh procedure. Cardiol. Young **25**(4), 698–704 (2014)

Fully-Automatic Segmentation of Cardiac Images Using 3-D MRF Model Optimization and Substructures Tracking

Georgios Tziritas[✉]

Department of Computer Science, University of Crete, Heraklion, Greece
tziritas@csd.uoc.gr

Abstract. We present a fully-automatic fast method for heart segmentation in pediatric cardiac MRI. The segmentation algorithm is a two step process. In the first step a 3-D Markov random field (MRF) model is assumed for labeling the MR images into four intensity classes, the two of them corresponding to the blood pool areas. The intensity distribution of the four classes is estimated by an unsupervised method. In the second step the resulting regions are, maybe further segmented and, classified in the three main categories: blood pool, myocardium and background. The classification is obtained by tracking the cardiac substructures that can be clearly distinguished in detected specific slices. The whole process is driven by the data analysis and by generic models on 2-D regions and 3-D volumes, without a deformation model, which eventually might be fitted. The algorithm is evaluated on the HSVMR 2016 data set in Congenital Heart Disease.

Keywords: Cardiac image segmentation · MRF optimization · Heart substructures tracking

1 Introduction

Automatic or semi-automatic heart segmentation is a challenging problem. A recent review [1] of the main existing algorithms for the whole heart segmentation shows that the state-of-the art methods use prior models, either atlas-based or generic deformable models. These approaches do not cover a wide range of pathological cases. The case of congenital diseases is particularly difficult. Therefore generic, robust and computationally inexpensive algorithms are needed for addressing patient-specific heart segmentation. These algorithms should be automatic or semi-automatic and would be considered as a tool minimizing the necessary user interaction. Another review on short axis left ventricle segmentation shows also the importance of prior knowledge [2], and therefore it concludes that the problem is challenging in absence of priors and when the borders are ill-defined.

The initial segmentation in our work is based on discrete optimization using a 3-D Markov Random Field (MRF) model. A comprehensive survey of MRFs

© Springer International Publishing AG 2017
M.A. Zuluaga et al. (Eds.): RAMBO 2016/HVSMR 2016, LNCS 10129, pp. 129–136, 2017.
DOI: 10.1007/978-3-319-52280-7_13

in computer vision and image understanding is given in [3]. This modelization has been also used in medical image analysis for image registration [4] or segmentation.

In absence of priors the data analysis provides guidelines for segmenting the volume and particularly for classifying the resulting segments. Our approach explores the potentiality of low and intermediate level methods in capturing the unknown structure of the data. The method is still under development and this paper reports the first achievements and explores methodologies that could be useful for obtaining fast algorithms with less user intervention.

Our algorithm is a two step process, the first one being a segmentation step, where the segmentation is considered as a discrete labeling problem at low-level. The second step is a tracking process on regions, based mainly on the assumptions used in the first step, but on structural information too, applying connectivity principles and relative location knowledge. The two sections of the paper present the methodology of the two algorithmic steps.

2   3-D Image Segmentation

The whole 3-D data set is segmented in four classes for facing the variability and inhomogeneity of the data. In particular the blood pool has not the same appearance in the vessels and in the ventricles. The distinction of two classes for the blood pool would facilitate the localization of the heart substructures.

The segmentation is posed as a probabilistic optimization problem using a discrete Markov random field (MRF) in order to obtain a regularized label field. In this manner, we aim at capturing the local interactions between voxels and the coherence of the segmentation 3-D map. The problem can be formulated as follows: we seek to assign a class label $l(v)$ to each node (voxel) of a graph $v \in \mathcal{V}$, so that the following cost is minimized:

$$\sum_{v \in \mathcal{V}} c_l(v) + \sum_{(v,u) \in \mathcal{E}} w(l(v), l(u)), \tag{1}$$

where $\mathcal{E}$ is the set of the graph edges. In this work for a 3-D volume a first order model with 6 connections is employed. The graph is composed by the whole regular 3-D grid of voxels.

The singleton potentials, or priors, are based on the voxel-wise computed probability density functions. Then the dissimilarities of pixels to the clusters l are given by

$$c_l(v) = -\ln p_l(X(v)), \tag{2}$$

where $X(v)$ is the voxel intensity.

The pairwise potentials are set according to the Potts function, with all weights w set equal to a constant w_0, in case of different classification, and zero potential when the two neighboring 3-D points are assigned the same class. The regularization constant w_0 is data adapted, having as relevant statistics the average value on the minimum dissimilarities at each point.

For minimizing the MRF energy in Eq. (1), we make use of the *primal-dual* method [5], which casts the MRF optimization problem as an integer programming problem and then makes use of the duality theory of linear programming in order to derive solutions that have been proved to be almost optimal.

The probability density functions $p_l(X)$ are computed from the data. A Rayleigh distribution is assumed for the first class, while the data for the three other classes are assumed to be distributed according to the Gaussian model. Because of the inhomogeneities encountered in the data set an automatic clustering risks to be inaccurate. For computing the probability density functions we propose to combine data quantization and spatial coherence.

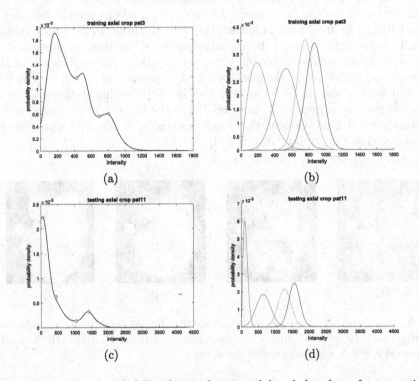

(a) (b) (c) (d)

Fig. 1. The estimated probability density function of the whole volume for two patients with the quantization boundary values given by the markers ((a) and (c)), and the corresponding probability density functions for the four intensity classes ((b) and (d)).

The quantizer results from the analysis of the whole volume, based on the localization of the modes of the global distribution. The global distribution is estimated using the kernel method given in [6]. In the HSVMR 2016 data set two situations appear: two modes, for all the volumes in the Testing data set, or three modes, more frequently in the Training data set. In the last case the three modes could be considered as corresponding to the three main classes. In this case the best choice for the quantizer intervals seems to be the two local minima of the global probability density function and the last peak. In Fig. 1 is depicted the estimated density for such a volume, where are also given the quantization boundary values. In Fig. 1(b) are given the four estimated density functions for the four intensity classes. In case of two modes the quantization boundary values are estimated from the modes location, possibly the inflection points of the probability density function, and an adaptation for obtaining a sufficient myocardium area. Such an example is also depicted in the same Figure, plots (c) and (d).

For each quantization interval the computation of the probability density function is based on the connected components of the corresponding interval, under the condition that the connected components are large enough, containing at least 10% of the total number of voxels attributed a priori to the corresponding class. This simple rule ensures the spatial coherence of the distribution estimator.

Having estimated the probability density functions the application of the optimization algorithm is straightforward. A segmentation result is given in Fig. 2(b) for the slice in (a). The objective in the following section will be to filter non relevant regions using rules related to the features of the main cardiac substructures. A final segmentation result is depicted in Fig. 2(c) which should be compared to the ground truth in 2(d).

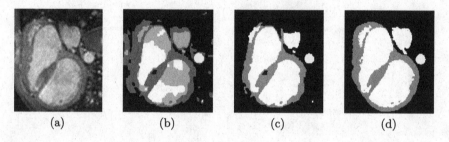

    (a)   (b)   (c)   (d)

Fig. 2. The initial segmentation result (b) for the slice in (a) with the classification result (c) and the ground truth (d) for the slice s_V (patient 0 of HVSMR data set). Horizontal is the X axis and vertical the Z axis.

3   Blood Pool and Myocardium Classification

We have considered two intensity classes for the blood pool for the initial segmentation step, because of the existing inhomogeneity and variability in its appearance. Now we have to segment in the main classes of blood pool and myocardium. The two classes of large intensity value are both labeled as "blood pool". A very important rule applied for classifying the extracted by the segmentation step regions is the requirement to have one 3-D connected component for the blood pool and one for the myocardium, and also for their union.

In our method the classification procedure is done slice by slice according to the Y axis. A global model of slice sequence segmentation is used which is identified by tracking the detected substructures, mainly those belonging to the "blood pool" class. Are identified going in the opposite direction of the Y axis, slice s_0 where the myocardium appears, slice s_V, where the two ventricles are well distinguished, slice s_M of maximum blood pool area, slice s_A at the superior level of the atria and slice s_F, where the myocardium disappears in the slice sequence. Therefore the whole heart is localized between slices s_0 and s_F. The global localization of the heart, as well as the localization of the substructures, might be useful for fitting a deformable model for each subsequence. It could be a possible extension of the current work.

The first step of the classification process is that of identifying the potential components for the blood pool. In Fig. 3 is illustrated the blood area as measured from the segmentation result for two volumes, the first one considered as typical, without obvious false detections, while for the case in (b), are detected regions with strong intensity not belonging to the "blood pool" class. These regions are detected and excluded from the "blood pool" class.

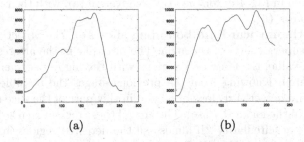

(a)   (b)

Fig. 3. The slice sequence of the potential blood area for two volumes with different content.

Hereafter are described the process modules for segmenting the Y axis slice sequence and classifying the detected regions.

Location of slice with best left and right ventricle appearance. It is known that the two ventricles appear and are well distinguished in many slices of the sequence segment after slice s_M. In this part of the sequence are detected those slices, where two "blood pool" regions appear clearly and continuously. A preference is given to the slice s_V, where the two ventricles are larger, that is as near as possible to the s_M slice.

Forward tracking the myocardium area from slice s_V. Having localized the left and right ventricles in slice s_V, the regions are tracked from slice to slice based on their location. The myocardium is also localized by the neighbouring region labeled as such according to the MRF segmentation result. When the tracking process fails to track any ventricle, slice s_0 is detected giving a Y bounding slice for the myocardium and the whole heart.

Tracking the myocardium from slice s_V to slice s_M. This tracking step is operated backwards. In each slice are localized the two "blood pool" candidate regions that are more similar to the two already detected in the previously processed slice. The similarity is measured by the Jaccard index. For both detected regions the major axis length feature is measured, that is the major axis of the ellipse that has the same normalized second central moments as the region. In case where one of the two axes and the whole 'ventricle' area grow with a rate higher than 10%, the tracking process is stopped. It is assumed that this slice is situated where the heart substructures are not separated by physical tissues. From this slice to slice s_M, one or two substructures are tracked, as obtained from the initial segmentation, independently of their growing rate. These slices are considered to be in the part of the heart where only anatomical knowledge could detect the substructure boundaries. For the myocardium localization the region neighbouring the "blood pool" regions is detected. Using distance measures of the detected "blood pool" regions to the 'background' class region, a maximum myocardium width is estimated for restricting the myocardium region, as often the initially segmented 'myocardium' regions are larger than the true ones. A segmentation result is given in Fig. 4(c) for the s_M slice given in (a), with the result of MRF optimization in (b).

Location of the myocardium bounding slice s_F. The objective now is to locate the superior level of the atria. The intensity in the arteres has almost surely high value, therefore only regions with the highest segmentation label are considered. Knowing from the previous stages the possible position of the heart, are detected regions of label 4 in this part of the slice subsequence before s_M (in the forward sense). The area of these regions is measured, as well as a feature of 'circularity'. If almost all the detected regions are positioned in the same region on the (X, Z) plane the region at the centroid position is detected. If the regions are dispersed, the cluster which is nearest to the origin of the (X, Z) is extracted and again the centroid position is estimated, but only for this group of regions. The region detected is tracked until a similar region in neighboring position can be found. The s_F slice is located where the tracking fails.

Tracking the myocardium from slice s_F to slice s_A. The region detected in slice s_F as the atria boundary, is tracked forwards. The Jaccard index is used for measuring similarity for tracking. When the tracking fails, slice s_A is located. At the same time is tracked the myocardium using also an estimation of its width.

Interpolation of the myocardium from slice s_M to slice s_A. In this sequence segment the myocardium is partially occluded. Therefore it is not possible to track it without a deformation model. We adopted a simpler low level approach of interpolation, as it is known that from slice s_A to slice s_M the myocardium area is growing. We consider a sequence of constant rate growing area candidate myocardium regions with the same shape as that of slice s_A. The myocardium region is localized as the intersection of the region with voxels labeled '1' by the MRF segmentation, the above defined candidate region and the convex hull of the myocardium region at slice s_M.

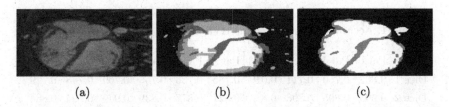

(a)   (b)   (c)

Fig. 4. The initial segmentation result (b) for the slice in (a) with the classification result (c) for the slice s_M (patient 11 of HVSMR data set). Horizontal is the X axis and vertical the Z axis.

In addition to the above modules, are used modules for locating the Descending Aorta and for filtering false detections of "blood pool" regions slice by slice. Finally, the application of the requirement to have exactly one 3-D connected component of myocardium and one for blood pool provides the final segmentation result. Two slices are depicted in Figs. 2(c) and 4(c).

4 Results and First Conclusions

We give now in Table 1 (resp. Table 2) the score measures, Dice coefficient and average surface distance, of our results on the 3-D cardiovascular magnetic resonance images of the HVSMR 2016 Training (resp. Testing) data set [7]. Label 1 is for the myocardium and 2 for the blood pool. Our model of Y slice sequence segmentation is correctly applicable to all 20 volumes, except for patients 15 and 16 in the Testing data set. Only for the last one it was necessary to use a backup solution, when the location of s_V and s_A slices failed. The tracking was then applied in two subsequences, where it was not possible to distinguish substructures. In the evaluation results for these volumes is reflected the failure of the model.

We consider our results as preliminary and encouraging. There exist some directions of possible improvements, as well as some methodological limitations. Even if the main steps of the algorithm are stable and generic, the need of post-processing could be considered as a weak point. At the same time many of our intermediate results of data analysis could be also helpful in other approaches. We consider that the introduction and fitting of a deformable model will be the best approach. The model fitting might be facilitated by the slice sequence segmentation and the first global segmentation results.

An important strong point of our algorithm is its computational cost. Processing a 4 million voxels volume on a laptop Intel Core i-7 2.6 GHz takes about one minute, the classification step taking 2 min or less for the whole training data set with a non-optimized implementation.

It should be noticed that there is place for learning algorithms for some important parameters of the classification modules. On the other hand, as the parameters tuning is often the work of an expert, it would be possible to extend this approach in an interactive mode.

Table 1. Accuracy measures for the HVSMR 2016 training phase data set.

	Pat 0	Pat 1	Pat 2	Pat 3	Pat 4	Pat 5	Pat 6	Pat 7	Pat 8	Pat 9
Dice 1	0.802	0.750	0.711	0.610	0.785	0.736	0.755	0.769	0.748	0.729
Dice 2	0.903	0.895	0.898	0.876	0.821	0.877	0.839	0.949	0.894	0.884
Adb 1	0.837	1.270	2.391	2.939	0.992	1.143	1.171	1.123	1.047	2.233
Adb 2	1.210	1.634	1.937	1.572	1.487	1.030	1.319	0.562	1.180	1.771

Table 2. Accuracy measures for the HVSMR 2016 testing phase data set.

	Pat 10	Pat 11	Pat 12	Pat 13	Pat 14	Pat 15	Pat 16	Pat 17	Pat 18	Pat 19
Dice 1	0.529	0.704	0.681	0.815	0.594	0.536	0.252	0.713	0.757	0.540
Dice 2	0.901	0.905	0.847	0.884	0.850	0.857	0.740	0.897	0.901	0.885
Adb 1	2.286	1.324	1.331	1.064	1.744	3.123	4.344	1.577	0.937	2.683
Adb 2	1.606	1.739	1.754	2.375	2.308	2.396	3.406	2.179	1.707	2.100

References

1. Zhuang, X.: Chalenges and methodologies of fully automatic whole heart segmantation: a review. J. Healthc. Eng. **4**, 371–407 (2013)
2. Petitjean, C., Dacher, J.-N.: A review of segmentation methods in short axis cardiac MR images. Med. Image Anal. **15**, 169–184 (2011)
3. Wang, C., Komodakis, N., Paragios, N.: Markov random field modeling, inference and learning in computer vision and image understanding: a survey. Comput. Vis. Image Underst. **117**, 1610–1627 (2013)
4. Glocker, B., Komodakis, N., Tziritas, G., Navab, N., Paragios, N.: Dense image registration through MRFs and efficient linear programming. Med. Image Anal. **12**, 731–741 (2008)
5. Komodakis, N., Tziritas, G.: Approximate labeling via graph cuts based on linear programming. IEEE Trans. Pattern Anal. Mach. Intell. **29**, 1436–1453 (2007)
6. Botev, Z.I., Grotowski, J.F., Kroese, D.P.: Kernel density estimation via diffusion. Ann. Stat. **38**, 2916–2957 (2010)
7. Pace, D.F., Dalca, A.V., Geva, T., Powell, A.J., Moghari, M.H., Golland, P.: Interactive whole-heart segmentation in congenital heart disease. In: Navab, N., Hornegger, J., Wells, W.M., Frangi, A.F. (eds.) MICCAI 2015. LNCS, vol. 9351, pp. 80–88. Springer, Heidelberg (2015). doi:10.1007/978-3-319-24574-4_10

HSVMR: Atlas-Based Strategies

Strengths and Pitfalls of Whole-Heart Atlas-Based Segmentation in Congenital Heart Disease Patients

Maria A. Zuluaga[1]([✉]), Benedetta Biffi[2,3], Andrew M. Taylor[3],
Silvia Schievano[3], Tom Vercauteren[1], and Sébastien Ourselin[1]

[1] Translational Imaging Group, Centre for Medical Image Computing,
University College London, London, UK
maria.zuluaga@gmail.com
[2] Department of Medical Physics and Biomedical Engineering,
University College London, London, UK
[3] Centre for Cardiovascular Imaging, UCL Institute of Cardiovascular
Science & Great Ormond Street Hospital for Children, London, UK

Abstract. Atlas-based whole-heart segmentation is a well-established technique for the extraction of key cardiac structures of the adult heart. Despite its relative success in this domain, its implementation in whole-heart segmentation of paediatric patients suffering from a form of congenital heart disease is not straightforward. The aim of this work is to evaluate the current strengths and limitations of whole-heart atlas based segmentation techniques within the context of the Whole-Heart and Great Vessel Segmentation from 3D Cardiovascular MRI in Congenital Heart Disease Challenge (HVSMR). Obtained results suggest that there are no significant differences in the accuracies of state-of-the-art methods, reporting maximum Dice scores of 0.73 for the myocardium and 0.90 for the blood pool.

1 Introduction

Congenital heart disease (CHD) has a reported incidence that varies between 4–10 per 1000 births [8]. In the last decades, the survival of CHD patients has increased thanks to improvements in diagnosis, medical treatment and surgical repair [13]. This has led to new challenges for follow-up, reinvestigation and reoperation [13].

Imaging plays a key role in the diagnosis of CHD and it is required at all stages of patient care [9]. It outlines anatomy and physiology, assists the intervention planning, helps to refine management, evaluates the consequences of interventions and facilitates prognosis [9]. At all stages of the CHD assessment pipeline, delineation and extraction of the whole heart, which includes the four chambers and eventually the great vessels, are crucial to achieve a successful outcome. To date, the process requires a significant amount of manual labour involving many hours of work [5] and it is prone to inter- and intra-observer variations.

© Springer International Publishing AG 2017
M.A. Zuluaga et al. (Eds.): RAMBO 2016/HVSMR 2016, LNCS 10129, pp. 139–146, 2017.
DOI: 10.1007/978-3-319-52280-7_14

Cardiovascular magnetic resonance (CMR) has emerged as a major alternative to echocardiography (the by default modality of choice in paediatric patients) as an imaging tool within the CHD assessment pipeline [9,11], due to its non-invasiveness, lack of ionizing radiation, and its higher anatomical resolution and extra cardiac information. Moreover, the vast literature in CMR analysis tools [14] proposes a large set of semi- and fully-automated methods for adult whole-heart segmentation that could be adapted and applied to paediatric CMR images to ease and improve the delineation and extraction of the heart.

Among fully-automated segmentation methods, atlas-based techniques are largely popular due to their robustness and high reported accuracies [6,15,17]. However, when applied in the context of CHD patients, they are not as successful. This might be explained by the substantial changes in heart topology and high anatomical variability in CHD that lead to poor segmentations [2,10,16]. In an ideal scenario, this could be solved by using as many atlas databases as pathological conditions. This is, however, difficult to achieve in practice. If atlas-based techniques were to be used for CHD assessment, there is a need to develop algorithms which are robust enough to topological and anatomical variations without the requirement of pathology-specific databases.

In the context of the Whole-Heart and Great Vessel Segmentation from 3D Cardiovascular MRI in Congenital Heart Disease Challenge (HVSMR) [10], this work focuses on atlas-based segmentation techniques and aims to assess the strengths and limitations of these methods in CHD patients. In the remaining of this paper, Sect. 2 provides a more detailed overview of atlas-based approaches, Sect. 3 describes the materials and methods used and Sect. 4 presents the obtained results. Finally, Sect. 5 discusses the results and presents the conclusions.

2   Background: Atlas-Based Segmentation

An atlas, in its simplest form, is made up by an intensity image and its corresponding annotated image. The final goal of atlas-based segmentation is to use the relationship between the labels of the annotated image and the intensities of the corresponding CMR image to assign labels to the voxels of an unseen (or target) image. Typically, this is achieved by registering the atlas into the unseen image space and then applying a technique to convert the labelled images into a final segmentation.

In whole-heart segmentation, atlas-based methods generally follow a two-stage registration approach to transform the atlas into the target image space. At the first stage, the atlas is registered using an affine transformation to the unseen image to achieve a rough alignment. After the affine alignment step, a non-rigid deformation registration is applied to align the atlas with the unseen image. The resulting transformation is finally used to resample the atlas' labels into the unseen image. Differences in methods making use of this two-stage framework can be found in: (1) the atlas database that is used, (2) the labels and (3) the algorithm used to convert the transformed atlas labels into the unseen image segmentation. In the following, a brief description of each is provided.

Atlas Database. In its simplest form, an atlas consists of a single pair of images. This *simple atlas* [15] can be composed of a CMR image and its associated label image or, more often, by a mean intensity image, which is obtained from the registration and averaging of several CMR images, and a label image. The associated label image can be formed by binary labels [15] or by a probabilistic image [7], reflecting the chance of a voxel to belong to a specific label/class. Alternatively, if a database of intensity images is available, it is possible to have multiple annotated images and propagate them to the unseen image [4,6,17]. This approach is referred to as multi-atlas segmentation.

Labels. The most common approach in cardiac segmentation seeks to not only identify the heart, but also its different structures [6,7,15,17]. Only a few works have focused on the heart as a unit by providing a single binary mask of the whole heart [4]. When a simple atlas is used, the use of multiple labels is straightforward. In multi-atlas segmentation, there is the need for specific methods (fusion algorithms) which can handle potential overlapping of different labels once the images are transformed into the target image space.

Fusion Algorithm. Methods using a simple atlas obtain the final segmentation by directly transforming the labelled image into the unseen image space [15]. When probabilistic images are used, it is common to have a post-processing stage to refine the propagations [7]. When multiple atlases and/or labels are used, it is mandatory to implement a merging technique which can combine the labels from multiple images into a final consensus segmentation. This is commonly denoted a fusion algorithm. Common combination rules applied to cardiac segmentation include majority voting [6] and weighted decision functions [4,17].

3   Materials and Methods

In this section, we describe the images and the experimental setup used to evaluate the strengths and limitations of atlas-based methods (Sect. 2) when aiming at highly accurate whole-heart segmentations of CHD patients.

3.1   Materials

CMR images provided by the challenge organisers[1] were acquired during clinical practice at Boston Children's Hospital (Boston, USA). Cases include a variety of congenital heart defects. Some subjects have undergone interventions. Imaging was done in on a 1.5 T scanner (Phillips Achieva) without contrast agent using a steady-state free precession (SSFP) pulse sequence. Image dimension and image spacing varied across subjects, and average $390 \times 390 \times 165$ and $0.9 \times 0.9 \times 0.85$ mm, respectively, in the full-volume training dataset.

Manual segmentation of the blood pool and ventricular myocardium was performed by a trained rater, and validated by two clinical experts. The annotated data is composed of two labels: blood pools and myocardium. The blood

---

[1] http://segchd.csail.mit.edu/index.html.

pool class includes the left and right atria, left and right ventricles, aorta, pulmonary veins, pulmonary arteries, and the superior and inferior vena cava. The myocardium class includes the thick muscle surrounding the two ventricles and the septum between them. Coronaries are not included in the blood pool class, and are labelled as myocardium if they travel within the ventricular myocardium.

3.2   Methods

As described in Sect. 2, state-of-the-art whole-heart segmentation frameworks mainly differ in the type of atlas, the number of labels and the type of fusion scheme. In this section, we describe the different strategies that were considered for the evaluation of these elements.

Although there exist several tools and schemes to implement the two-stage registration pipeline typically used in whole-heart segmentation we have selected the registration scheme described in [16] for its performance and because sit contains the necessary information to be reproduced. The effect of the registration algorithm in whole-heart atlas-based segmentation is out of the scope of this work.

Simple Atlas vs. Multi-atlas. In order to evaluate the performance of a simple atlas w.r.t a multi-atlas approach, mean intensity atlases were constructed using the CMR images of the training data through co-registration to a reference image within the training set. Binary labels, rather than probabilistic ones, were obtained via majority voting and manual correction of the results. For multi-atlas evaluation, no additional processing of the data was required: the training data provided was used as the atlas.

Single vs. Multi-label. An additional atlas using a single label was constructed by combining the two original labels, blood pool and myocardium, into a single one, denoted whole-heart. When evaluating these two schemes, it was the accuracy in segmenting the whole heart rather than each individual class what was assessed. For this purpose, in the multi-label case all the labels were used during the propagation and fusion process, but the resulting labels in the final segmentation were considered as one when comparing to the single label approach.

Fusion Schemes. We evaluated three different fusion schemes for the merging of the labels when using multiple labels or atlases. These are: majority voting (MV), STEPS [1] and the STAPLE algorithm [12]. Both MV and STEPS have been successfully applied in whole-heart segmentation [6,17]. STAPLE has not been applied in this domain but, given its large success in brain image segmentation, we included it in the fusion schemes to consider.

Post-processing. The label fusion result does not necessarily represent the final segmentation; sometimes it is fed to another algorithm to estimate the output labels [3]. In whole-heart segmentation, this kind of post-processing techniques have not been that popular and are rarely used [7]. However, we have included this step within the evaluated framework as it could be used to improve the segmentation obtained from the fusion, which can be prone to errors due to the existing pathologies. In this work we evaluated the use of the label fusion result as initialisation for parameter estimation of a Gaussian mixture model using expectation maximisation (EM) algorithm.

4   Experimental Results

Evaluation of the different settings involved in the implementation of an atlas-based segmentation pipeline was performed using the Dice score coefficient (DSC), as suggested by the challenge organisers.

4.1   Training Data

Table 1 summarises the results obtained when using a simple atlas. Results are reported using multiple labels and a single one. In the latter, when no post-processing is applied, only the whole heart DSC is reported. Table 2 presents the results for the multi-atlas based segmentation using different labels, fusion schemes and post-processing. A comparison of the results from both tables shows that multi-atlas segmentation is superior to that one using a single atlas.

4.2   Testing Data

The best performing pipeline, as reported in Table 2 was submitted to the HVSMR Challenge. For this matter, 10 additional cases were segmented. The full training data set was used as atlas. Average DSC of 0.73 and 0.90 were obtained for the myocardium and blood pool, respectively. These values are very similar to those obtained when performing cross-validation over the training set. The full set of results are reported in the HVSMR website[2].

Table 1. Mean DSC ($\pm$ std. deviation) using a simple atlas to segment the whole heart (single label) and the multiple labels. Results are also reported with no post-processing and post-processing through EM refinement.

	Whole-heart	Myocardium	Blood pool
No post-processing	0.61 ± 0.08	0.43 ± 0.08	0.54 ± 0.08
EM refinement	-	0.65 ± 0.08	0.75 ± 0.08

5   Discussion and Conclusions

In this work we have evaluated the use of standard atlas-based segmentation techniques for the extraction of the blood pool and the myocardium in CHD patients. The results demonstrate that, as it had been suggested in previous works, atlas-based methods show lower accuracies in the presence of

----

[2] https://challenge.kitware.com/#submission/57dc2c02cad3a51cc66c8b12.

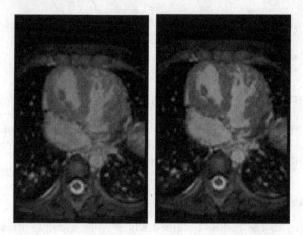

Fig. 1. Poor segmentation (case 4) using a multi-atlas, single label and STEPS fusion approach with post-processing (right) and without post-processing (left). A large section of the myocardium is missed originally and this cannot be recovered by the post-processing.

high anatomical variations that can not be captured by the registration algorithm. Nevertheless, the results demonstrate the potential of atlas-based methods within the CHD assessment pipeline.

Overall the presented results suggest to prefer the use of multiple atlases over a simple atlas. However, when in a multi-atlas based scheme the results have suggested that there is not a specific pipeline configuration that performs significantly better than the others. In the same way that no differences were encountered when evaluating different multi-atlas schemes, the authors believe that no significant differences should arise when using different registration algorithm implementations (under the assumption it has been properly tuned). However, it should be noted that registration is out of the scope of this work. Based on these findings, we believe there is room for improvement by exploiting the way the information of the atlases is structured (*e.g* single vs multiple atlas or labels). To date, most of the efforts have been directed towards the development of novel registration and fusion algorithms rather than towards the development of novel atlas generation strategies, e.g. data augmentation to simulate CHD atlases, with enriched information and features.

The obtained results also suggest that the use of a post-processing scheme can improve the results of the atlas-based segmentation. For instance, the best performing pipeline was obtained through the use of the EM algorithm. However, it should be noted that when the initial segmentation is not good enough (Fig. 1), there is not much that can be improved through the post-processing. Finally, if a single technique had to be recommended to be used currently in the CHD pipeline assessment, then we would recommend to prefer multiple atlases and the use of a single label to locate the heart, in combination with the EM algorithm.

Table 2. Mean DSC (± std. deviation) using a multi-atlas approach. Results are reported for all the possible configurations. (SL) denotes the use of a single label for fusion and the results from the best performing pipeline are highlighted in bold.

Fusion	Segmentation	No post-processing	EM refinement
Majority voting	Whole heart (SL)	0.89 ± 0.05	-
	Whole heart	0.88 ± 0.04	-
	Myocardium (SL)	-	0.74 ± 0.09
	Myocardium	0.72 ± 0.13	0.74 ± 0.09
	Blood pool (SL)	-	0.90 ± 0.05
	Blood pool	0.88 ± 0.04	0.90 ± 0.05
STEPS	Whole heart (SL)	**0.90± 0.03**	-
	Whole heart	0.90 ± 0.04	-
	Myocardium (SL)	-	**0.74 ± 0.09**
	Myocardium	0.73 ± 0.07	0.73 ± 0.08
	Blood pool (SL)	-	**0.90 ± 0.03**
	Blood pool	0.89 ± 0.03	**0.90 ± 0.03**
STAPLE	Whole heart (SL)	0.87 ± 0.09	-
	Whole heart	0.85 ± 0.09	-
	Myocardium (SL)	-	0.68 ± 0.14
	Myocardium	0.70 ± 0.09	
	Blood pool (SL)	-	0.87 ± 0.08
	Blood pool	0.86 ± 0.09	0.88 ± 0.06

Acknowledgements. This work was supported through an Innovative Engineering for Health award by the Wellcome Trust [WT101957]; Engineering and Physical Sciences Research Council (EPSRC) [NS/A000027/1]. BB is funded by UCL EPSRC Centre for Doctoral Training in Medical Imaging Scholarship Award. AMT and SS receive funding from Heart Research UK, the British Heart Foundation and the National Institute for Health Research Biomedical Research Centre at GOSH and UCL. SO receives funding from the National Institute for Health Research University College London Hospitals Biomedical Research Centre (NIHR BRC UCLH/UCL High Impact Initiative BW.mn.BRC10269) and the EPSRC (EP/K005278/1).

References

1. Cardoso, M.J., Leung, K., Modat, M., Keihaninejad, S., Cash, D., Barnes, J., Fox, N.C., Ourselin, S.: Steps: similarity and truth estimation for propagated segmentations and its application to hippocampal segmentation and brain parcelation. Med. Image Anal. **17**(6), 671–684 (2013)
2. Gilbert, K., Cowan, B.R., Suinesiaputra, A., Occleshaw, C., Young, A.A.: Rapid D-Affine biventricular cardiac function with polar prediction. In: Golland, P., Hata, N., Barillot, C., Hornegger, J., Howe, R. (eds.) MICCAI 2014. LNCS, vol. 8674, pp. 546–553. Springer, Heidelberg (2014). doi:10.1007/978-3-319-10470-6_68

3. Iglesias, J.E., Sabuncu, M.R.: Multi-atlas segmentation of biomedical images: a survey. Med. Image Anal. **24**(1), 205–219 (2015)
4. Išgum, I., Staring, M., Rutten, A., Prokop, M., Viergever, M., van Ginneken, B.: Multi-atlas-based segmentation with local decision fusion application to cardiac and aortic segmentation in CT scans. IEEE Trans. Med. Imaging **28**(7), 100–1010 (2009)
5. Jacobs, S., Grunert, R., Mohr, F.W., Falk, V.: 3D-imaging of cardiac structures using 3D heart models for planning in heart surgery: a preliminary study. Interact. Cardiovasc. Thorac. Surg. **7**(1), 6–9 (2008)
6. Kirisli, H.A., Schaap, M., Klein, S., Papadopoulou, S., Bonardi, M., Chen, C., Weustink, A., Mollet, N., Vonken, E.P.A., Geest, R., Walsum, T., Niessen, W.: Evaluation of a multi-atlas based method for segmentation of cardiac CTA data: a large-scale, multicenter, and multivendor study. Med. Phys. **37**(12), 6279–6292 (2010)
7. Lorenzo-Valdes, M., Sanchez-Ortiz, G., Elkington, A., Mohiaddin, R., Rueckert, D.: Segmentation of 4D cardiac MR images using a probabilistic atlas and the EM algorithm. Med. Image Anal. **8**, 255–265 (2004)
8. Marelli, A.J., Mackie, A.S., Ionescu-Ittu, R., Rahme, E., Pilote, L.: Congenital heart disease in the general population changing prevalence and age distribution. Circulation **115**, 163–172 (2007)
9. Ntsinjana, H.N., Hughes, M.L., Taylor, A.M.: The role of cardiovascular magnetic resonance in pediatric congenital heart disease. J. Cardiovasc. Magn. Reson. **13**(51) (2011)
10. Pace, D.F., Dalca, A.V., Geva, T., Powell, A.J., Moghari, M.H., Golland, P.: Interactive whole-heart segmentation in congenital heart disease. In: Navab, N., Hornegger, J., Wells, W.M., Frangi, A.F. (eds.) MICCAI 2015. LNCS, vol. 9351, pp. 80–88. Springer, Heidelberg (2015). doi:10.1007/978-3-319-24574-4_10
11. Prakash, A., Powell, A.J., Geva, T.: Multimodality noninvasive imaging for assessment of congenital heart disease. Circulation **3**, 112–125 (2010)
12. Warfield, S., Zou, K., Wells, W.: Simultaneous truth and performance level estimation (staple): an algorithm for the validation of image segmentation. IEEE Trans. Med. Imaging **23**(7), 903–921 (2004)
13. Wren, C., O'Sullivan, J.: Survival with congenital heart disease and need for follow up in adult life. Heart **85**, 438–443 (2001)
14. Zhuang, X.: Challenges and methodologies of fully automatic whole heart segmentation: a review. J. Healthc. Eng. **4**, 371–407 (2013)
15. Zhuang, X., Rhode, K., Razavi, R., Hawkes, D., Ourselin, S.: A registration-based propagation framework for automatic whole heart segmentation of cardiac MRI. IEEE Trans. Med. Imaging **29**(9), 1612–1625 (2010)
16. Zuluaga, M.A., Burgos, N., Mendelson, A., Taylor, A., Ourselin, S.: Voxelwise atlas rating for computer assisted diagnosis: application to congenital heart diseases of the great arteries. Med. Image Anal. **26**(1), 185–194 (2015)
17. Zuluaga, M.A., Cardoso, M.J., Modat, M., Ourselin, S.: Multi-atlas propagation whole heart segmentation from MRI and CTA using a local normalised correlation coefficient criterion. In: Ourselin, S., Rueckert, D., Smith, N. (eds.) FIMH 2013. LNCS, vol. 7945, pp. 174–181. Springer, Heidelberg (2013). doi:10.1007/978-3-642-38899-6_21

Automated Cardiovascular Segmentation in Patients with Congenital Heart Disease from 3D CMR Scans: Combining Multi-atlases and Level-Sets

Rahil Shahzad$^{(\boxtimes)}$, Shan Gao, Qian Tao, Oleh Dzyubachyk,
and Rob van der Geest

Division of Image Processing (LKEB), Department of Radiology,
Leiden University Medical Center, Leiden, The Netherlands
r.shahzad@lumc.nl

Abstract. This paper presents an automatic method that enables segmentation of the whole heart and the great vessels from 3D MRI scans. The proposed method is built upon a multi-atlas-based segmentation approach and consists of a number of intermediate steps to enable accurate segmentation of the ventricular myocardial tissue, intra-cardiac blood pool, and the aorta. The method was tested on the datasets provided by the HVSMR 2016 MICCAI challenge organizers. Results on the testing data show that, the proposed method achieved an average Dice index of 0.89 for the blood pool and 0.75 for the ventricular myocardial tissue. The corresponding average surface distance error were 1.6 mm and 1.1 mm, respectively.

Keywords: Atlas-based segmentation · Registration · Tissue maps · Hough transform · Level-sets

1 Introduction

Cardiac segmentation is a very important step in understanding the condition of the heart. Various important clinical parameters can be derived from accurately segmented heart structures. A number of imaging modalities, such as magnetic resonance imaging (MRI), computed tomography (CT) and ultrasound (US) are used for diagnostic purposes and understanding the cardiac physiology. Cardiac MR (CMR) is the most accurate 3D non-invasive imaging modality used nowadays. With advances in technology, accurate 3D CMR images that visualize the cardiac anatomy in fine detail can be acquired. However, manual segmentation of the cardiac structures on these scans is a challenging and time-consuming process.

In this work, we propose an automatic method to segment the heart and the great vessels. The proposed workflow consists of four steps: (i) Whole heart

© Springer International Publishing AG 2017
M.A. Zuluaga et al. (Eds.): RAMBO 2016/HVSMR 2016, LNCS 10129, pp. 147–155, 2017.
DOI: 10.1007/978-3-319-52280-7_15

segmentation using an atlas-based registration approach; (*ii*) Separation of the myocardial tissue and the blood pool from the whole heart segmentation using probabilistic tissue classes; (*iii*) Segmentation of the descending aorta using circular Hough transform; and (*iv*) A level-set approach to refine the segmentations.

2   Data and Methods

2.1   Data

The data used in this paper were acquired at Boston Children's Hospital (Boston, MA, USA). The data provided include a variety of congenital heart defects. Scans were acquired on a 1.5T Phillips Achieva MR scanner (Phillips, Best, The Netherlands) using a steady-state-free-precession (SSFP) pulse sequence. The scans were acquired using ECG and respiratory-navigator gating, no contrast agent was used.

In total, ten datasets (axial slices, with cropped FOV) were provided with annotated reference standard for training purposes. The reference standard consisted of ventricular myocardium and blood pool (from the heart and the major vessels). In addition, ten test datasets were also provided for evaluating the proposed method.

2.2   Multi-atlas-based Cardiac Segmentation

Multi-atlas-based segmentation is a very popular technique and has been successfully used in segmenting cardiac scans: cardiac chambers [1], coronary artery territories [2], whole heart [3], and left atrium [4]. In this paper, eight manually delineated CT cardiac angiography (CTA) scans from the work of Kirisli *et al.* [1] are used as atlases to segment the unseen CMR dataset. The CTA scans have the following labels: the whole heart (WH), left atrium (LA), left ventricle (LV), right atrium (RA), right ventricle (RV), and the aortic root (AR). Figure 1 shows an example of using the CTA multi-atlas-based approach to segment a CMR dataset.

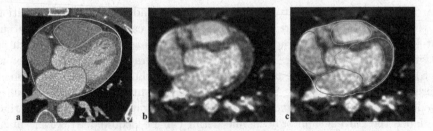

Fig. 1. Multi-atlas based segmentation on a CMR dataset. Axial slice from one of the atlas CTA scan (a), corresponding slice from a random subject (b), resulting segmentations (c). Different colours represent the various cardiac structures.

Image registration is used to spatially align the atlas (CTA) scans and the subjects (CMR) scan. Registration process is represented as:

$$\hat{\mathbf{T}} = \arg \min_{\mathbf{T}} \mathcal{C}\left(\mathbf{T}; I_f, I_m\right),$$

where $\mathbf{T}$ is the transformation parameter, $\mathcal{C}$ is the cost function, and I_f and I_m are the fixed and moving images respectively.

For the registration strategy used in this paper, the CMR scan was used as the fixed image and the CTA scan as the moving image. A two-stage registration approach consisting of an affine transformation followed by a non-rigid B-spline transformation, was used. Mutual information was used as the similarity measure for the cost function. Optimization was performed using adaptive stochastic gradient descent. A three-stage multi-resolution coarse-to-fine scheme was used. All registrations were performed using elastix [5].

Once all eight CTA atlases are registered to the CMR subject scan, the resulting transformed labels are combined using majority voting to obtain the final segmentation. In the current work, only the WH, LV, RV and AR labels from the atlas scans are used. The multi-atlas-based segmentations did not require extensive registration parameter tuning using the training datasets.

2.3   Segmentation of Descending Aorta

As the descending aorta (DA) appears as an approximate circular structure in an axial volume, a Circular Hough Transform (CHT) based segmentation was applied to automatically extract the DA. The proposed method has three main stages, described in the remainder of this section.

Accumulator Calculation: The circle detection technique relies on a 3D accumulator defined over the CHT parameter space. The coordinates in the Hough space are represented as (c_x, c_y, r_k): a circle with center (c_x, c_y) and radius r_k. The center location of a potential circle is given as:

$$\begin{cases} c_x = x - r_k \cos(\pi + \theta), \\ c_y = y - r_k \sin(\pi + \theta), \end{cases}$$

where θ is the gradient direction at position (x, y). The radius candidate r_k lays within the 4–12 mm range.

The CHT calculation has two steps: voting and accumulation. For a radius candidate r_k, a vote is added to the Hough space at coordinate (c_x, c_y, r_k) when an edge pixel (x, y) in the MR image is detected. After all edge pixels in the MR image on slice n were calculated, vote accumulation was performed at each coordinate of the Hough space to compute the cell value $A_n(c_x, c_y, r_k)$ of the 3D accumulator. To enable the CHT to detect imperfect circles, the final CHT response map for slice n can be calculated as:

$$M_n(c_x, c_y) = G_\sigma * \sum_{k=1}^{K} A_n(c_x, c_y, r_k),$$

where G is a 2D Gaussian smoothing kernel of width σ (here $\sigma = 3$ pixels was used) and K is the total number of radius candidates. More details of the CHT calculation can be obtained from the study of Gao *et al.* [6].

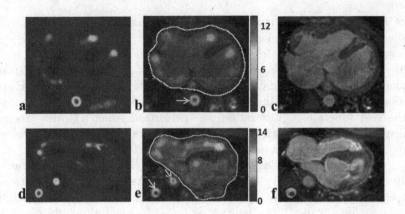

Fig. 2. Illustration of initial DA localization performed on subject 1 (a–c) and subject 2 (d–f). The median CHT calculated from the axial slices (a, d). The mid-heart CMR slice with the corresponding CHT map overlayed on it (b, e), the white contour indicates the whole heart segmentation on the current slice, yellow arrows show the DA candidates which lie within the lower half of the FOV (red dashed line). Segmented DA (red contour) on the CMR slice (c, f). (Color figure online)

Initial DA Position Detection: The result of the whole heart segmentation was used to aid the DA localization. As the DA runs vertically, median of the CHT maps from all the axial slices within the ROI of the whole heart was calculated (see Fig. 2a, d). A number of candidates (local maxima in Fig. 2b, e) were obtained by thresholding the median CHT, the threshold value (T_D) was set to 65% of the global maximum value. Using knowledge about the anatomy and the imaging protocol, we know that potential candidates are located in the lower half of the axial slice (see Fig. 2b, e). Most of the non-target candidates can be effectively excluded by using the above assumptions. The remaining peaks in the median CHT are produced by DA and vertebral foramen. Further distinguishing DA from vertebral foramen was performed at the mid-heart slice (see Fig. 2b, e): candidate with the shortest distance to the segmented heart was retained as DA (see Fig. 2c, f).

DA Segmentation: When estimating the centerline of DA, we assume that the position of the DA is gradually changing in subsequent axial slices. If there are n_d slices that include the DA, a set of n_d points $(P_1, P_2, \ldots, P_{n_d})$ on the centerline will be the center of DA in a series of 2D images, where each point P_n is represented by its x and y coordinate. With known center point position at the mid-heart slice $P_{n_{mh}}$, the centerline tracking was achieved by propagating it in both directions in a slice-by-slice manner according to the following equation:

$$P_n = \arg\max_p \begin{cases} M_n(p) - D(p, P_{n+1}), & n = n_{mh} - 1, \ldots, 1, \\ M_n(p) - D(p, P_{n-1}), & n = n_{mh} + 1, \ldots, n_d, \end{cases}$$

where $D(p_1, p_2)$ is the Euclidean distance between points p_1 and p_2. This term imposes a constraint on the amount of displacement of DA in adjacent slices.

For the scans used in this paper, the DA always begins at slice one, but the last slice (n_d) of DA needs to be detected using the following equation:

$$n_d = \arg\min_n \left\{ \max_p \{M_n(p) - D(p, P_{n-1})\} \leq T_D \right\} - 1.$$

For an axial slice, the radius of DA can be estimated once the accumulator A_n is calculated and the DA center P_n is detected. The best radius at the slice n is calculated as:

$$R_n = \arg\max_{r_k = 1 \ldots K} A_n(P_n, r_k).$$

With the detected centers and radii, we fit optimal circles to the axial slices to obtain the DA segmentation.

2.4   Probability Tissue Maps

Since the task of the segmentation in this case is to separate the blood pool and the myocardial tissue, we generate probabilistic images for the blood and tissue classes. Coherent Local Intensity Clustering (CLIC) algorithm [7] is used for this process. Class membership functions calculated by the CLIC algorithm were used as probability tissue maps. Initially, the scans were smoothed using a 3×3 median filter followed by 50 iterations of the CLIC algorithm. Other parameter values for the CLIC algorithm were: number of classes $n_c = 2$, standard deviation of the Gaussian kernel $\sigma_c = 10$, fuzzyfier $q = 2$. Figure 3b shows an example of the obtained probabilistic image.

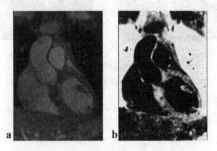

Fig. 3. Coronal slice of a random subject (a). Image representing the probabilistic myocardial tissue map (b), dark regions represent low probability values, in this case blood and grey regions belong to the myocardial tissue.

Using the WH, LV and RV segmentation obtained as described in Sect. 2.2 as the region of interest, the corresponding blood and ventricular myocardial regions are extracted by thresholding the probabilistic images.

2.5 Refinement of Blood-Pool Segmentation by Level-Set Approach

The obtained blood pool and myocardial segmentations have two main issues. (*i*) Optimal circles were fitted for the segmentation of the descending aorta, which does not always provide accurate segmentation. (*ii*) Since the multi-atlas-based segmentation approach did not provide labels for the pulmonary veins, pulmonary arteries, and the superior and inferior vena cava they were not segmented. In this step, we used a level-set approach [8] to refine and grow the initial segmentation into the great vessels by using local image details.

A level-set function is defined in a 3D space such that it has positive values inside and negative values outside the surface. The dynamics to evolve the 3D surface can be imposed in its normal direction, by image forces derived from the original CMR image. In this work, the image force was defined as a combination of image gradient and region information to evolve the implicit surface (blood pool), as described in [9]. A characteristic property of the level-set method approach is that it does not have prior assumptions on the object geometry and can deal with complex shapes such as the pulmonary arteries and veins, and the aorta. Which is especially suitable for cases of congenital heart disease, where considerable variability in the cardiac anatomy is encountered. Figure 4 shows an example of the refinement step and Fig. 5 shows the final result of our complete pipeline.

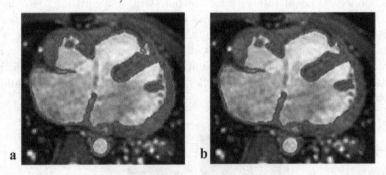

Fig. 4. Example of the level-set refinement: before refinement (a), after refinement (b). Automatically obtained segmentations in green, compared with the ground-truth segmentation in red. (Color figure online)

3 Results

The parameters used by our pipeline were optimized using the training datasets provided by the challenge organizers. On the training dataset, our proposed

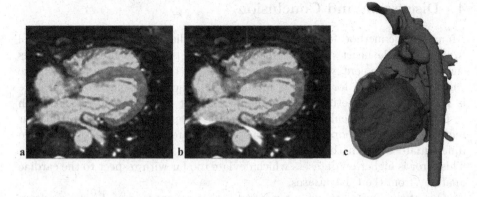

Fig. 5. Axial slice with the ground truth segmentation (a), corresponding slice with the automatic segmentation results (b), automatic segmentation represented as 3D surface (c). Red and blue colours represent the blood pool and the ventricular myocardium, respectively. (Color figure online)

Table 1. Performance of our method on the training and testing datasets in terms of average distance of boundaries (Adb), Hausdorff distance of boundaries (Hdb). Label 1 indicates the myocardial tissue and 2 indicates the blood pool.

Subjects	Adb1	Adb2	Dice1	Dice2	Hdb1	Hdb2	Kappa
Average training	2.19	1.61	0.69	0.86	12.04	9.10	0.92
Subject 10	0.96	0.97	0.73	0.93	3.30	5.12	0.96
Subject 11	1.32	1.39	0.63	0.91	7.28	7.02	0.95
Subject 12	1.13	2.41	0.79	0.83	6.87	13.83	0.95
Subject 13	1.06	1.85	0.84	0.89	3.79	15.43	0.96
Subject 14	0.89	1.49	0.75	0.86	3.20	8.24	0.94
Subject 15	1.09	1.83	0.70	0.86	4.46	10.07	0.94
Subject 16	1.55	1.52	0.62	0.86	8.04	11.31	0.93
Subject 17	0.83	1.32	0.86	0.91	3.71	8.13	0.96
Subject 18	0.95	1.47	0.79	0.90	5.22	7.33	0.95
Subject 19	1.21	1.27	0.75	0.90	5.03	7.40	0.95
Average testing	1.10	1.55	0.75	0.89	5.09	9.41	0.95

method obtained a Dice index of 0.69 for the ventricular myocardium and 0.86 for the blood pool. On the test dataset, our proposed method obtained a Dice index of 0.75 for the ventricular myocardium and 0.89 for the blood pool. Detailed results are presented in Table 1.

4   Discussion and Conclusion

An automatic method for segmenting the myocardial tissue and the blood pool from the whole heart and the great vessels has been presented. The results show good agreement with the ground truth for the blood pool, the average value of Dice index for which is around 0.89. The main source of error here is inability of the method to completely segment all the great vessels. With respect to the ventricular myocardium the average dice obtained is 0.75, our method performs suboptimal, meaning that our proposed pipeline is unable to differentiate between the ventricular myocardium and the atrial myocardium. This error is higher on datasets which deviate too far with respect to the cardiac anatomy from the CTA atlases.

One of the limitations of our method is that we are using CTA atlases from adults to segment paediatric CMR scans. This results in inaccurate chamber segmentation in a few scans. The reason for this is that the atlas scans used in this paper are not a representative set for congenital heart defects. The atlas scans have rather normal heart anatomy, hence the transformed labels of the other structure do not always map accurately. However, from the results we can observe that the proposed framework works quite well on CMR images with congenital heart defects. This demonstrates robustness of our proposed method.

In the future, our method can be further improved by including a wide range of CMR atlas scans that cover a broad range of congenital heart defects.

References

1. Kirişli, H., Schaap, M., Klein, S., et al.: Evaluation of a multi-atlas based method for segmentation of cardiac CTA data: a large-scale, multicenter, and multivendor study. Med. Phys. **37**(12), 6279–6291 (2010)
2. Shahzad, R., van Walsum, T., Schaap, M., et al.: Vessel specific coronary artery calcium scoring: an automatic system. Acad. Radiol. **20**(1), 1–9 (2013)
3. Shahzad, R., Bos, D., Metz, C., et al.: Automatic quantification of epicardial fat volume on non-enhanced cardiac CT scans using a multi-atlas segmentation approach. Med. Phys. **40**(9), 091910 (2013)
4. Tao, Q., Ipek, E.G., Shahzad, R., et al.: Fully automatic segmentation of left atrium and pulmonary veins in late gadolinium-enhanced MRI: towards objective atrial scar assessment. J. Magn. Reson. Imaging **44**, 346–354 (2016)
5. Klein, S., Staring, M., Murphy, K., Viergever, M., Pluim, J.: Elastix: a toolbox for intensity-based medical image registration. IEEE Trans. Med. Imaging **29**(1), 196–205 (2010)
6. Gao, S., van't Klooster, R., Brandts, A., et al.: Quantification of common carotid artery and descending aorta vessel wall thickness from MR vessel wall imaging using a fully automated processing pipeline. J. Magn. Reson. Imaging, **45**(1), 215–228 (2016)
7. Li, C., Xu, C., Anderson, A.W., Gore, J.C.: MRI tissue classification and bias field estimation based on coherent local intensity clustering: a unified energy minimization framework. In: Prince, J.L., Pham, D.L., Myers, K.J. (eds.) IPMI 2009. LNCS, vol. 5636, pp. 288–299. Springer, Heidelberg (2009). doi:10.1007/ 978-3-642-02498-6_24

8. Osher, S., Sethian, J.A.: Fronts propagating with curvature-dependent speed: algorithms based on Hamilton-Jacobi formulations. J. Comput. Phys. **79**(1), 12–49 (1988)

9. Zhang, Y., Matuszewski, B.J., Shark, L.K., et al.: Medical image segmentation using new hybrid level-set method. In: Fifth International Conference on BioMedical Visualization, MEDIVIS 2008. IEEE, pp. 71–76 (2008)

HSVMR: Random Forests

Automatic Heart and Vessel Segmentation Using Random Forests and a Local Phase Guided Level Set Method

Chunliang Wang[1(✉)], Qian Wang[2], and Örjan Smedby[1]

[1] School of Technology and Health (STH),
KTH Royal Institute of Technology, Stockholm, Sweden
chunliang.wang@sth.kth.se
[2] School of Biomedical Engineering, Med-X Research Institute,
Shanghai Jiao Tong University, Shanghai, China

Abstract. In this report, a novel automatic heart and vessel segmentation method is proposed. The heart segmentation pipeline consists of three major steps: heart localization using landmark detection, heart isolation using statistical shape model and myocardium segmentation using learning based voxel classification and local phase analysis. In our preliminary test, the proposed method achieved encouraging results.

Keywords: Image segmentation · Level set · Coherent propagation · Local phase analysis · Shape model

1 Introduction

Automatic segmentation of the heart chamber and myocardium from a 3D cardiovascular magnetic resonance image (MRI) is an essential step in building patient-specific heart models for surgery planning of children with complex congenital heart disease (CHD). Unlike cardiac imaging in adults, the heart of children with CHD can show considerable anatomical variation from patient to patient (such as transposition of the great arteries, single ventricle defect etc.). This relatively large variation may confuse conventional segmentation methods that rely on statistical shape models or standard atlases [1]. On the other hand, due to the similar intensity between the myocardium and liver parenchyma, methods that rely merely on the local features may also fail to deliver satisfactory results. In early studies, a number of researchers have found that phase-based active contour methods deliver relatively accurate segmentation results in heart chamber segmentation [2, 3]. To further improve the segmentation accuracy, the local phase information can also be combined with a statistical shape model, which takes both global and local image features into account [4]. In this study, we implemented a similar approach by combining the probability map outputted from a patch-based voxel classifier with shape-model-guided phase analysis to drive the propagation of the active contour. In addition, a robust random-forest-based anatomy landmark detection method was used to estimate the location of the heart in any given image. In our preliminary test, the proposed method achieved encouraging results.

© Springer International Publishing AG 2017
M.A. Zuluaga et al. (Eds.): RAMBO 2016/HVSMR 2016, LNCS 10129, pp. 159–164, 2017.
DOI: 10.1007/978-3-319-52280-7_16

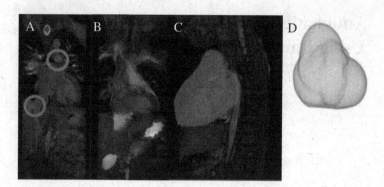

Fig. 1. A. Training image with landmark labels. B. Detected landmarks. C. Estimated heart location. D. Mean shape of the hearts

2 Method

The proposed automatic heart segmentation pipeline consists of three major steps: heart localization, heart isolation and myocardium segmentation. A detailed description of each step is given in the following sections.

2.1 Heart Localization Using Landmark Detection

To estimate the location of the heart, four random-forest-based classifiers are trained to detect four anatomical landmarks: the aortic arch, the pulmonary artery bifurcation, the inferior vena cava root and the vertebral body at the level of the cardia. Figure 1A shows an example of training images. Image patches of $64 \times 64 \times 64$ are used as input to the classifiers. Each classifier contains 100 randomly trained decision trees, and each tree contains 8 levels. At each node, 5000 randomly generated first and second order Haar-like features are used for the training. Figure 1B shows the probability map generated by different classifiers after applying them to an unseen image using a sliding window. Possible locations are selected by first applying a threshold and then finding the center of each connected component. To eliminate false positive detections, a modified pictorial structure method [5], similar to the method proposed in [6], is implemented to find the most plausible combination of detected landmarks. In this framework, body parts are seen as nodes that are constrained by spring-like connections. Given any pair of body parts, $l_i(x_i, y_i, s_i)$ and $l_j(x_j, y_j, s_j)$, the probability distribution of the relative location of these two parts can be estimated using the relative connection parameters $c_{ij} = (\mu_{ij}, \Sigma_{ij})$.

$$p(l_i, l_j | c_{ij}) = \mathcal{N}(x_i - x_j, \mu_x, \sigma_x)\mathcal{N}(y_i - y_j, \mu_y, \sigma_y)\mathcal{N}(s_i - s_j, \mu_s, \sigma_s) \quad (1)$$

Here x, y represent the center position of the body part, and s represents the scale of the body part. Using the training images, c_{ij} can be estimated. $p(l_i, l_j |, c_{ij})$ is used to represent the strength of the connection of two detected landmarks. To find the most likely structure groups for a number of detections, we will remove the connection between two body parts if the Mahalanobis distance of the pair is outside the 95% tolerance interval of the normal distribution defined by c_{ij}. After applying such a threshold, the detected nodes can be organized into a number of connected graphs. The graph with the highest confidence score is identified by summing the probability of each detected node. In cases where there are multiple nodes with the same landmark label, the best one is chosen by finding the node that has the shortest summed Mahalanobis distance to all other landmarks (with different labels) in the graph. A rigid transformation matrix can be calculated between a testing and a training image by matching the corresponding detected landmarks with the ground truth in the training set.

2.2 Heart Isolation Using Statistical Shape Model and Model Guided Local Phase Analysis

While the internal structure of hearts with CHD may vary considerably, the overall shape of its outer surface appears relatively similar from patient to patient. Based on this observation, we performed a heart isolation step using a statistical shape model guided level set method. The heart shape model contains both the heart chambers and the main branches of great vessels as shown in Fig. 1D. The overall shapes of the training datasets were smoothed with morphology operators before being used to generate the statistical shape model. Instead of using the image intensity or gradient to guide the propagation of the active contour, learning-based image features are used by training classifiers to predict the probability of each voxel belonging to the heart or the background. A more detailed explanation of the voxel classification is given in Sect. 2.3. Since the trained classifier may become confused at the basal part of the heart, where it meets the liver, and suggest the probability to be 50:50 for the voxel belonging to the heart or the background, we introduced the local phase as an additional feature to prevent the active contour from leaking into the liver.

Local phase is a measurement that indicates whether the local structure of the image is more similar to an edge-like structure or to a ridge-like structure [7]. It is calculated from the output of a pair of quadrature filters, which combine a ridge-picking filter with an edge-picking filter in the spatial domain. The output of this pair of filters is represented by a complex number where the output of the ridge-picking filter is seen as the real part and the output of the edge-picking filter as the imaginary part. The argument of this complex number in the complex plan is referred to as the *local phase* [7]. The magnitude of the complex number is called the *local energy*. Local phase is orientation dependent. To make it better suited for the purpose of stopping the active contour at the border of the heart, we adapted the model-guided local phase analysis method reported in [4]. The advantage of this method is that it makes a clear differentiation between a black-to-white edge and a white-to-black edge, which can be used to design a speed function that stops the contour before it enters the liver. All three types of forces (model, phase and probability) are combined using an adaptive weighting scheme that is described in [4]. Figure 2 shows an example of the probability and local phase terms and the heart isolation result. In this step, the position of the left atrioventricular (AV) plane is also estimated by mapping the AV plane marked in the mean shape model to the target shape.

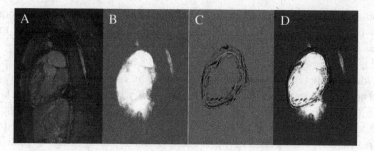

Fig. 2. A. Input image. B. Probability term. C. Phase term. D. Combined external speed function

2.3 Myocardium Segmentation Using Learning-Based Voxel Classification

To segment the myocardium and blood pool of the heart, we used a learning-based voxel classification scheme. A multi-class random-forest-based classifier is trained to classify each voxel into one of 3 classes, i.e. blood, myocardium or background. The classifier contains 20 randomly trained trees and each tree contains 12 levels. First and

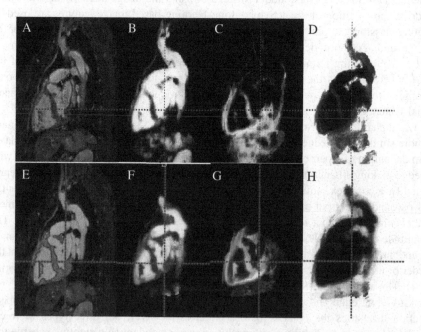

Fig. 3. A. Input Image. B, C, D. Probability maps of the blood pool and vessels, the myocardium and the background from the multi-class classifier, using only Haar-like features. E. Segmentation results. F, G, H. Probability maps of the blood pool and vessels, the myocardium and the background from the multi-class classifier, adding distances to AV plane and shape model as additional features

second order Haar-like features collected from an image patch of $32 \times 32 \times 32$ voxels centered at the voxel are used for the classification. In addition, the distance to the AV plane and the heart shape model estimated in the previous step are also used for training and testing. Figure 3 shows the probability maps of the three components generated from a trained classifier. After applying the heart mask from the previous step, we apply a level set based segmentation on the remaining to get the final myocardium segmentation. A similar approach is used to create the segmentation of the heart chambers and the large vessels.

3 Experiments and Results

The proposed method was tested on the HVSMR whole-heart and great vessel segmentation challenge [8]. The landmark detectors and voxel classifier were trained on 10 training datasets and tested on 10 testing dataset. The statistical shape model was trained using 7 thoracic CT scans from adults that were collected for a different study. The quantitative evaluation of the proposed method is summarized in Table 1. The average processing time for segmenting all components was about 15–20 min per case on an ordinary PC with a quad-core CPU.

Table 1. Evaluation of the proposed method

	Average distance of myocardium	Average distance of vessels	Dice coefficient of myocardium	Dice coefficient of vessels	Hausdorff distance of myocardium	Hausdorff distance of vessels
Case 10	1.332	1.408	0.692	0.890	4.773	6.410
Case 11	2.012	2.159	0.527	0.860	9.575	10.926
Case 12	1.841	2.441	0.619	0.810	10.080	1.841
Case 13	2.216	1.631	0.733	0.874	14.531	2.216
Case 14	1.482	1.952	0.639	0.845	6.904	1.482
Case 15	.491	1.433	0.669	0.872	6.563	6.258
Case 16	1.795	2.460	0.617	0.807	8.817	21.622
Case 17	1.513	2.509	0.746	0.853	5.185	16.332
Case 18	1.557	2.031	0.618	0.851	5.600	10.014
Case 19	1.248	1.410	0.778	0.895	4.540	6.903
Average	1.649	1.943	0.664	0.856	7.657	10.785

4 Discussion and Conclusion

The hearts of children with CHD may have a significantly different anatomical shape from healthy subjects. Therefore, the landmarks that we used to locate the heart are actually not inside the heart, but the anchor points of the heart. Using a combination of multiple landmarks further improves the success rate. We have found the proposed heart detection method to be relatively robust on the given training datasets.

The proposed method has a number of limitations. The most common segmentation error occurs in the upper part of the heart, where the soft tissue around the great vessels is classified as myocardium. This is probably due to similar appearance between these two types of tissue. Using the distance to the AV plane as an additional feature for the classification improved the segmentation accuracy. However the estimation of the AV plane is not very accuracy in the current setting.. We also noticed that the trained classifier has difficulties to recognize the myocardium in the cases with pericardial effusion, which may be related to insufficient training data as there are very few cases with pericardial effusion in the training group.. The results might potentially be improved by using more training cases. In addition, adding some auto-contexting iterations could be helpful to improve the segmentation accuracy.

In conclusion, an automatic whole heart and great vessel segmentation method is proposed. Encouraging results were achieved with a relatively small number of training samples.

References

1. Zheng, Y., Barbu, A., Georgescu, B., Scheuering, M., Comaniciu, D.: Four-chamber heart modeling and automatic segmentation for 3-D cardiac CT volumes using marginal space learning and steerable features. IEEE Trans. Med. Imag. **27**, 1668–1681 (2008)
2. Belaid, A., Boukerroui, D., Maingourd, Y., Lerallut, J.-F.: Phase-based level set segmentation of ultrasound images. IEEE Trans. Inf. Technol. Biomed. **15**, 138–147 (2011)
3. Wang, C., Smedby, Ö.: Model-based left ventricle segmentation in 3d ultrasound using phase image. In: presented at the MICCAI Challenge on Echocardiographic Three-Dimensional Ultrasound Segmentation (CETUS), Boston (2014)
4. Wang, C., Smedby, Ö.: Multi-organ segmentation using shape model guided local phase analysis. In: Navab, N., Hornegger, J., Wells, W.M., Frangi, A.F. (eds.) MICCAI 2015. LNCS, vol. 9351, pp. 149–156. Springer, Heidelberg (2015). doi:10.1007/978-3-319-24574-4_18
5. Felzenszwalb, P.F., Huttenlocher, D.P.: Pictorial structures for object recognition. Int. J. Comput. Vis. **61**, 55–79 (2005)
6. Wang, C., Lundström, C.: CT scan range estimation using multiple body parts detection: let PACS learn the CT image content. Int. J. Comput. Assist. Radiol. Surg. **11**, 317–325 (2016)
7. Knutsson, H., Granlund, G.H.: Signal Processing for Computer Vision. Springer, Heidelberg (1994)
8. http://segchd.csail.mit.edu/index.html

Total Variation Random Forest: Fully Automatic MRI Segmentation in Congenital Heart Diseases

Anirban Mukhopadhyay(✉)

Zuse Institute Berlin, Berlin, Germany
anirban.akash@gmail.com

Abstract. This paper proposes a fully automatic supervised segmentation technique for segmenting the great vessel and blood pool of pediatric cardiac MRIs of children with Congenital Heart Defects (CHD). CHD affects the overall anatomy of heart, rendering model-based segmentation framework infeasible, unless a large dataset of annotated images is available. However, the cardiac anatomy still retains distinct appearance patterns, which has been exploited in this work. In particular, Total Variation (TV) is introduced for solving the 3D disparity and noise removal problem. This results in homogeneous appearances within anatomical structures which is exploited further in a Random Forest framework. Context-aware appearance models are learnt using Random Forest (RF) for appearance-based prediction of great vessel and blood pool of an unseen subject during testing. We have obtained promising results on the HVSMR16 training dataset in a leave-one-out cross-validation.

Keywords: Total Variation · Random Forest · Congenital heart disease · 3D cardiac MRI · Automatic segmentation

1 Introduction

Segmenting the whole heart from high resolution pediatric cardiac MRIs is a crucial step since it provides a segmentation map of contiguous and meaningful regions. For children with Congenital Heart Defects (CHD), segmentation can improve the surgical planning by creating individualized heart models. Building whole heart model necessitates the delineating/labeling of all the cardiac structures in a patient's MRI. Manual and semi-automatic delineation of cardiac structures including blood pool, epicardial surface and great vessels introduce significant latency in the whole process. In this work, we are proposing a fully automatic whole heart segmentation technique to resolve these issues.

Whole-heart segmentation is a challenging problem even when the subjects are in normal condition. However, model-based segmentation can be exploited in those cases due to the typically regular anatomy of heart [1]. On the contrary, CHD affects the heart anatomy resulting the use of model-based segmentation impractical (unless a large repository of already segmented CHD affected hearts are available). Though motion has also been considered as an important cue for

© Springer International Publishing AG 2017
M.A. Zuluaga et al. (Eds.): RAMBO 2016/HVSMR 2016, LNCS 10129, pp. 165–171, 2017.
DOI: 10.1007/978-3-319-52280-7_17

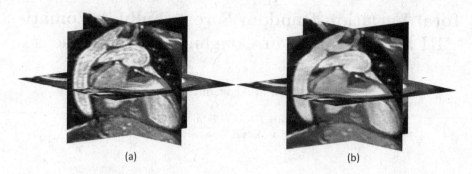

(a)   (b)

Fig. 1. Exemplar raw (a) and TV inhomogeneity removed (b) images.

cardiac segmentation [6], being static, HVSMR16 dataset does not allow to perform motion based segmentation. Finally, the de-facto standard of modern fully automatic segmentation - Atlas based methods [9] fail due to large anatomical variability and only semi-automatic atlas-based segmentation techniques can be employed for this problem [7] (Fig. 1).

Our proposed Total Variation Random Forest (TVRF) method is driven by the key observation that high-resolution of HVSMR16 dataset ensures homogeneous intensities in general within an anatomy. But, MR acquisition and reconstruction has introduced inhomogeneities in these datasets. Typical sources of inhomogeneity can be noise, acquisition artifacts etc. Even though there are many denoising tools available for 3D MR images, none of them consider 3D inhomogeneity removal. However, successful removal of intensity inhomogeneity within certain anatomies can ensure better performance by fully automatic appearance-based multi-label learning algorithms. To this end, we introduce Total Variation as an important preprocessing step for inhomogeneity removal, followed by Random Forest for multi-label appearance learning.

The main contributions of this paper are twofold. First, we introduce Total Variation based inhomogeneity removal in cardiac image analysis context. Second, we present a complete pipeline where Total Variation can be combined with Random Forest for multi-label appearance-based fully automatic segmentation. The remainder of the paper is organized as follows: Sect. 2 presents the proposed method, whereas the implementation details are described in Sect. 3. Results are described in Sect. 4 and finally, Sect. 5 offers discussions and conclusion.

2   Method

Our proposed TVRF method for fully automatic whole heart segmentation is described here in details.

2.1   Total Variation

Even though the raw data of HVSMR16 shows overall homogeneity of appearance within cardiac anatomical structures, the quality of data is affected by the acquisition related noise. Furthermore, these MR images also get affected by inhomogeneity related problems e.g. partial volume effect.

Even though many filtering techniques can be employed for 3D noise removal, they are in general incapable of refining inhomogeneity. Here, we have employed the $L1$-norm Total Variation ($L1$-TV) using Augmented Lagrangian method introduced in [2] for solving both the problems together. The energy function we have used for this particular minimization problem is:

$$\underset{f}{\text{minimize}} \ \frac{\mu}{2}\|u - v\|_1 + \| \bigtriangledown u\|_2$$

where v is the input 3D image and u is the processed image. The main reason behind choosing $L1$-norm over $L2$ is the fact that appearances 3D MR of different anatomies are piece-wise constant functions with quantized levels within a certain anatomy and there are sharp edges across anatomical boundaries.

2.2   Random Forest

The problem of segmenting great vessel and blood pool from background is posed here as a multi-class classification problem, which is well-suited for random forest classifier. This section describes the way in which Random Forest is utilized as an appearance classifier.

Training: Given a set of pre-processed (inhomogeneity removed) 3D training images and corresponding ground truth labels (i.e. great vessel and blood pool), content of each image can be represented by three classes $c \in \{BG, GV, BL\}$, related to background, great vessel and blood pool respectively. A RF is employed to determine class c for a given spatial input $p \in \Omega$ from spatial domain Ω. Each spatial point is associated with a feature vector f_p containing appearance and context-based information, described in details in Sect. 2.3. RFs are an ensemble of decision trees $t \in [1, T]$, where each tree t is a weak classifier.

Features and the manually labeled associated classes $\{f_p, c_p\}$ across all the spatial location p are given as input for training the RF. During classification, each node contains a set of training examples and a class predictor. Starting from root, at each node a splitting is performed based on the well-known information gain criteria which results in left and right child node. The splitting continues iteratively until a pre-specified depth D is reached. The probability of each class c is stored at each leaf node.

Testing: Feature vectors similar to previous section is computed at a data point x that needs to be classified. This features vector f_x is pushed through each tree t by applying the learnt split functions. When the feature reaches a particular leaf, the associated posterior probability of the classes for the leaf is assigned to the data point. The probabilities are accumulated for all the trees in the forest and final decision is made based on the highest overall probability.

2.3 Feature Description

We have considered contextual features, relative location and posterior probabilities of Gaussian mixture model together as the input feature vector for each pixel. In particular, contextual features are learnt by finding the difference between pixel intensities of the current position and the location within a certain pre-specified distance d_C away from the current location in all six neighborhoods as described in Fig. 2. Gaussian mixture model with 2 components are learnt for each class, resulting in a concatenated feature vector of 16 dimension, which is considered as input for RF, similar to [10].

2.4 Initialization

During testing, proper initialization is necessary for two reasons: it can reduce the search space and focuses on cases

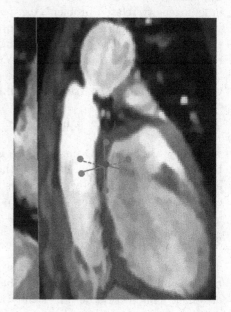

Fig. 2. 3D Contextual features used for training Random Forest.

where decision making is most difficult. We have used Demons registration [8] strategy for initialization. In particular, all the training data are registered to the testing data using [8]. Top 2 registered cases, based on the mutual information of the moving image and the testing image is used to initialize the search space. The ground truth mask of top 2 cases are also transformed and the union of the two transformed masks is considered as the initial region of interest.

3 Implementation

We have used the ADMM Lagrangian solver developed in [2] for TV based inhomogeneity removal. The Demon implementation of [5] is used for registration-based initialization. [4] is used for training the RF and testing on new data. Spatial regularization over the output of RF is achieved by solving a slice-by-slice MRF problem using graph cut [3], where the log-likelihood of posterior probabilities from RF is used as the input data term. The final segmentation result also contained some small artifacts, which has been removed using connected component analysis to get the final segmentation mask of both great vessel and blood pool.

4 Results

The aim of the proposed TVRF method is to fully automatically segment whole heart (great vessel and blood pool) from 3D MR Images. To validate the segmentation quality of TVRF, all the experiments on the training dataset is performed

Table 1. Dice overlap comparison for different subjects in Axial view.

Subjects	Training		Testing	
	Great vessel	Blood pool	Great vessel	Blood pool
0	0.705	0.876	0.447	0.816
1	0.658	0.795	0.456	0.854
2	0.508	0.899	0.669	0.833
3	0.402	0.828	0.652	0.805
4	0.590	0.766	0.338	0.719
5	0.707	0.842	0.44	0.727
6	0.604	0.804	0.255	0.702
7	0.788	0.938	0.566	0.815
8	0.571	0.821	0.585	0.822
9	0.648	0.812	0.537	0.846
Average	0.618	0.838	0.495	0.794

using strict leave-one-subject-out cross validation. Experiments on the testing dataset is performed by learning from the whole training dataset.

4.1 Parameter Settings

For all experiments, $\mu = 1$ is chosen for TV. A RF of $T = 30$ trees each of depth $D = 15$ is trained during training, where $d_C = 4$ is chosen ofr generating the context features input of RF. For the Graph-cut, a 4-connected neighborhood and Pott's model is considered to employ slice-by-slice spatial smoothness.

4.2 Quantitative Analysis

Quantitative experimental results of TVRF segmentation technique is reported in Tables 1 and 2. Volumetric dice overlap is considered as the metric to represent segmentation quality. For all 10 subjects, segmentation is performed in both axial and short axis view and the dice accuracy of for both great vessel and blood pool and reported in Tables 1 and 2 respectively. An average Dice accuracy of 0.618 and 0.838 is achieved for great vessel and blood pool in Axial view whereas an average 0.575 and 0.827 is achieved in Short Axis view of the training dataset. On the testing dataset, average Dice accuracy of 0.495 and 0.794 is achieved for Axial cases whereas 0.359 and 0.766 is achieved for the SA view.

Considering the difficulties associated with CHD segmentation, fully automatic TVRF segmentation method achieves good dice accuracy. Experimental observation suggests that the general performance and dice accuracy score has been affected by certain slices where appearance-based TVRF strategy grossly over-estimated great vessel area. This kind of over-estimation can generally be avoided by model-based post-processing, but here the inherent problem of CHD-affected heart has hindered the use of model-driven post-processing.

Table 2. Dice overlap comparison for different subjects in Short Axis (SA) view

Subjects	Training		Testing	
	Great vessel	Blood pool	Great vessel	Blood pool
0	0.661	0.875	0.267	0.821
1	0.587	0.788	0.237	0.814
2	0.544	0.895	0.484	0.769
3	0.4	0.83	0.453	0.775
4	0.567	0.731	0.295	0.740
5	0.635	0.847	0.267	0.821
6	0.554	0.808	0.377	0.714
7	0.688	0.938	0.383	0.791
8	0.508	0.782	0.417	0.762
9	0.603	0.78	0.297	0.759
Average	0.575	0.827	0.359	0.766

4.3 Qualitative Analysis

The quality of the segmentation mask generated by our proposed method is compared with manually segmented mask in Fig. 3. It is important to note the quality of TVRF segmentation by the smoothness and similarity of the segmented mask w.r.t. the manually segmented one.

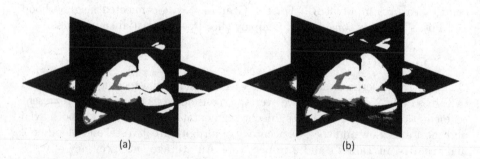

(a)   (b)

Fig. 3. Exemplar whole heart segmentation for qualitative comparison between the segmentation of TVRF (b) and manual segmentation (a).

5 Discussions and Conclusion

This study results in promising Dice accuracy for both great vessel and blood pool in the training dataset. Moreover, it is shown that our design is general enough to be applied for both axial and short axis view. Introducing TV as a pre-processing step for intensity inhomogeneity removal can have far reaching consequences towards overall accuracy and design choices of appearance-based algorithms. Moreover, by introducing semi-automatic steps, the results can be significantly improved due to the homogeneity of tissue appearance introduced by TV. In future, we are planning to investigate in the direction of 3D graph cut and better feature description for the improvement of overall segmentation results.

References

1. Assen, H.C., Danilouchkine, M.G., Behloul, F., Lamb, H.J., Geest, R.J., Reiber, J.H.C., Lelieveldt, B.P.F.: Cardiac LV segmentation using a 3D active shape model driven by fuzzy inference. In: Ellis, R.E., Peters, T.M. (eds.) MICCAI 2003. LNCS, vol. 2878, pp. 533–540. Springer, Heidelberg (2003). doi:10.1007/978-3-540-39899-8_66
2. Chan, S.H., et al.: An augmented Lagrangian method for total variation video restoration. IEEE Trans. Image Process. **20**(11), 3097–3111 (2011)
3. Delong, A., et al.: Fast approximate energy minimization with label costs. Int. J. Comput. Vision **96**(1), 1–27 (2012)
4. https://github.com/karpathy/Random-Forest-Matlab
5. http://de.mathworks.com/matlabcentral/fileexchange/39194-diffeomorphic-log-demons-image-registration
6. Mukhopadhyay, A., Oksuz, I., Bevilacqua, M., Dharmakumar, R., Tsaftaris, S.A.: Unsupervised myocardial segmentation for cardiac MRI. In: Navab, N., Hornegger, J., Wells, W.M., Frangi, A.F. (eds.) MICCAI 2015. LNCS, vol. 9351, pp. 12–20. Springer, Heidelberg (2015). doi:10.1007/978-3-319-24574-4_2
7. Pace, D.F., Dalca, A.V., Geva, T., Powell, A.J., Moghari, M.H., Golland, P.: Interactive whole-heart segmentation in congenital heart disease. In: Navab, N., Hornegger, J., Wells, W.M., Frangi, A.F. (eds.) MICCAI 2015. LNCS, vol. 9351, pp. 80–88. Springer, Heidelberg (2015). doi:10.1007/978-3-319-24574-4_10
8. Vercauteren, T., Pennec, X., Perchant, A., Ayache, N.: Symmetric log-domain diffeomorphic registration: a demons-based approach. In: Metaxas, D., Axel, L., Fichtinger, G., Székely, G. (eds.) MICCAI 2008. LNCS, vol. 5241, pp. 754–761. Springer, Heidelberg (2008). doi:10.1007/978-3-540-85988-8_90
9. Zhuang, X.: Challenges and methodologies of fully automatic whole heart segmentation: a review. J. Healthc. Eng. **4**(3), 371–408 (2013)
10. Zikic, D., et al.: Decision forests for tissue-specific segmentation of high-grade gliomas in multi-channel MR. In: Ayache, N., Delingette, H., Golland, P., Mori, K. (eds.) MICCAI 2012. LNCS, vol. 7512, pp. 369–376. Springer, Heidelberg (2012). doi:10.1007/978-3-642-33454-2_46

Author Index

Alberola-López, Carlos 58
Amin, Zahir 3
Atkinson, David 3

Bayly, Philip V. 24
Biffi, Benedetta 139
Brau, Anja C.S. 70
Brooks, Rupert 48
Burschka, Darius 70
Bustin, Aurélien 70

Chouhan, Manil 3
Cordero-Grande, Lucilio 58

Dzyubachyk, Oleh 147

Ebner, Michael 3

Felblinger, Jacques 70

Gao, Shan 147
Gomez, Arnold D. 24
Gómez, Pedro A. 37
Gueziri, Houssem-Eddine 48

HajiRassouliha, Amir 14
Heng, Pheng-Ann 103
Heuveline, Vincent 121

Išgum, Ivana 95

Janich, Martin A. 70

Krahmer, Felix 37

Lamata, Pablo 83
Laporte, Catherine 48
Leiner, Tim 95
Li, Jinpeng 111
Lösel, Philipp 121

Martin-Fernandez, Marcos 58
Menini, Anne 70
Menze, Bjoern H. 37
Menzel, Marion I. 37

Montana, Giovanni 83
Mukhopadhyay, Anirban 165

Nash, Martyn P. 14
Nielsen, Poul M.F. 14

Odille, Freddy 70
Ourselin, Sébastien 3, 139

Patel, Premal A. 3
Pham, Dzung L. 24
Poudel, Rudra P.K. 83
Prieto, Claudia 58
Prince, Jerry L. 24
Punwani, Shonit 3

Qin, Jing 103

Read, Samantha 3
Royuela-del-Val, Javier 58

Schievano, Silvia 139
Shahzad, Rahil 147
Shi, Lin 111
Simmross-Wattenberg, Federico 58
Smedby, Örjan 159
Sperl, Jonathan I. 37
Stone, Maureen 24

Taberner, Andrew J. 14
Tao, Qian 147
Taylor, Andrew M. 139
Taylor, Stuart 3
Tremblay, Sebastien 48
Tziritas, Georgios 129

Ulas, Cagdas 37
Usman, Muhammad 58

van der Geest, Rob 147
Vercauteren, Tom 3, 139
Viergever, Max A. 95

Wang, Chunliang 159
Wang, Defeng 111

Wang, Qian   159
Wolterink, Jelmer M.   95
Woo, Jonghye   24

Xing, Fangxu   24

Yang, Xin   103
Yu, Lequan   103

Zhang, Rongzhao   111
Zuluaga, Maria A.   139

Printed in the United States
By Bookmasters